P9-CLX-080

Academic Freedom

after September 11

Academic Freedom after September 11

Edited by Beshara Doumani

ZONE BOOKS · NEW YORK · 2006

Printed in the United States of America.

Distributed by The MIT Press,
Cambridge, Massachusetts, and London, England

Designed by Bruce Mau and Julie Fry
Typeset by Archetype

COVER IMAGE: Yale students, wearing camouflage gags, march
at Yale University, New Haven, CT on Friday, Oct. 4, 2002 in
protest against U.S. military recruiters participating at Yale
Law School's fall interview program. The gags symbolize the
military's "don't ask, don't tell" policy (AP/Wide World Photos).

SPINE AND INSIDE BACK COVER: David McLain/Getty Images

INSIDE FRONT COVER: Doug Menuez/Getty Images

LIBRARY OF CONGRESS CATALOGING-IN-PUBLICATION DATA

Academic freedom after September 11 / edited by Beshara
Doumani
    p. cm.
    Papers presented at the conference, "Academic freedom
after September 11," held on Feb. 27, 2004, at the
University of California at Berkeley.
    Includes bibliographical references.
    ISBN 1-890951-62-5 – ISBN 1-890951-61-7 (pbk.)
    1. Academic freedom – United States – Congresses.
2. Education, Higher – United States – Congresses.
I. Title: Academic freedom after September eleventh.
II. Doumani, Beshara, 1957–

LC72.2.A295 2006
328.1'213–dc22
                                    2005051449

To

Reginald Zelnik (1936–2004)

and

Edward Said (1935–2003)

each in his own way

Contents

Acknowledgments

This book is dedicated to Reginald Zelnik and Edward Said in honor of their lifelong commitment to the causes of freedom, social justice, and peace. Each in his own way contributed mightily to and became a symbol of free speech. Tragically, both were taken from us at the moment we needed them the most. To me, they embody, through their words and personal example, what a scholar and a teacher must possess: a deeply ethical pursuit of knowledge and understanding; the moral courage to begin with a critique of one's own national identity and to speak truth to power; and an unflagging commitment to making a difference as public intellectuals. They did not just enjoy academic freedom: they did something with it.

The dictum "pessimism of the intellect, optimism of the will" has never been more apt. There is much to be pessimistic about when it comes to the future of academic freedom in the United States. At the same time, I draw a great deal of hope and inspiration from the colleagues, students, friends, and loved ones who made this edited volume possible. It is difficult to express the depth of my gratitude. Suffice it to say that the list is long, the debt is huge, and the shortcomings are mine alone.

This edited volume, like so many others of its ilk, began as a conference. "Academic Freedom After September 11" — convened on February 27, 2004, at the University of California at Berkeley — was generously supported by grants from the Center for Middle Eastern Studies (CMES), Townsend Center for Humanities, Institute of International Studies, Human Rights Center, and UC Berkeley's Department of History. The support of the CMES team — Nezar AlSayyad, CMES'S director; Emily Gottreich, the associate director and conference organizer; Amanda Leung, the manager; and Lily Cooc, the administrative assistant — were crucial to its success.

All the conference papers were original commissioned essays. Unfortunately the contributions of David Hollinger on what it means to be "balanced," George Bisharat on the Sami al-Arian case, Snehal Shingavi on academic freedom in the age of empire, and Michael Hindi and Tanya Suleiman on international education could not be included in this volume. I thank them for their ideas and critical comments, as I do the panel discussants, Kerwin Klein and Laura Nader.

My research assistant, Osamah Khalil, scoured the Internet for sources on the major academic-freedom controversies since 9/11. Mayssoun Sukarieh and Faisal Ghori have taken an interest in my work and continue to fill my e-mail inbox with much appreciated links to related articles on subjects ranging from the sublime to the absurd. Ramona Naddaff, who edited this volume for Zone Books, made two strategic interventions that considerably strengthened the final product.

I owe a large debt to David Hollinger, with whom I have been engaged in a continuing conversation on academic freedom over the past two years. His intimate knowledge of academic culture in the U.S., his long-standing commitment to the protection of academic freedom, and his judicious temperament helped me negotiate new and unfamiliar terrains. Finding one's voice is one thing; keeping and honing it over long periods of time is another. Invaluable in this regard have been the generosity and support of Judith Butler, Thomas Laqueur, Carla Hesse, and Thomas Brady. As always, my greatest debt is to the women in my life: my partner, Ismat, and my daughters, Tala and Yara. I cannot imagine life without them.

Beshara Doumani
Berkeley, May 27, 2005

Between Coercion

and Privatization:

Academic Freedom in the

Twenty-First Century

Beshara Doumani

Academic freedom is facing its most serious threat since the McCarthy era of the 1950s. In the aftermath of the attacks of September 11, 2001, government agencies and private advocacy and special-interest groups have been subjecting institutions of higher learning to an increasingly sophisticated infrastructure of surveillance, intervention, and control. This bold campaign of censorship and intimidation comes at a time when the academy is in the midst of a transformation driven by the increasing commercialization of knowledge. Buffeted between the conflicting but intimately related forces of antiliberal coercion and neoliberal privatization, colleges and universities are more vulnerable than ever to the myriad ways outside political and economic forces are reshaping the landscape of intellectual production.

It is an open question whether the dark clouds hovering over academic life in the United States betoken a passing storm — with "Islamic terrorism" replacing Soviet Communism as the evil and the source of fear — or whether they are the harbingers of a structural shift in the production of knowledge. Much depends on whether a new contract among the academy, society, and the government (both state and federal) can be configured so as to overcome the stifling and corrupting forces unleashed in times of war and privatization. In the meantime, much also depends on how effectively and vigorously academic freedom is defended, for it is vital to a robust democratic public culture; to the pursuit of knowledge for the social good; and to the promotion of a public culture of tolerance, justice, and understanding.

Movement on both fronts depends, in turn, on the answers to two sets of questions. The first has to do with the clarity of the concept itself. Is academic freedom primarily an individual right, best based on the First Amendment to the United States Constitution, that guarantees free speech, as most have come to believe and expect since the 1950s? Or is it a professional privilege based on a codification of a set of understandings governing employer-employee relations that allows faculty members to regulate their affairs according to their own standards? Can either of the above be truly considered academic freedom in the absence of fundamental critiques of professional norms, national identity, and hierarchal power relations?

The jury is still out on these issues. So much so, in fact, that Part One of this volume provides three carefully considered, strongly argued, and not easily reconcilable essays that more or less reflect the range of approaches mentioned in the previous paragraph. Taken together, the chapters by Robert Post, Judith Butler, and Philippa Strum constitute a solid platform for informed discussions of the legal structures, philosophical foundations, and political dimensions of academic freedom. The authors — all committed defenders of academic freedom — provide a sweeping overview as well as in-depth analysis of what is at stake. What deserves the greatest attention is not the rhetorical home of these arguments but the careful parsing of the issues involved as well as the points of conflict and agreement in the assumptions and positions the three authors take.

The second set of questions has to do with the historical context and specific nature of the challenges to academic freedom. How has the institutional transformation of universities — in terms of sources of funding, organizational culture, public mission, academic programs, and the social demographics of the faculty and the student body — shaped the ways academic freedom is understood and practiced? And how have the relationships between the academy, on the one hand, and private advocacy groups and the U.S. government, on the other, changed as a result of September 11? Kathleen J. Frydl addresses the first question through a richly illustrated case study of the transformation of the University of California into a "multiversity" following the Second World War. She forcefully reminds us that in the new configuration, the real front line of academic freedom is not who is fired but who is hired. In an understated but gripping narrative, Amy Newhall considers the dilemma faced by the government when it seeks, at one and the same time, to promote language acquisition and area studies while attempting to control the uses that this knowledge is put to. Finally, Joel Beinin draws on his long experience in the embattled field of Middle East studies to analyze the techniques and goals of the self-appointed private groups attempting to police thought in the academy.

These six thoughtful and tightly argued essays lay the groundwork for informed discussion on a subject sure to occupy an ever greater space in public debates over the coming years. The authors bring insights from a variety of disciplines as well as geographic areas of expertise. They also occupy different locations on the front lines, so to speak, of the defense of academic freedom. Their differing perspectives and practical experiences make for a rich yet cohesive conversation, for the authors respond to each other's arguments and bring their expertise to bear on a common set of examples. All the authors, for instance, ponder the implications of their arguments for possible strategies for tackling current challenges to academic freedom, such as House Resolution 3077, the International Studies in Higher Education Act, thus providing the reader with clear points of comparison.[1] What they have to say is crucial to rethinking the concept of academic freedom, to developing the most effective and ethical means to protect the free pursuit of knowledge, and to keeping the mission of higher education focused on service to the public good.

In this introduction, I want to depart from the conventional editorial essay that summarizes and loosely strings together the chapters by the contributors. Instead, I will embed brief discussions of the authors' contributions in a longer narrative that attempts to understand the significance and the exceptionalism of the post-9/11 moment when it comes to the roller-coaster history of academic freedom. This narrative is divided into three parts. The first argues at some length that the global war on terrorism is distinct from previous wars in ways that do not bode well for the future of academic freedom; that the unprecedented curtailment of civil liberties following the passage of the USA Patriot Act in October 2001 has affected academic freedom structurally; and that unlike in the McCarthy era, private advocacy and special-interest groups are playing the lead role in national campaigns to undermine academic freedom by replacing professional norms with arbitrary political criteria. The second part steps back from the alarm-bell immediacy of the first yet casts an even more somber gaze on the changing political economy and institutional infrastructure of higher education, which arguably pose the greatest challenges to the continuation of the academy as a semi-autonomous sphere of critical inquiry. The third considers the contested nature of this concept in terms of its conflicting sources of authority and the compromises involved in pursuing various strategies of praxis, both of which raise difficult questions about what visions of academic freedom must be defended and about the most effective ways of doing so.

Academic Freedom after September 11

Academic freedom suffered serious setbacks after September 11, 2001. The hasty passage of the bill with the Orwellian name, the USA Patriot Act, has compromised privacy protections, eroded civil liberties, and chilled dissent, prompting civil libertarians from both the left and the right to loudly voice their concerns.[2] In addition, several government agencies have instituted a series of intrusive restrictions on the free flow of information, inspiring stubborn protests by scientists and university officials, among others. Major funding organizations, such as the Ford and Rockefeller foundations, added new language about terrorism to contracts that must now be signed by all grant recipients, although several modifications in response to pressure from civil-rights organizations and elite universities have lessened the original impact of this language. Perhaps more pernicious have been aggressive "take back the campus" campaigns by well-funded and politically connected private advocacy organizations that mobilize politicians, donors, alumni, and the local and national press. These campaigns aim to influence the production of knowledge by promoting certain lines of inquiry while delegitimizing others. One outcome of these campaigns is the introduction of legislation on the federal and state levels that would impose political tests on faculty members and students — although their possible passage and implementation are still hotly contested. Meanwhile, some radical right-wing groups are using sophisticated techniques of intimidation, ranging from posting lists of "un-American" professors on the

Internet to coordinating attacks on specific scholars, course offerings, and programs of study. While in the past such challenges have been mounted in disciplines such as biology, history, and comparative literature as well as gender, ethnic, and cultural studies, they have focused with greatest intensity in the post-9/11 moment on Middle East and Islamic studies. Critics of the foreign policies of the Bush administration, especially those students and faculty members connected academically or culturally to Muslim countries, the Middle East, or both, tend to be identified as suspect, both in their loyalties to the United States and in their ethical commitment to the pursuit of knowledge and understanding.

It is to be expected that threats to academic freedom will increase when a national crisis inspires fear, hypernationalism, and intolerance, as September 11 did.[3] The (1919–20) Red Scare following the Bolshevik Revolution in Russia, the internment of American citizens of Japanese descent during the Second World War, and the mid-century McCarthy inquisitions are cases in point. It is also to be expected that attacks on academic freedom will meet with determined resistance that can have the paradoxical effect of making this concept even more deeply rooted in the public consciousness. Indeed, the two most authoritative statements on academic freedom in the United States were each articulated by the Association of American University Professors (AAUP) one year after the outbreak of a major war. The first was the "1915 Declaration of Principles on Academic Freedom and Academic Tenure." The second was the "1940 Statement of Principles on Academic Freedom and Tenure" (see the Appendix for the text of the latter).

But this war, unlike previous ones, may have the potential to inflict long-term damage to academic freedom, if not to transform the hitherto fairly open system of knowledge production and transmission around the world. Why? Partly, this is because of the virulently anti-intellectual nature of both the 9/11 attacks and the war launched in response. Mostly, however, it is because 9/11 crystallized three long-term processes. First, the emergence of the United States after the end of the Cold War as the uncontested global economic and military power. Second, the political triumph of a highly ideological coalition of evangelical religious fundamentalists, militant nationalists, and neoconservatives that now dominates, among others, the presidency, the Congress, and the top civilian ranks of the Pentagon and is imposing itself on the intelligence services. Third, the privatization and commerciali- zation of knowledge in an information age, which has greatly re- duced the degree of intellectual autonomy within universities and magnified the influence of private donors and corporations. In this larger context, the vigorous campaign to discipline the acad- emy unleashed after 9/11 can be seen as part of a sustained effort to shift public discourse in favor of four major agendas in foreign and domestic policies: dominating the globe through the doctrine of preemptive military intervention with special focus on the Middle East, dismantling the New Deal society, reversing the gains of the various civil-rights and environmental movements, and blurring the line between church and state.

It is still too early to tell whether these agendas will be fully realized. But it would not be an exaggeration to say that the pub- lic sphere since 9/11 has been characterized by a use of the big stick and the discursive shift. The shock of 9/11, the "Pearl Har- bor of the twenty-first century," has been cynically used by the Bush administration to silence critical and informed discussion at home and to justify a radical "clean break" foreign policy of military intervention abroad. At the same time, the White House has initiated elaborate public-relations campaigns to change the frameworks by which people view major issues, such as the inva- sion of Iraq, the Palestinian-Israeli conflict, and the future of Social Security.[4]

Academic Freedom in a Time of War
It is a truism that war and truth do not go well together, but we usually take comfort in the fact that wars end while the pursuit of knowledge is endless. Herein, however, lies the danger of this new and unique global war on terrorism. To begin with, it is a war without end, for it is not against a specific country or regime, but against an ill-defined enemy: shadowy groups usually referred to as "Islamic terrorists" or "Islamic militants" that can be any- where and can appear at any time.[5] These groups are to be hunted at home and given no safe haven abroad, even if that means sus- pending hard-earned civil liberties to keep the homeland secure or flouting international law by invading countries that pose no imminent threat to the United States but are suspected of "har- boring" terrorists.

Thus far, this should sound familiar to students of the Cold War, but there is an important difference: Terrorists are portrayed by the Bush administration as driven not by a rational and competing ideology of modernity that seeks to seize state power, such as communism, but by an irrational and purely evil hatred for "our way of life." Indeed, the representation of this war is based on a virulently anti-intellectual stand that insists that the enemy cannot be understood through the conventional interpretative concepts and units of analysis that the academy generates. Consequently, and again unlike in the Cold War period, the expertise of area specialists in particular and most scholars in the humanities and social sciences in general are made irrelevant. President Bush's repeated statements that the war against terrorism is but a part of a larger war to spread God-given freedom to the world best illustrate the irrelevance of rational inquiry. The operative assumption in his speeches is that freedom is not a product of history but God's gift to humanity.[6] Furthermore, the United States is ordained to carry out the sacred mission of extending it. That is, the United States has a religious and moral duty as the most powerful country in the world to use its power through diplomatic and economic pressures and, if necessary, military force, in order to spread God's freedom to oppressed people everywhere. The overtones of a religious crusade are difficult to ignore, for in this worldview freedom, like terrorism, is located outside history and society.

The often unstated vision undergirding the banishment of terrorism and freedom from the realm of reason is that of an unending clash between an undemocratic and fanatical Islamic civilization, on the one hand, and its Judeo-Christian opposite, on the other.[7] Pat Robertson, Jerry Falwell, and other leaders of the evangelical Christian right-wing organizations that constitute the core constituency of the Bush administration routinely refer to the Prophet Muhammad as a terrorist and to the Islamic religion as war-like.[8] This vision literally renders the academy as we know it — for example, as a product of the Enlightenment — superfluous, except as a servant to those who subscribe to this worldview. This is why the naive but important question "Why do they hate us?" has yet to be systematically explored and discussed. And this is why academics who publicly speak about the roots or political contexts of 9/11 are either ignored or attacked as "un-American."

The black-and-white warning by President Bush, "Either you are with us, or you are with the terrorists," does not only ask other countries to surrender their foreign policy. It also asks academics to give up what they hold most dear: the use of critical reason in the free pursuit of knowledge.[9]

The ways the global war on terrorism has undermined academic freedom are very similar to the ways it has been used to undermine other pillars of democracy: constitutional protections of civil liberties, the independence of the judiciary, freedom of the press, and the system of Congressional checks and balances to the executive branch of government.[10] With the national media and the Congress unable or unwilling to fulfill their role as watchdog of the most powerful presidency in living memory, the spotlight soon turned to the academy, which, as the bastion of socially valued dissent, found itself attracting a great deal of unwanted negative attention. As the next two sections argue, 9/11 has heralded structural, not just passing changes in the relationships among the academy, the government, and society.

"Be Careful": The Academy and the Government

After 9/11, official government constraints on academic freedom must be seen as part of a much larger and ongoing process of erosion along the entire spectrum of civil liberties. Although many objectionable constraints on academic freedom by the federal government predate 9/11, the legal groundwork for this radical and qualitative shift in the relationship between the state and the academy was laid with the passage of the Patriot Act.[11] Some provisions of the even more dangerous "Patriot II" — which was proposed by then–Attorney General John Ashcroft in January 2003 but never became law in its entirety due to vigorous opposition — were attached to the bill reorganizing the nation's intelligence agencies in 2004.[12]

Post-9/11 regulations that undermine academic freedom are usually presented as technical, value-free measures designed solely for the purposes of homeland security and the global war on terrorism. In fact, they were brewed in the most ideologically motivated administration since that of Ronald Reagan, if not in all of recent U.S. history. The broad categories of these regulations are surveillance, control of the circulation of information, restrictions on foreign students and scholars and on the conduct of scientific research, and proposed legislation on both the federal and the state level to facilitate political intervention on campus, especially in area studies and foreign policy. In 2003, a measured and carefully worded preliminary assessment by the AAUP on the threats to academic freedom after 9/11 concluded, "Sufficient proscriptions *are already in place* to justify grave concerns and deep apprehension."[13] After September 11, one has to be careful.

Be careful what books you buy or borrow from the library. The Department of Homeland Security, under the terms of Section 215 of the Patriot Act, could monitor you. A further "gag order" provision of that law threatens criminal prosecution of anyone alerting you to government inspection of your selections. In response, the American Library Association adopted a strongly worded resolution that described this section of the Patriot Act as "a present danger to the constitutional rights and privacy rights of library users" and urged noncooperation by its members.[14] The response was so overwhelming that many news stories spoke of an "uprising" by librarians.[15]

Be careful what articles you accept for publication. Several scientific journals found themselves on the wrong side of the law due to a February 2004 declaration by the U.S. treasury department's Office of Foreign Assets Control to the effect that American presses could not publish works authored in nations under trade embargoes. These countries include Iran, Sudan, and Cuba. The consequences are fines up to $1 million and jail terms of up to ten years.[16] Enforcement of this law has resulted in banning the publication of the memoirs of Nobel Peace Prize winner and human-rights activist Shirin Ebadi, an Iranian national, among others.[17]

Be careful if you are a scientist or a university that depends on government contracts for scientific research. Several of the tightened or new restrictions on circulation of scientific research constitute "a needless clampdown on academic freedom — including moves to bar non-citizens, and even foreign-born U.S. citizens, from participating in an ever-expanding list of science and engineering research projects."[18] The situation worsened in 2004 when the inspectors general of the commerce, state, energy, and defense departments released a report that broadened the definition of "deemed exports" (information and technical data that require licenses even though they do not have to leave the U.S. but might be seen or shared with a non–U.S. citizen working on a scientific project) while, simultaneously, narrowing the definition of basic research, that which allows universities to conduct scientific inquiries openly and freely.

Be careful if you are a scientist whose research findings or political opinions do not fit with the ideological positions of the Bush administration. Many scientists recruited to serve on government advisory panels were subjected to political litmus tests, including questions about their views on abortion and their voting records. The findings of others were ignored or deliberately erased from Web sites. The blatant arm-twisting reached such a point that in 2004 hundreds of scientists, including twenty Nobel laureates, signed a statement condemning the White House for deliberately and systematically distorting scientific fact in the service of policy goals and warning of great potential harm to future generations (see Appendix). The statement is part of a report by the Union of Concerned Scientists that details how the White House censors and suppresses its own scientists, stacks advisory committees, and disbands government panels for political and not academic reasons.[19]

Be careful if you are a non–U.S. citizen who is coming to the U.S. to teach, learn, or participate in scientific research. Barriers to entry or reentry based on political "profiling" (selective implementation of new restrictive policies depending on one's national, ethnic, or religious background) have called into question the entire international dimension of knowledge production in the U.S. Your visa could also be revoked if you have views that are even mildly critical of U.S. foreign policy. According to the American Civil Liberties Union (ACLU), Section 411 of the Patriot Act has been used to exclude foreign scholars because of their political views. Citing a "serious and growing threat to academic freedom," the ACLU issued a press release on March 16, 2005, announcing that it had filed a Freedom of Information Act request to investigate this matter further.

The case of Tariq Ramadan, a Swiss citizen and an influential public intellectual who writes on Islam and modernity, is instructive. After "careful vetting" by the University of Notre Dame, Tariq Ramadan was invited in 2003 to serve as the Henry B. Luce Professor of Religion, Conflict, and Peace Building at the Kroc Institute for International Peace Studies. Ramadan's visa was approved early in 2004, and his children were enrolled in local schools. However, at the request of the Department of Homeland Security and nine days before he was to depart for the United States, the State Department informed Ramadan that his visa had been revoked.[20] State Department representatives cited two sections of the Immigration and Nationality Act. The first section bars entry to those who have used a "position of prominence within any country to endorse or espouse terrorist activity." The second section cited those whose entry may have "potentially serious adverse foreign policy consequences for the United States."[21] Prior to this incident, Ramadan had visited the United States more than thirty times, including a fall 2003 trip during which he gave a lecture on European Muslims to diplomats and officials from the FBI and CIA at the U.S. State Department.[22] Despite concerted efforts by Ramadan, concerned scholars, and various human-rights and academic-freedom organizations, the decision was not reversed.[23]

Visa restrictions after 9/11 have sharply lowered the number of foreign students in the U.S. For example, applications of graduate students — who are critical to higher education in the U.S., especially in the sciences and engineering — dropped 28 percent in 2004 alone, though the decline slowed to 5 percent in 2005.[24] These restrictions also have serious economic and political consequences. The more than 570,000 foreign students in the U.S. pump more than $13 billion a year into the economy.[25] They also cause a public-relations problem, as the United States is alienating future leaders of other countries.

Although this crisis has eased as of 2005, those who are admitted to the U.S. are heavily monitored, and universities are required to submit regular reports on them to government agencies. There is hardly a university administrator involved in foreign-student affairs who has not banged her head against the wall while working with Student and Exchange Visitor Information System (SEVIS), mandatory information-tracking software set up to feed data to the Department of Homeland Security. Like many other government regulatory programs, SEVIS is a complex bureaucratic structure that is not very responsive to the rich diversity of university environments. The glitches and delays alone have wreaked havoc and made the lives of thousands of foreign students miserable, contributing to a significant decline in enrollment.[26]

Be careful what you teach. In September 2003, the House of Representatives unanimously passed HR 3077, which would establish an advisory board to monitor area-studies centers in order to ensure that they advance the "national interest" (see the Appendix). While the law would apply to all 123 centers funded under the federal Title VI program, the target is clearly the nation's 17 centers for Middle East studies. The AAUP, the ACLU, the Middle East Studies Association of North America (MESA), and most professional educational organizations have raised alarms about this unprecedented government invasion of the classroom. Among their concerns are the board's sweeping investigative powers, lack of accountability, and makeup, for it would be composed in part from two national security agencies. If HR 3077 is passed by the U.S. Senate, a government-appointed investigative body will be allowed to police the classroom by deciding, for example, what constitutes a "diverse" or "balanced" lecture. This would effectively replace professional academic standards with arbitrary political criteria.

HR 3077 brings to the surface the contradictory relationship between the academy and the government — one that, since the Second World War, has been primarily based on the exchange of money for expertise and training. On the one hand, financial largesse has been and continues to be the most powerful instrument in the hands of the state for shaping the production of knowledge. If the spending spree on U.S. campuses by the Department of Homeland Security is any indication, September 11 will probably be seen as having spurred government investment in science and technology, though not with the same intensity or the same benefit to primary research as the Soviet launch of Sputnik.[27] Indeed, there is no shortage of entrepreneurial administrators and faculty members milking this cow.[28]

On the other hand, government investment paradoxically creates an ambiguous space that allows for the emergence of critical perspectives.[29] Instructive here is Amy Newhall's crisp and gripping history of the ups and downs in the sometimes open, sometimes secret, but always symbiotic relationship between the academy and security agencies when it come to federally funded area-studies and language-acquisition programs. Newhall argues that the structural failure to teach foreign languages (especially the Less Commonly Taught Languages [LCTLs]) in the primary and secondary school system has led to a devil's bargain of sorts between the government, which has long used universities as a site to produce the experts it needs, and the academy, which has received from the government the necessary money to maintain area- and language-studies programs. This relationship was not without problems, especially as academics asserted the right to choose their own research questions and to voice their opinions. In the early 1970s, for example, the Nixon administration, stung by area-studies scholars' criticisms of its policy in Vietnam, sought to eliminate Title VI programs altogether, using arguments similar to those of advocates of HR 3077 upset by academics' criticism of U.S. policies in Iraq and of Israeli military occupation of Palestinian Lands. Since then, a clear pattern has emerged of giving security agencies, such as the Department of Defense, more and more power over the use of language-acquisition funds. Still, the devil's bargain is unraveling, Newhall concludes, as the government, in a very short-sighted move, decided after 9/11 to use the stick of control even though the only possible outcome of coercion is even greater shortages of qualified and informed experts. Such a shortage, of course, was one reason why the crisis occurred in the first place.

"A Clear and Present Danger": The Academy and Private Advocacy Groups

It is of signal importance that the storms of controversy currently sweeping American campuses are not a result of internal activism or clashes. Compared to the 1960s, campuses have been unusually quiet since 9/11, despite the significant popular opposition to the war on Iraq and the domestic policies of the Bush administration. Rather, the escalating tensions are a product of calculated and professionally organized external interventions by well-funded private advocacy groups intimately tied to the coalition of forces currently walking the corridors of power in Washington, D.C. In contrast to the McCarthy era, private groups — not the government — are playing the lead role in the campaigns to quarantine dissent, to dominate the framing of public discourse, and to re-channel the flows of knowledge production.

Take, for example, the release in 2002 of the report *Defending Civilization: How Our Universities Are Failing America and What Can Be Done About It*, by the American Council of Trustees and Alumni (ACTA).[30] Founded by Lynn Cheney (the former head of the National Endowment for the Humanities and spouse of Vice President Richard Cheney) and the Democratic senator Joseph Lieberman (Al Gore's vice-presidential candidate in 2000), among others, ACTA accused the universities of being the weak link in the war against terror and a potential fifth column.[31] The report contrasted the responses to 9/11 of American political leaders and U.S. citizens participating in public opinion polls with those of academics. It cautioned that "when a nation's intellectuals are unwilling to sustain its civilization" the enemy is emboldened.[32] Specifically, the report criticized universities for adding courses on "Islamic and Asian cultures" rather than "ensuring that students understand the unique contributions of America and Western civilizations."[33] As if the general hint at treason were not enough, an appendix to the report listed the names of 117 "un-American" professors, staff members, and students, and the offending statements they had allegedly made.

ACTA's report may have been precipitated by the events of 9/11, but the ideological agenda that informed it is familiar to anyone knowledgeable about the hard-fought battles on U.S. campuses during the so-called culture wars of the 1990s, which revolved around issues such as affirmative action, postmodernism, and "political correctness."[34] One of the iconic moments of that period was Lynn Cheney's opposition to the adoption of new national history standards for high-school textbooks that gave greater attention to the experiences of Native Americans, African Americans, and other historically oppressed groups.[35] Indeed, the true "Axis of Evil" for ACTA and similar private advocacy groups is not the foreign one composed of the "rogue" states of Iraq, Iran, and North Korea that President Bush outlined in his famous post-9/11 State of the Union address. Rather, it is a domestic one: the liberal government that taxes the self-reliant and spends on the socially undeserving; the liberal media and the entertainment industry, which lie and spread moral corruption everywhere; and the liberal universities that brainwash our young and fill them with hatred for their own country and for Western civilization as a whole. All three are blamed for bringing about what many of these groups perceive as the calamities that have befallen the United States in the twentieth century: the New Deal, the civil-rights and feminist movements, the anti–Vietnam War protests, and environmental regulations, among others.

The role of private groups in exerting external pressures on the academy may have been energized by the events of 9/11, but it is rooted in a four-decade-long, massive investment by right-wing groups in a national network of institutions: think tanks, policy institutes, grassroots faith-based organizations, law firms, social advocacy groups, corporate lobbying outfits, media outlets (radio, television, newspapers, the Internet), tracking organizations, and pressure groups of various kinds.[36] The long period of gestation is reflected in the strategic goal of ACTA: to fundamentally transform the structure, mission, and role of universities from the top down by achieving a commanding presence among trustees and alumni. Although keen on mobilizing donors (private and corporate) as well as government officials and agencies on the local, state, and national levels, ACTA operatives eschew the push for legislating political orthodoxy in favor of exerting pressure through the administrative structures of universities.[37] This long-term strategy seeks to turn back the clock to the time when conditions of "at-will" employment prevailed in institutions of higher education. Ironically, these conditions, often characterized by politically motivated, heavy-handed interference from above, gave impetus to the first major statement on academic freedom, in 1915 (see the chapter by Post in this volume). At stake is academics' hard-earned right to regulate the production of knowledge according to their own professional norms.

The attacks of September 11 created a very wide opening for these socially conservative, right-wing institutions to work hand-in-hand with the Bush administration to implement long-cherished goals on several fronts at once. In addition to groups like ACTA, two other distinct but related sets of organizations became part of a loose coalition crystallized by the events of 9/11: neoconservative and "muscular nationalist" policy advocacy groups primarily concerned with foreign policy issues, such as the Project for the New American Century; and pro-Israel lobbying groups, such as the American-Israel Public Affairs Committee, who been heavily invested since the early 1970s in policing what can be said about Israel on campus and in public discourse.

The organizations in this broad alliance that are involved in "take back the campus" campaigns are not of one mind or one strategy. They are all, however, politically connected, amply funded, and well organized. An important uniting factor, especially since 9/11, is unstinting support for the increasingly symbiotic relationship between the Bush administration and right-wing groups in Israel. This close relationship is based on disparate and sometimes conflicting motivations, ranging from a millennialist religious worldview promoting the ingathering of Jews in preparation for the Apocalypse to a view of Israel as a pioneer of defiant and uncompromising war against Islamic terrorism and of a foreign policy based on military preemption.[38] This partially explains these organizations' severe allergy to any criticisms of Israeli government policies in the media or the academy and the centrality of Israel-related issues to most of the campus controversies that have attracted national attention. There is also a technological glue of sorts: this loose coalition's increasingly coordinated national "take back the campus" campaigns are powered by the Internet. Web sites, e-mail lists, and chat groups have proven to be effective vehicles of information transfer and political mobilization that are almost unfettered by volume, time, and space. This makes it possible to exert enormous pressure on several target points quickly and simultaneously.

It is too early to tell whether the events of 9/11 will tip the balance of power in the culture wars in the academy. What is clear is that the challenges posed to academic freedom are structural, not cosmetic, in intent, as they emanate for the most part from worldviews that aim at fundamental changes in the mission of higher education. It is also clear that these challenges are not about to go away any time soon. In fact, instead of declining as the aftershocks of 9/11 have subsided, the campaigns have actually picked up steam with each passing year. The rest of this section considers three distinct but related types of challenges to academic freedom driven by the efforts of private advocacy groups: the targeting of specific individuals and curricular offerings, the attempt to codify political intervention through legislative initiatives at the state and federal levels, and the pressure to change the requirements of major funding organizations so as to delegitimize certain lines of inquiry and to promote others.

In the aftermath of 9/11, a variety of private advocacy groups initiated dozens of campaigns targeting specific professors, courses, and programs of study. The University of North Carolina at Chapel Hill, for instance, was sued in 2002 by a right-wing Christian group, the Family Policy Network, for assigning a brief introductory text about Islam to incoming students. The state legislature soon became involved and voted 64–10 to forbid the university to use public funds to teach the book.[39] With predictable hyperbole, Bill O'Reilly of Fox News said that assigning such a text was similar to forcing students to read Hitler's *Mein Kampf* in 1941.[40] The university held firm, and the court of appeals dismissed the suit, despite additional attacks by local politicians and some university trustees.[41]

Enforcing a narrow range of permissible speech through direct intervention instead of working through the university system usually does not yield good results. Generally speaking, the more impatient the strategy, the more resistance it meets from the academy. The least effective tactics are those that resort to ad hominem attacks and other techniques of intimidation. After 9/11, various private groups started openly recruiting students and faculty members to inform on their colleagues, who were then publicly "outed" on Web sites as un-American, anti-Semitic, or pro-terrorist.[42] As ACTA quickly found out, it was not its descriptions of universities as a fifth column but its list of 117 un-American professors that drew the greatest attention. Angry protests forced ACTA to take this list off its Web site and to delete it from the report *Defending Civilization*.[43] The infamous Campus Watch Web site was forced to do the same. After all, virulent smear campaigns against academics who enjoy good reputations among their peers are, ultimately, a sign of weakness, an admission that politically motivated denunciations have no purchase in the academy as a whole.

That said, intimidation campaigns have increased exponentially since 9/11, precipitating a rapid degradation of the academic climate on numerous campuses.[44] The worsening climate has been exacerbated by the weak response of university officials, who are constantly looking over their shoulders at corporate backers, politicians, alumni and individual donors, and mainstream media outlets. Controversies that attracted national attention — such as those at Columbia University, the University of Colorado, the University of California at Berkeley, and the University of North Carolina at Chapel Hill — have had an especially corrosive effect on the intellectual atmosphere in this country and set dangerous precedents that bode ill for the future of academic freedom.

As Joel Beinin argues in his chapter in this volume, the George W. Bush administration has rescued the marginal voices of the extreme right from the wings and put them on center stage. Although there have been numerous efforts to police discussion on the Middle East since the late 1960s, the post-9/11 moment has crystallized a new political context, ideological climate, and web of institutional alliances. This has greatly strengthened the hand of the individuals and organizations waging campaigns of intimidation against scholars and students connected culturally or academically to the Middle East or considered insufficiently pro-Israel. Specifically, Beinin traces the historical evolution of what he calls the "American Likud" — those who tend to see the world from the prism of the Israeli right wing — and analyzes the tactics they have used to stifle dissenting voices and impose a political orthodoxy on campuses.

The politically motivated attacks on several scholars of the Middle East at Columbia University — Joseph Massad, Hamid Dabashi, George Saliba, and Rashid Khalidi — are a case in point. Since 2001, enormous resources have been expended in making examples of these professors and in conducting two high-profile internal investigations (the first one initially kept secret) that are deeply injurious to the cause of academic freedom.[45] (See the Appendix for the NYCLU's letter to Columbia University president Lee Bollinger concerning the case of Joseph Massad.) The following quote from an investigative report in *The Nation* provides the flavor of the affair:

> The roots of the Columbia conflict can be traced back to campus political developments in 2001 and early 2002. In March 2002 a network of national Jewish organizations met to evaluate what they saw as an alarming rise in anti-Israel activity on campus. From those meetings emerged the Israel on Campus Coalition (ICC), which is a partnership of Hillel and the Charles and Lynn Schusterman Family Foundation. (The three organizations share a building in Washington.) According to a 2002 article for the *Jewish Telegraphic Agency*, a Jewish-oriented news service, top-flight talent was brought in to advise the ICC and assemble a battle plan. "Pro-Israel professionals from the elite consulting firm McKinsey & Company offered pro-bono services," the article noted. Those professionals created a document for the ICC arguing that "the primary goal for this year

should be to 'take back the campus' by influencing public opinion through lectures, the Internet and coalitions." The ICC — which recently received a $1,050,000 grant from the Schusterman Foundation, and whose speakers list includes Daniel Pipes — has an impressive array of "members": AIPAC, ADL, Americans for Peace Now and the Zionist Organization of America, among others.[46]

The capitulation of Columbia University president Lee Bollinger, a noted First Amendment scholar, to outside political pressures calling for investigations of faculty members based on politically motivated accusations that clearly lacked substance sent a chill throughout the academy. So did the earlier warning by Harvard University president Lawrence Summers, who, in a much publicized statement, effectively equated criticism of Israeli policies on campus with anti-Semitism.[47] In addition to creating a climate of intimidation and fear, these developments have accompanied demands for withdrawing funding from centers for Middle East studies and for increasing funding for chairs, fellowships, and programs in Israel studies.[48]

The Columbia professors are but a few of the many faculty members and students who have been subjected to humiliating and damaging investigations by their own universities. More often than not, these investigations were conducted not because there was substantive cause for concern but in order to deflate pressure from some donors, politicians, trustees, alumni, and media outlets mobilized by advocacy groups that are right-wing, pro-Israel, or both. Colleges and universities are privileged institutions, and the voices of faculty members, especially tenured professors, enjoy more protection than most others in society; still, the tepid responses of university officials invariably lead to a slippery slope of concessions that becomes more difficult to reverse over time. The smear campaigns at Columbia, for example, opened the door to a whole new level of attacks on academic freedom, such as the banning by the New York City Department of Education of another Columbia professor, Rashid Khalidi, from a teacher training program because of his reported views on Israeli government policies.[49] Jonathan R. Cole, a former provost and the dean of faculties at Columbia University from 1989 to 2003, strongly cautions university leaders about responding to outside attacks. He writes, "There are a few matters on which universities must stand on absolute principle. Academic freedom is one of them. If we fail to defend this core value, then we jeopardize the global preeminence of our Universities.... Whenever academic freedom is under fire we must rise to its defense with courage — and without compromise."[50]

The second major front that poses a challenge to academic freedom is the nationwide push by several private advocacy groups to codify political intervention in the academy through legislative initiatives on the federal and state levels. The two most important examples are HR 3077 in the Congress (discussed earlier) and the Academic Bill of Rights, which had been introduced in over a dozen states as of early 2005.[51] The net effect of these initiatives, if they all passed, would be to shift pedagogical authority from the academy to politicians and the courts. A statement by the AAUP charges that the campaign for the Academic Bill of Rights

> undermines the very academic freedom it claims to support. It threatens to impose administrative and legislative oversight on the professional judgment of faculty, to deprive professors of the authority necessary for teaching, and to prohibit academic institutions from making the decisions that are necessary for the advancement of knowledge.[52]

The language being deployed to sell these and other initiatives cynically appropriates the liberal terminology of the New Deal and civil-rights eras. Code words such as balance, fairness, diversity, accountability, tolerance, and, not least, academic freedom are used to justify the enforcement of a political orthodoxy that undermines these very values. This terminology abounds in the screeds by pro-Israel right-wing activists targeting Middle East studies and faculty members.[53] Identical terminology is used in the renewed debate on teaching evolution. For example, in over a dozen states, policy makers are considering proposals that seek to legislate the marginalization of the theory of evolution in science classes and to promote alternatives such as "intelligent design" and other creationist concepts.[54] According to an article in the *Washington Post*,

> Sen. Rick Santorum (R-Pa.), a Christian who draws on Discovery Institute material, drafted language accompanying the law that said

students should be exposed to "the full range of scientific views that exist." "Anyone who expresses anything other than the dominant worldview is shunned and booted from the academy," Santorum said in an interview. "My reading of the science is there's a legitimate debate. My feeling is let the debate be had."

In the same article, Stephen C. Meyer of the Discovery Institute describes the legislation as "an academic freedom proposal. What we would like to foment is a civil discussion about science. That falls right down the middle of the fairway of American pluralism.... We are interested in seeing that spread state by state across the country."[55] Considering the ideological imperatives behind this language, it is not entirely inconsistent that the same Santorum sought to limit debate when he announced in April 2003 that he intended to introduce legislation that would cut off federal funding to institutions of higher learning that allowed students or faculty members to openly criticize Israel, on the assumption that such criticism is necessarily anti-Semitic.

Exposing the ideological agenda and coordinated efforts behind these and other attempts at politically codifying the middle or balance point of the spectrum of knowledge on any issue is emphatically not an argument for insulating the academy from social forces espousing specific points of view or a claim that knowledge is generated solely by academic experts. That would be a guarantee of irrelevance and a breach of the larger aim of serving the public good, a task that can hardly be accomplished without a certain degree of responsiveness and accountability to the needs of society on the part of the academy.[56] However, it is difficult to sustain a rational and productive discussion when criticisms of U.S. or Israeli government policies are routinely stigmatized as treasonous or anti-Semitic. In the post-9/11 political climate, there is no field more radioactive than Middle East studies and nothing more frowned upon than expressions of support for Palestinian rights.[57] This is especially clear when it comes to the third front in the challenges to academic freedom by private advocacy groups: the successful pressures brought on the Ford and Rockefeller foundations to change their grant language.

Decisions by big foundations about what lines of inquiry to fund and what to ignore have a major influence on research trends and academic programs. In the heyday of the Cold War, the big

foundations, elite universities, and intelligence agencies constituted a veritable ménage à trois, at least when it came to language
and area studies.[58] Until fairly recently, however, the importance
of universities was such that there was a wide space for a politics of
"moral ambiguity," as John Lie calls it, which allowed area-studies
experts and other academics a certain freedom to ask their own
questions and even to take up public political positions that challenged U.S. foreign policies.[59] Foundations, elitist and patronizing
as some can be, have been instrumental in expanding this space,
especially during the civil-rights and anti–Vietnam War periods.

After 9/11, that distance seems to have closed considerably, as
evidenced by the new language that has been added to standard
grant letters. In the case of the Ford Foundation, for instance,
grantees must sign a document that forbids them to promote or
engage in "violence, terrorism, bigotry or the destruction of any
state." (See the Appendix.) Those familiar with public debates
on the Palestinian-Israeli conflict long before September 11 will
instantly recognize the phrasing, for it is identical to the public-
relations language of pro-Israel advocacy groups. This is no sur-
prise, for the new language came about as a response to criticisms
from (and then in lengthy consultations with) several major Jewish organizations upset that some of the human rights groups at
the 2001 World Conference Against Racism, Racial Discrimination, Xenophobia and Related Intolerance, in Durban, South
Africa, who criticized Israeli policies had received funds from the
Ford and Rockefeller foundations.[60]

This language introduces a different form of ambiguity, one
that can be used not to create a safe haven for counterhegemonic
projects but to filter them out. Can universities and colleges be
sued or lose their funds if a student or faculty member affiliated
with a sponsored project speaks out in favor of the right of indige-
nous people to use violence against a foreign military occupation?
Would a lecture advocating the right of Islamist organizations such
as the Hezbollah Party to participate in the Lebanese political system be construed as promoting terrorism, since Hezbollah is
officially listed as a terrorist organization by the U.S. State Department? Would signing a petition calling for divestment from companies involved in the Israeli military occupation be considered
a form of anti-Semitism, hence bigotry? Would research that argues
for the establishment of a binational state in Israel/Palestine

instead of a two-state solution be accused of promoting the destruction of a state? Several private elite universities objected to the foundations' new language, prompting some minor changes.[61] These changes were so minor, in fact, that in 2004 the ACLU, the major civil-rights organization in the U.S., turned down a $1 million grant from Ford and a $150,000 grant from Rockefeller. The ACLU press release stated that it was "a sad day when two of this country's most beloved and respected foundations feel they are operating in such a climate of fear and intimidation that they are compelled to require thousands of recipients to accept vague grant language which could have a chilling effect on civil liberties."[62]

Before 9/11, government constraints set off the loudest beeps on the academic-freedom radar screens of most individuals and organizations. After 9/11, I think it is fair to say, these radars should be retuned to track the prominent role of private advocacy groups, especially those engaged in enforcing the agendas of right-wing Christian and pro-Israel organizations on campus. For several reasons, the increasingly weighty involvement of these groups over the past decade poses a more complex if not greater challenge to the autonomy of the academy and the future of academic freedom than the specter of government intervention. For one thing, the lack of a unifying symbol, or at least one as convenient as "The Government," makes it very difficult to effectively mobilize faculty members and students in the face of multiple and simultaneous challenges from a variety of advocacy groups to academic appointments, programs of study, individual instructors, and legitimate forms of student activism on campus. Furthermore, private groups have, and rightly, numerous protections under the law and greater latitude of action when compared to governments that are, at least in theory, accountable to the people who elected them. Most important, perhaps, the privatization of knowledge, one aspect of which is the growing power of a managerial administrative structure at the expense of shared governance with the faculty and the student body, has rendered institutions of higher education more vulnerable than ever to intervention from without by powerful interest groups.[63] Corporations, donors, and advocacy groups have become adept at institutionalizing relations of dependence with this managerial class, mostly through financial and political means, in ways that are transforming the very structure and mission of higher education.

The Multiversity and the Privatization of Knowledge

When one is busy dodging sticks and stones, it is easy to forget that what is at stake in the battles for academic freedom is the survival of institutions of higher education as a regulated public trust. One's sense of shock at the level of coercion in the post-9/11 moment stands in inverse relationship to one's appreciation for the changing political economy of knowledge. Simply put, as the commercialization of knowledge expands, the space accorded to academic freedom contracts.

To understand the significance of the post-9/11 moment, therefore, it is important to locate it in the context of the rapid institutional transformation of the academy that began in earnest after the Second World War, when the United States emerged as the main military and economic power in a devastated world. And that was just the beginning of a golden era of unprecedented economic expansion that lasted two decades. The rise of managerial capitalism, which replaced family-run empires with a rationalized hierarchy of experts — a development that university administrations would later be patterned after — was especially fortunate for the academy. Large sums of money from the government and corporations flowed into public and private research universities, which were popularly perceived as knowledge factories that produced the human resources, technological advances, and ideological environment that undergirded the United States' economic and military prowess.

Kathleen J. Frydl ties the many strands of this volume together by exploring the relationship between the changing meanings of academic freedom and the changing institutional structure and political economy of the academy after the Second World War. She analyzes how the University of California, the trendsetting model of the new "multiversity," experienced two formative and iconic episodes: the loyalty-oath controversy of 1949 and the Free Speech Movement in the 1960s. Even though both were popularly seen as extramural battles over free speech, they actually reflected fundamental transformations in the student body and in the services provided by the university.

According to Frydl, universities were pried open after the Second World War in two ways. First, they came to reflect more closely the demographic landscape of the United States, and second, they became much more integrated with larger market

Robert Post is David Boies Professor of Law at the Yale Law School. From 1992 to 1994 he was general counsel of the American Association of University Professors (AAUP), and he is now a member of Committee A of the AAUP. He is the author of *Constitutional Domains* and *Prejudicial Appearances* and the editor of *Censorship and Silencing: Practices of Cultural Regulation*. He is a recognized expert in the area of First Amendment jurisprudence.

Amy Newhall teaches in the Department of Near Eastern Studies at the University of Arizona. She also serves as the executive director of the Middle East Studies Association of North America.

Philippa Strum is Director of the Division of United States Studies at the Woodrow Wilson International Center for Scholars, and Emerita Broeklundian Professor of Political Science at the City University of New York. She is the author of numerous prize-winning books and articles, including *Women in the Barracks: The VMI Case and Women's Rights*; *When the Nazis Came to Skokie: Freedom for the Speech We Hate*; *Privacy: The Debate in the United States Since 1945*; *Louis D. Brandeis: Justice for the People*; *The Supreme Court and "Political Questions"*; and *Presidential Power and American Democracy*.

forces that would prove very difficult to resist. Universities were no longer the preserve of a tiny elite, as had been the case a century before, nor were they limited to the classical curriculum of liberal arts and the sciences. The multiversity became home to a much larger and more diverse student body, and its mission expanded to serve a stunningly wide range of intellectual, research, and service objectives. The golden age of the research multiversity also signaled increasing dependence on joint ventures with corporations and on government funds for research projects and academic programs. Paradoxically, it also made possible a socially engaged process of knowledge production that spoke truth to power, especially at the height of the Vietnam War. Within this larger historical context, Frydl argues, policing thought might be an ugly and painful business, but the hidden and mundane process of establishing sovereignty over research, teaching, and learning matters more.

There is by now a large amount of scholarship on the impact of the commercialization of knowledge on the academy, on how corporate culture has permeated the top administrative ranks of the university, and on the ways neoliberal assumptions are shaping the consciousness of the young generation of students.[64] But two brief personal vignettes will suffice to convey, by way of texture and symbolism, the nature of the new environment. My first semester as an employee of the University of Pennsylvania in the late 1980s opened with speeches by the university's president and provost to newly hired assistant professors like me. The president gestured elegantly in an attempt to persuade the young crowd — very much aware of the dictum "publish or perish" — that it could reach great heights in both teaching and research, neither at the expense of the other. This rosy and uplifting rhetoric did not prepare us well for the devastatingly honest and straightforward first line of the next speaker. The provost extended his arm, pointed his finger, and, after making a sweep from one end of the room to the other, exclaimed with authority: "There is one thing you have to remember about the University of Pennsylvania: we are a $1.2 billion corporation!"

During Parents' Weekend that same year, I sat near the statue of Benjamin Franklin — a proud symbol of Quaker tolerance, the scientific method, critical thinking, and revolutionary politics — strategically located between the administration building and the library on the main campus lawn, observing students giving tours to their proud parents. I saw one of the students point at a large, plain metal sculpture of the ubiquitous 1960s peace sign planted on the grass lawn and say: "And this is the Mercedes sign in front of the Van Pelt Library." There could not be a more stark contrast between the two contenders for sovereignty over the house of knowledge: the corporation, on the one hand, and the subversive symbol of the anti–Vietnam War movement, on the other. Of course, it is not really much of a contest: the former was already hegemonic in the imagination of the student who, as it turned out, was hurriedly walking to the Wharton School of Business, whose resources and reputation have come to dwarf those of its poor liberal-arts cousin. The role of the university as the producer of knowledge for the greater good, symbolized by Benjamin Franklin — one of the founding fathers of United States as well as of the University of Pennsylvania — is in danger of becoming a thing of the past.[65]

These two vignettes sketch the parameters of the conditions of possibility for higher education in the twenty-first century. As Frank Newman and his colleagues argue, the special privileges that universities and colleges have long enjoyed — such as tax exemption and state funding, autonomy and academic freedom, and public respect and trust — all depend on a host of historically layered expectations about their perceived contributions to the greater social good.[66] But the meaning of "social good" and the ways these institutions have been structured to deliver it have changed over time. In class terms, these institutions, whose modest initial goal was to deliver cultivated future civic and church leaders from among the elite, became factories producing a new middle class of experts, technocrats, and scientists, and were then, until recently, vehicles of social mobility for hitherto locked-out groups, such as the working classes, women, and people of color.

The latter no longer obtains. Institutions of higher education are going through a dizzyingly fast, intense, and irreversible transformation. Pushed farther and farther away from the intimate embrace of public regulation, universities and colleges are finding themselves in a merciless open market, very much like phone and utility companies of old.[67] They are engaged in cutthroat competition and driven by the bottom line. Some university administrators act and are paid like CEOs; many faculty members steer away from controversy and learn how to become entrepreneurs to further their careers; and students are surrounded by shops, restaurants, and chain bookstores in shopping-mall campuses, where they are encouraged and expected to negotiate a consumer-culture environment whose motto is "Keep the customer satisfied." Meanwhile, knowledge is being commercialized and sold on the open market as a product for the private good by a fantastically large array of nonprofit public and private institutions and for-profit multinational corporations operating both in brick-and-mortar settings and in cyberspace.[68] This is all taking place in an increasingly deregulated environment, in which politicians clamor for accountability and flexibility, corporations and special-interest groups for control of the product, and academic administrators for more autonomy and money. Can critical thought — the beating heart of academic freedom — survive in such a corporatized environment?

Although the system of higher education in the United States is still, by and large, the best in the world, the concerns outlined above are real, and ignoring them is folly. In the words of David Kirp,

> Many institutions have abandoned the high ground that has given higher education a claim on the public resources of the society, forgetting that their purpose is speaking truth to power.... With Public Universities relying less on state funds, and for-profit schools like DeVry and Phoenix coming into their own, the very idea that institutions of higher learning have a mission beyond promoting their members' individual private good can no longer be taken for granted.... How much academic freedom is available to professors at a place like the University of Virginia's business school, who cannot use course materials that they have prepared for executive training courses in their regular classes? What is the meaning of the community of scholars when a single corporation can patent the research products of an entire department, as Novartis was essentially able to do at Berkeley?[69]

As the University of Pennsylvania speeches mentioned above symbolize, there is a wide gap between the rhetoric of public purpose and the reality of private good. Typical of the consequences of privatization everywhere, there is a growing class and race divide, as current admissions policies favor affluent children with access to good schools at the grade- and high-school levels.[70] In a sober and restrained analysis, Frank Newman, Lara Couturier, and Jamie Scurry summarize the situation as follows:

> The rhetoric describes devotion to student learning, while in reality the student bears principal responsibility.... The rhetoric describes devotion to teaching, while in reality...faculty are devoted to research, publishing, and outside consulting. The rhetoric calls for service to the community, while attention is focused on improving rankings.... The rhetoric proclaims the importance of fundamental and trustworthy scholarship that serves society, while in fact impartiality is undercut by growing corporate control of research and faculty conflicts of interest.[71]

The commercialization of education is producing a culture of conformity decidedly hostile to the university's traditional role as a haven for informed social criticism. In this larger context, academic freedom is becoming a luxury, not a condition of possibility for the pursuit of truth.

Knowledge production driven by market forces that reflect the hierarchy of power slowly restructures institutions of higher learning by promoting certain lines of inquiry and quietly burying others. Over time, the process becomes hegemonic, in the sense that unwritten rules about what is fundable and what is not are bureaucratically internalized and modalities of self-censorship act as a filter for condoning or shunning proposed research, teaching, and extramural utterance. For example, most scholars of the Middle East, especially graduate students and untenured professors, understand very well that there is a heavy price to pay for publicly supporting Palestinian national aspirations and very little support for research projects that do not fit into the policy-driven priorities of most funding agencies.

The similarities between this self-censorship in Middle East studies and that of teaching evolution in high schools are striking. While it is very unfortunate that many local boards of education are attempting to prevent the teaching of evolution, an even greater concern is that large numbers of teachers who believe in evolution and who are free to teach it still choose not to discuss it in class. "It is just too much trouble," said one such teacher in reference to the repressive social atmosphere.[72] It is well to keep in mind here the power of popular beliefs in U.S. society. The United States, in fact, is an oddity among all industrialized nations in that one-half of its population explicitly rejects evolution, compared to only a minuscule number elsewhere. This speaks volumes about a public culture that is becoming less tolerant of the worldviews that sustain practices such as academic freedom. Relevant here is the finding, in the largest study of its kind, that the overwhelming majority of high-school students in the United States are ignorant of the contents of the First Amendment. More troubling, when the exact text was read to them, three out of four said that it goes "too far" in the rights it guarantees.[73]

In this environment of repressive political culture and tightening economic pressures, there can be no adequate defense of academic freedom based on what Kathleen J. Frydl calls "freedom from" strategies. Academic freedom has to be invested with new meanings, and new strategies of "freedom to" need to be articulated. There is no alternative to political engagement by faculty members, students, and institutions of higher education as a whole if they are to preserve some autonomy and shape the radical and ongoing transformation of higher education. But how is this to be done?

Rethinking Academic Freedom
The legal structures, philosophical foundations, and ethical practices of academic freedom have taken on different roles and meanings over time. Over the course of the twentieth century, especially after the Second World War, social and intellectual movements as well as legal developments expanded and confused the meanings of academic freedom: courts became involved, especially on matters relating to individual rights of academics and free-speech issues; skepticism about objectivity and truth increased; and universities became complex and varied institutions much more intimately connected to corporations and government agencies.

When talking about academic freedom, one needs to be specific about the institution and the kind of activity in question and the location of the individual within the institution. It matters whether one is talking about private or public universities, nonprofit or for-profit systems, or the variety of corporate and multinational organizations that offer degrees, certificates, and licenses.

The invocation of professional norms may be the best defense for the freedom of research and teaching by faculty members but not necessarily the most effective when it comes to extramural utterance, especially for students and staff members. There are conflicting interests between tenured and nontenured faculty members and certainly between the academic freedom of the individual and the special freedoms attached to academic institutions. What visions of academic freedom can we defend and what strategies should we adopt in light of the structural changes to the academy over the past few decades, as well as the challenges of the post-9/11 moment?

Philippa Strum's analysis of cases heard before the U.S. Supreme Court in this volume shows that the individual right of faculty members to free speech under the First Amendment has become an important, albeit still ambiguous, part of the legal structure of academic freedom. In a concise, accessible, and smoothly structured exposition of case law, Strum persuasively argues that the Supreme Court has thus far upheld this right by using the pragmatic rationale of "social benefit," but only when it comes to public institutions. It is also unclear whether this right resides in individuals or institutions, as the court has frequently referred to both. She warns that in light of the fairly brief history of academic freedom in American constitutional law, the very conservative makeup of the current Supreme Court, and the increasing weight of security considerations during a time of war, the very same pragmatic bent can be used to politically redefine social benefit to sacrifice liberty for security and critical thinking for national unity. At the same time, Strum argues strongly that academic freedom can and must be seen as an individual right, especially if we are to include private institutions as well as students and independent scholars under the First Amendment umbrella.

In his chapter, Robert Post, who served as legal adviser for the AAUP's academic freedom committee, focuses on the historical moment at the turn of the twentieth century when the basic structural foundations of academic freedom were laid. Post argues that, just as justice is best advanced by judges who are technically government employees yet have the right to freely exercise their judgment according to the law, not the whim of the government, knowledge as a public good is best served by the unfettered pursuit by faculty members of three key areas: research and writing, teaching, and extramural utterance. Professional academic standards and norms, in short, constitute the shield that protects academic freedom while internally regulating and constraining it. These structures have succeeded so brilliantly that academic freedom is now part of the institutional woodwork of higher education. Paradoxically, their very success has made them more limited in scope, orthodox in content, and estranged from a popular imagination that, in a historical wrong turn, planted the flag of academic freedom on the steps of the First Amendment.

The invocation of professional norms may indeed be the most effective immediate defense. But does not this strategy privilege those who have already been admitted into the guild of tenured professors, reinforcing a hierarchy of knowledge production that can undermine the "public good"? And is not this defense attractive to university administrators eager to draw an impermeable line between the "free speech" of students and the academic-freedom issues of faculty members? And what about public universities and the epistemological problem of how norms are defined?

In her contribution to the volume, Judith Butler argues that if professional norms have a history, as they must, then academic freedom is the product of ongoing critical scrutiny and reinterpretation of the norms themselves, combined with an ethical practice that negotiates among multiple norms in contestation with each other. It is important, she continues, to deconstruct and historicize the notion of professional norms in order to provide greater freedom for extramural political speech, so that the lines between areas of expertise and political commentary, between individual rights and institutional prerogative, and between the public good and the institutional autonomy are not too rigidly drawn.

It is difficult to imagine real academic freedom existing in the absence of the skeptical approach to professional norms that lies at the very heart of what it means to be an academic. The fluidity and intellectual migrations that Butler insists on are key to reconfiguring the concept of academic freedom so it can meet the challenges of a new wave of coercion and privatization that is sweeping not just academia but the whole world. This fluidity, in fact, is already apparent in the heated debates within and between disciplines about what questions ought to be asked and what methods ought to be used to answer them. These correction mechanisms of academic inquiry have always been part of the intellectual process, and resistance to them provides a reminder that professional norms can sometimes constrain freedom of thought more than administrative and external pressures. But to what degree is it possible to conduct a relentless critique of enlightenment categories of knowledge — such as the assumption that truth exists and can be objectively discovered — that give academic freedom as we know it its specific structures, while maintaining professional standards stable enough to act as pillars for academic freedom? If the ambiguities extend too far beyond the boundaries of what it might be politically feasible to defend as the autonomous territory of professional inquiry, what compass would we use to navigate that terrain? At stake is the very language that frames perceptions, codes knowledge, and determines the possibilities of political action.

Butler essentially agrees with Joan W. Scott, the former head of the Committee on Academic Freedom of the AAUP, who argues persuasively for the need to put ethical praxis at center stage. "Academic freedom," Scott writes, "lives in the ethical space between an ideal of the autonomous pursuit of understanding and the specific historical, institutional, and political realities that limit such pursuits."[74] Scott deliberately substitutes "understanding" for "truth" in order to stake a middle ground between knowledge and interpretation. It is precisely in that distance between contradictory spaces — ideal/history, knowledge/power, disciplinary norms/criticism — that academic freedom operates.[75] Academic freedom, in other words, is built, reinforced, and changed, one controversial case at a time, through an ethical practice that eschews dogmatism and appreciates the historical specificity of the moment.

For Scott's bridging proposal not to err too much on the side of conservative pragmatism and accommodation, a particular understanding of what it means to be an intellectual needs to be emphasized: Edward Said's understanding of academic freedom as a "ceaseless quest for knowledge and freedom" based on an autocritique of one's own national identity, even if, as in the case of the Palestinians, of which he is one, national self-determination has yet to be achieved.[76] Adopting the image of the academic as a traveler who "depends not on power, but on motion," instead of that of the academic as potentate who "survey[s] all ... with detachment and mastery," he defines academic freedom "as an invitation to give up on identity in the hope of understanding and perhaps even assuming more than one." "We must always view the academy," he continues, "as a place to voyage in, owning none of it, but at home everywhere in it."[77] This insistence on a compassionate, universalist, and ultimately humanist autocritique has the virtue of anchoring ethical praxis inside the academic world while guiding political action outside of it.

Conclusion

It is unlikely that a single conception or strategy of academic freedom can be equally effective in the ever-changing political and institutional terrains of higher education in the United States. In light of the concerted attacks on academic freedom and the great vulnerabilities stemming from the commercialization of higher education, it is clearly no longer sufficient for tenured and tenure-track faculty members to circle the wagons and cling to long-standing structures of cognitive authority. At the same time, it is not feasible to abandon the effective defense of professional autonomy so as to line up with other individuals, inside and outside of the academy, under the ideologically more intuitive but legally and politically leaky umbrella of the First Amendment.

Fortunately, time moves very slowly inside the academy, and the culture of academic freedom has become firmly embedded legally, ethically, and politically over the past century. Institutions of higher learning occupy a privileged and protected place in our society, and it seems unlikely that they will easily give up their hard-earned autonomy and freedoms. Academic freedom may be violently shaken by willfully blind and destructive political alliances, such as that between neoconservatives and "End of Days" evangelical Christian groups, but it will likely outlast them.

There is still time to have a civil and reasoned discussion that can result in a new compact between the academy, society, and the government, before the forces of commercialization and political coercion become too toxic for the body politic. Ideally, the government would support education for all, instead of pushing universities and colleges down the river of privatization without so much as a boat, let alone a paddle; private capital would recognize that creativity and economic development require autonomy, freedom, and the free flow of information instead of ownership for a profit; administrators would accept meaningful shared governance with faculty members and students to create the best conditions for free inquiry and learning instead of pursuing the top-down managerial style (not to mention the privileges) of CEOs and engaging in cutthroat competition in service of the rich and powerful; and, finally, academics could retain their privileges by earning the public trust through an ethical pursuit of knowledge instead of hanging the sign "Have Knowledge, Will Travel."

But time is running out, and the tragedy of 9/11 has been cynically manipulated to create an environment that is less and less conducive to rational and civil discussion. The stick has never been wielded so heavily, massively, and effectively; and never has it been so freely available to so many private advocacy and special-interest groups ready to sacrifice the public good for their own narrowly conceived interests. Most important, never has the state/foundation/corporation/donor nexus been so intimate, so politically conservative, so kinetically charged and so woven into the institutional and cultural fabric of university administrations. At a moment when coercion is facilitated by privatization and vice versa, the neoliberal "free-market-of-ideas" framework offers no adequate defense against the attacks of antiliberal forces.

We are at a crossroads and need to think carefully about how to reconfigure the concept and praxis of academic freedom so that it can serve just as well in a world where war and information control have become the norm and peace and the free pursuit of knowledge the exception. At stake is the continuation of the academy as the bastion of informed, independent, and alternative perspectives crucial to a better understanding of the world we live in. If teachers and students cannot think and speak freely, who can? True, academics in most fields are not as openly and aggressively policed as those who study the Middle East, who are a small and marginal part of the academy. Also true, richly endowed universities are not threatened with extinction or as vulnerable to buyout as many others, especially those that serve the most needy. Still, what happens to Middle East studies faculty members or to small community colleges can have dangerous consequences. Narrowing access to knowledge and silencing the voices of dissent and critical thought through the stick of coercion or the carrot of funding creates chilling ripple effects. Complacency is even more dangerous. If we stand on the sidelines hoping not to be hit, we deprive society of independent and alternative perspectives.

Much depends on what academics and academic institutions do at this juncture. Regardless of whether academic freedom is an individual or an institutional right, one thing is clear: academics and the academy have to respond to the current challenges as a community. Systemic challenges require a systemic response. They also have to put the "social" back into the concept of social benefit and the "public" into public trust, for both are being eclipsed by a neoliberal vision that puts knowledge in the service of profit and the pursuit of the private good.

The question is not simply how to preserve academic freedom but rather what to do with it. Academics need to consistently engage students, parents, and citizens about why academic freedom is important to them and why it is not simply a guild issue of preserving special privileges for an elite. Academics and their institutions must open the gates and meet the world instead of locking down and hoping the storm will soon end. It is time to have a full and open discussion about the role of universities in this troubled world and to engage as public intellectuals the domestic and international movements for civil rights, democracy, and justice. Defending academic freedom is but a part of a larger effort to make the world a better place to live. Let us speak and act before it is too late.

NOTES

I am grateful to Philippa Strum, Kathleen J. Frydl, Mary Burgan, Ramona Naddaff, John Lie, Erika Gubrium, Lisa Hajjar, Joel Beinin, and Rashid Khalidi for their helpful comments on earlier drafts of this essay.

1. See below for an extended discussion of this subject. HR 3077 died in the U.S. Senate Committee on Health, Education, Labor and Pensions during the 108th Congress. As this book was going to press, the resolution was reintroduced in essentially the same form as HR 509 in the 109th Congress.

2. The Uniting and Strengthening America by Providing Appropriate Tools Required to Intercept and Obstruct Terrorism (USA Patriot) Act of 2001 passed in the Senate on October 11, 2001, and became law on October 26, leaving little time for lawmakers to read this act.

3. For a historical overview of free-speech issues at times of crisis, see Geoffrey R. Stone, *Perilous Times: Free Speech in Wartime from the Sedition Act of 1798*

to the War on Terrorism (New York: Norton, 2004). The extraordinarily long list of repressive but often short-lived measures imposed on the U.S. population is sobering and, in many ways, makes the post-9/11 period look tame in comparison. Time will tell, but the powerful technologies of surveillance and control available to governments these days, the Bush administration's obsession with secrecy, the decades-long crusade by the core constituency of this presidency to impose a radical right-wing agenda, and the unprecedented projection of U.S. military power in a unipolar world are but a few of the factors that have the potential to cause serious and long-term damage to civil liberties, both domestically and internationally.

4. The most infamous examples are the drum beats about weapons of mass destruction in Iraq and the systematic attempts to link Saddam Hussein to September 11. The effectiveness of this one-two punch despite abundant evidence to the contrary is such that even in 2005 a majority of Americans believed that the government of Saddam Hussein was behind the plot of September 11 and that it possessed weapons of mass destruction. An example of a similar campaign on the domestic front is the one unleashed by President George W. Bush during his inaugural address on January 20, 2005: to convince the U.S. public that the Social Security system is facing imminent collapse and that the best way to fix it for the poor, the middle classes, and African Americans is through the establishment of private savings accounts. The goal is to push through a program of privatization that would destroy the New Deal society and replace it with an "ownership" society. For the extreme lengths the current administration is willing to go to in selling Social Security reform, see Paul Krugman, "Kansas On My Mind," *New York Times*, February 25, 2005. Krugman draws on two works that explore how public debates are framed: George Lakoff, *Don't Think of an Elephant: Know Your Values and Frame the Debate; The Essential Guide for Progressives* (White River Junction, VT: Chelsea Green Publishing, 2004), and Thomas Frank, *What's the Matter with Kansas? How Conservatives Won the Heart of America* (New York: Metropolitan, 2004). For a detailed report on one of the Bush administration's strategies to frame news coverage on television, see David Barstow and Robin Stein, "Under Bush, a New Age of Prepackaged News," *New York Times*, March 13, 2005.

5. Stone correctly reminds us, "Declaring a 'war' on terrorism was more than a rhetorical device to rally the public, for it enabled the administation to assert the extraordinary powers traditionally reserved to the executive in wartime" (*Perilous Times*, pp. 554–55). That Bush went to claim that "the war against terrorism will never end" raises the frightening possibility that these extraordinary powers will be abused and not given up easily, as has happened before in the history of national crises in the United States.

6. This assumption was best articulated in Bush's inaugural address of January

20, 2004. Another typical phrase is "a universal right granted by a Higher Being."

7. Revealing in this regard is the detailed investigative report on how the Bush administration is attempting to foment an "Islamic Reformation" by quietly funneling tens of millions of dollars to "Islamic radio and TV shows, coursework in Muslim schools, Muslim think tanks, political workshop, or other programs that promote moderate Islam" in over two dozen countries. A key player in what is being called the Muslim World Outreach strategy is Karen Hughes, who was Bush's communications guru and is now the new head of the State Department's public diplomacy office. David E. Kaplan, "Hearts, Minds, and Dollars," *U.S. News and World Report*, April 25, 2005.

8. A scroll through the press-release archives of the Council on American-Islamic Relations (CAIR) website is very instructive here: http://www.cair-net.org/default.asp?Page=archive&theType=NR. On May 2, 2005, for example, CAIR called on political leaders in the U.S. to repudiate the statement by Pat Robertson that Muslims should not serve in the cabinet or the judiciary. The demonization of Muslims, Arabs, and Palestinians is generated by the increasingly intimate alliance between many pro-Israel advocacy groups and Christian evangelical organizations. This alliance has been the subject of numerous publications and documentaries. For an overview, see the segment of the Public Broadcasting Station show *NOW with Bill Moyers* called "God and Politics in the Holy Land," which aired on February 20, 2004. A case study of the political implications of this alliance on the Palestinian-Israeli conflict is Gershom Gorenberg, *The End of Days: Fundamentalism and the Struggle for the Temple Mount* (Oxford: Oxford University Press, 2002).

9. Useful here are the reflections on this issue in Judith Butler, "Explanation and Exoneration, or What We Can Hear," in *Precarious Life: The Powers of Mourning and Violence* (London: Verso, 2004), especially pp. 2–4 and 15.

10. See, for example, Eric Alterman, "Bush's War on the Press," *The Nation*, May 9, 2005.

11. Examples of pre-9/11 constraints on academic freedom include the Solomon Amendment of 1996, which penalizes colleges and universities that ban military recruiters or the Reserve Officers' Training Corps (ROTC) from campus; the 1996 federal statute making it a crime to offer "material support" (the term is not defined) to terrorists; the Federal Bureau of Investigation's "Carnivore" Program; and export controls on software. Some of these are discussed in the American Association of University Professors, "Academic Freedom and National Security in a Time of Crisis," *Academe* 89.6 (2003), p. 56. Also, see Amy Newhall's chapter in this volume, which provides a larger context, especially her discussion of the establishment of the National Security Education Program (NSEP). For more information, particularly about surveillance of the Arab and

Muslim communities in the United States, see Susan M. Akram and Kevin R. Johnson, "The Targeting of Arabs and Muslims," and Samih Farsoun, "Roots of the American Anti-Terrorism Crusade," in Elaine C. Hagopian (ed.), *Civil Rights in Peril: The Targeting of Arabs and Muslims* (Chicago: Haymarket, 2004).

12. See David Price's analysis of the little-noticed Section 18 of the Intelligence Authorization Act (2004), which budgets $4 million to the Pat Roberts Intelligence Scholars Program, whose purpose is to close the "human intelligence" gap identified as critical in preventing future terrorist attacks. The specifics, however, point to a grave breach of the open process of knowledge acquisition. The names of students and scholars recruited into the program are kept secret from university administrations, as are the names of the campuses at which they work. David H. Price, "The CIA's Campus Spies," *Counterpunch*, March 12, 2005. Price is also the author of *Threatening Anthropology: McCarthyism and the FBI's Surveillance of Activist Anthropologists* (Durham, NC: Duke University Press, 2004). In a followup article, Price argues that one goal of this program and of another one funded in December 2004, the Intelligence Community Scholars Program, might be to ensure that intelligence agencies do not relinquish control over the intellectual development of their assets during their college years, so as to decrease the chances of these assets' developing "undesirable" political opinions. See David Price, "CIA Skullduggery in Academia," *Counterpunch*, May 21, 2005.

13. American Association of University Professors, "Academic Freedom and National Security in a Time of Crisis," p. 57. Emphasis added. As noted in this report, the Patriot Act undermines several protections enacted to ensure the privacy of citizens and noncitizens alike, such as the Family Educational Rights and Privacy Act, the Electronic Communications Privacy Act, and the Foreign Intelligence Surveillance Act.

14. The resolution was adopted on January 29, 2003. See http://www.ala.org/ala/washoff/WOissues/civilliberties/theusapatriotact/alaresolution.htm.

15. See, for example, the Fox news report from May 7, 2003: http://www.foxnews.com/story/0,2933,86167,00.html.

16. Libya was on the list of sanctioned countries but was removed in 2004. See document GN071904.doc at http://www.ustreas.gov.

17. Jess Bravin, "Nobel Laureate Sues U.S. Over Ban," *Wall Street Journal*, November 1, 2004. According to this report, Cuban authors have suffered the most: "According to the university press association, suspended or cancelled publications include a book on Cuban archaeology to be published by the University of Alabama Press, a Cornell University Press edition of *Field Guide to the Birds of Cuba* and an *Encyclopedia of Cuban Music* from Temple University Press."

18. Barry Bergman, "Research Under Fire," *Berkeleyan*, January 26, 2005.

19. For an overview of tensions between scientists and the Bush administration, see Andrew C. Revkin, "Bush vs. the Laureates: How Science Became a Partisan Issue," *New York Times*, October 19, 2004.

20. Stephen Kinzer, "Muslim Scholar Loses U.S. Visa as Query is Raised," *New York Times*, August 26, 2004.

21. Tom Coyne, "Revoked Visa Bars Muslim Scholar at Notre Dame," Associated Press, August 25, 2004.

22. Deborah Sontag, "Mystery of the Islamic Scholar Who Was Barred by the U.S.," *New York Times*, October 6, 2004.

23. See Tariq Ramadan, "Scholar Under Siege Defends his Record," *Chicago Tribune*, August 31, 2004, "Too Scary for the Classroom?" *New York Times*, September 1, 2004, and the letter from the AAUP, http://www. aaup.org/newsroom/press/2004/Ramadan.htm.

24. "Still Fewer Foreigners Applying to American Graduate Schools," Associated Press, March 9, 2005. This has followed three years of decline, after a decade of increasing applications. See also Justin Pope, "Fewer Foreign Grad Students Enroll in U.S.," Associated Press, November 4, 2004.

25. "US Loses Foreign Students to Post-9/11 Competition," Reuters, March 24, 2005.

26. A simple correction can take months to process, leaving students in the lurch. For more information see the American Association of University Professors, "Academic Freedom and National Security," pp. 49–51. Many universities charge foreign students a fee for this "service," in essence making them pay for their own surveillance. See, for example, the case of University of Florida: http://www.alligator.org/edit/news/issues/stories/040407gauprev.html.

27. According to Steven Mikulan, "DHS's growing sugar-daddy role on American campuses . . . has begun to leave a deep boot print on academia. Primed with a $70 million scholarship and research budget, DHS represents the biggest intrusion into Americans' intellectual life by security agencies since the height of the Cold War." Mikulan also notes that unlike in the Cold War period, when the "CIA surreptitiously worked its magic" on U.S. campuses, the DHS's influence is a "broad-daylight affair." In September 2003, for example, the DHS funded one hundred fellowships to undergraduate and graduate students, who were expected to work for the agency later. Carnegie Mellon received $100 million, and the University of Southern California received a $12 million three-year grant to establish one of several DHS facilities across the United States. Steven Mikulan, "University of Fear: How the Department of Homeland Security Is Becoming a Big Man on Campus," *LA Weekly*, April 2, 2004.

28. For example, see the *Journal of Homeland Security and Emergency Management*, published by Berkeley Electronic Press, which was established by three

Boalt Hall School of Law professors at the University of California at Berkeley: http://www.bepress.com/jhsem/. See also the Web site of the National Academic Consortium for Homeland Security, which has a membership of over two hundred fifty colleges and universities: http://homelandsecurity.osu.edu/NACHS/.

29. John Lie, "Moral Ambiguity, Disciplinary Power, and Academic Freedom," *Bulletin of Concerned Asian Scholars* 29.1 (1997), pp. 30–33.

30. Jerry L. Martin and Anne D. Neal, *Defending Civilization: How Our Universities Are Failing America and What Can Be Done About It* (Washington, D.C.: American Council of Trustees and Alumni, 2001). The section on ACTA in this chapter has benefited from the research of Osamah Khalil.

31. http://www.goacta.org. ACTA was founded in 1995. Its stated goal is to "mobilize concerned alumni, trustees, and education leaders across the country on behalf of academic freedom, excellence, and accountability at our colleges and universities." Out of ACTA came the conservative National Scholars Association, which played a public role in the culture wars of the 1990s.

32. Martin and Neal, *Defending Civilization*, p. 7. The report referred to a 1933 Oxford Student Union debate on "whether it was moral for Britons to fight for king and country." The authors claimed that the result of the debate emboldened Adolf Hitler by convincing him that the West would "not fight for its survival."

33. *Ibid.*

34. These issues will not be discussed in any detail in this introduction. For a full consideration of how these battles have led to the rethinking of academic freedom, see Louis Menand (ed.), *The Future of Academic Freedom* (Chicago: University of Chicago Press, 1996).

35. Gary B. Nash, Charlotte A. Crabtree, and Ross E. Dunn, *History on Trial: Culture Wars and the Teaching of the Past* (New York: Knopf, 1997).

36. For social conservatives and militant nationalists, the turning point was the tumultuous 1960s, which witnessed the failed campaign of Barry Goldwater and the antiwar, civil-rights, and environmental movements. For the pro-Israel lobbying groups, who are also playing a lead role in policing thought on campus, the turning points were Israel's sweeping victories in the 1967 war and its ensuing "special relationship" with the United States.

37. The transformation of the State University of New York under Gov. George Pataki and the ways he effected many of these changes through an activist board of trustees is detailed in an article by Patrick D. Healy, "In Pataki's Time, SUNY Runs More Like Private Universities," *New York Times*, March 24, 2005.

38. See the discussion and reference in n.8 above for how this alliance

between groups that have disparate cultural politics and domestic agendas can be constructed through the identification of an external enemy: "militant Arab Islam." The electoral, economic, and strategic motivations behind the alliances between neoconservatives, the current leadership of the Christian right, and militant nationalists have received a great deal of attention. Still to be systematically explored is the possible set of connections around the transformation of race and class politics in the United States since the 1960s. The Jewish versus African American split that characterized the 1968 teachers' strike in New York is widely seen as a foundational moment for the neoconservative movement. Some of the major organizations in the Jewish American community, such as the Anti-Defamation League, have tried to vigorously counter the influence of nationalist, Islamic, and Third-Worldist political tendencies within the African American community, identified with Malcolm X, the Black Panthers, and Louis Farrakhan. At the same time, the right-wing takeover of the evangelical movement in the 1970s brought to power leaders with strong roots in the anti–civil rights movement, such as members of the John Birch Society. Two recent articles shed light on this set of connections: Chris Hedges, "Soldiers of Christ II: Feeling the Hate with the National Religious Broadcasters," *Harpers*, May 2005; and Hishaam D. Aidi, "Slavery, Genocide and the Politics of Outrage: Understanding the New 'Racial Olympics,'" *Middle East Report* 234 (2005), pp. 40–55. Aidi's article discusses the relationship between the Darfur crises and racial politics in the United States.

39. "Nation in Brief," *Washington Post*, August 9, 2002.

40. David Van Biema, "A Kinder, Gentler Koran," *Time*, August 19, 2002.

41. Alan Cooperman, "A Timely Subject — and a Sore One: UNC Draws Fire, Lawsuit for Assigning Book on Islam," *Washington Post*, August 7, 2002.

42. A group called Students for Academic Freedom placed ads in campus newspapers calling on students to report their professors. As an AAUP statement notes, the John Birch Society in the 1960s, Accuracy in Academia in the 1980s, and Campus Watch after 9/11 all assumed that role; Campus Watch focuses on professors of Middle East studies. For an overview of the issues and pending legislation, see http://www.aaup.org/Issues/ABOR/aborintro2.htm.

43. The new version, however, is perhaps even more threatening. By removing the names of individuals yet listing the department and institution for each objectionable comment, the report implicates a far larger group of people as accessories to apologists for terror. I thank Osamah Khalil for pointing this out.

44. Some Web sites, such as discoverthenetwork.org, are vulgar and take a "know your enemy" approach, spewing out venomous polemics along with deliberately distorted mug shots. Others are meant to intimidate, as is clear from the warning that Martin Kramer, one of the public figures in this campaign,

sent out after the launch of the Campus Watch Web site: "Well, academic colleagues, get used to it. Yes, you are being watched. Those obscure articles in campus newspapers are now available on the Internet, and they will be harvested. Your syllabi, which you've also posted, will be scrutinized. Your websites will be visited late at night. And to judge from the Campus Watch website, the people who will do the real watching will be none other than your students, those young people who pay hefty tuition fees to sit at your feet. Now they have an address to turn to, should they fall victim to intellectual malpractice." This quote was later removed, but it was available on his Web site as of September 18, 2002. The Campus Watch Web site also removed a passage in the introduction page that imputed disloyalty on the parts of Edward Said, Rashid Khalidi, and others because of their ethnic origins.

45. The report of the second investigation found no evidence of anti-Semitism: http://www.columbia.edu/cu/news/05/03/ad_hoc_grievance_committee_report.html. Massad's reply to the Ad Hoc Grievance Committee Report can be found at http://electronicintifada.net/v2/article3744.shtml. Still, a *New York Times* editorial on the report, provocatively titled "Intimidation at Columbia," called on the university to clamp down on the "anti-Israel bias" of some of its professors (April 7, 2005). It is highly unusual for such a major newspaper to call for intervention to correct perceived political bias in the classroom. Juan Cole, an eminent scholar of the Middle East, identifies the "lesson for academics, and American society as a whole: McCarthyism is unacceptable except when criticism of Israel is involved." Juan Cole, "The New McCarthyism," *Salon.com*, April 22, 2005.

46. Scott Sherman, "The Mideast Comes to Columbia," *The Nation*, April 4, 2005, http://www.thenation.com/doc.mhtml?i=20050404&s=sherman. This argument is consistent with press reports at the time. A fairly detailed example is Rachel Pomerance, "Jewish Groups Coordinate Efforts to Help Students 'Take Back Campus,'" *Jewish Telegraphic Agency*, August 27, 2002. See also Rachel Pomerance, "AIPAC Trains US Student Pro-Israel Activists on Campus," *Cleveland Jewish News*, December 31, 2002. On August 1, 2005, AIPAC's Web site stated that "AIPAC's mission in 2005–2006 is nothing short of repositioning the American campus to be a tangible asset to the pro-Israel movement" (http://www.aipac.org/NERO80105_Repositioning%20campus.htm).

47. For a careful and forceful rebuttal see Judith Butler, "No, It's Not Anti-Semitic," *London Review of Books*, August 21, 2003. According to a *New York Times* article, Summers "vocally supported bringing R.O.T.C. back to Harvard … And he supported Harvard's honoring the Solomon Amendment, which ties federal funding to universities' allowing military recruitment on campus, something students and faculty had protested." The article goes on to quote the

author Richard Bradley that "Summers explicitly linked the future of the United States in its fight against terrorism with the success of Harvard." Rachel Donadio, "The Tempest in the Ivory Tower," *New York Times*, March 27, 2005. See Richard Bradley, *Harvard Rules: The Struggle for the Soul of the World's Most Powerful University* (New York: HarperCollins, 2005). Many other university presidents were quick to issue statements calling for protection of academic freedom while in the same breath registering in the strongest terms their personal revulsion about specific views attributed to targeted faculty and students, such as calls for divestment of university funds from companies that profit from Israel's military occupation of Palestinian lands. What they give with one hand, in other words, they take away with the other hand, for these statements pull the political and moral rug from under the teachers and students they are supposed to defend. For example, Columbia University President Lee Bollinger is quoted as stating that he finds the views of Hamid Dabashi "deeply offensive." See N.R. Kleinfield, "Mideast Tensions Are Getting Personal on Campus at Columbia," *New York Times*, January 18, 2005. In contrast, see also the statement by University of Pennsylvania President Judith Rodin, who registers her opposition to divestment from Israel, yet resists the temptation that ensnared so many of her colleagues either to register personal revulsion or to rush into a public apology for the speech of a faculty member. "Judith Rodin: On Divestment and Hate," *Daily Pennsylvanian*, October 18, 2002, http://www.dailypennsylvanian.com/ vnews/ display.v/ART/3dafaccbea74e?in_ archive=1.

48. See, for example, Peter Berkowitz and Michael McFaul, "Studying Islam, Strengthening the Nation," *Washington Post*, April 12, 2005. The investigations of the Columbia professors came at the same time that a new chair in Israel Studies was announced.

49. One of the remarkable aspects of this incident is that the ban was imposed without any knowledge by those responsible about what these views actually were. Brock Read, "Columbia Professor Banned From Teacher Training," *Chronicle of Higher Education*, March 4, 2005.

50. Jonathan R. Cole, "Academic Freedom Under Fire," *Daedalus* 135.2 (2005), p. 13.

51. http://www.studentsforacademicfreedom.org/abor.html. If the bills fail, efforts by their backers are made to persuade individual universities to adopt the language.

52. http://www.aaup.org/statements/SpchState/Statements/ billofrights. htm.

53. For a deft disposal of the concept of "advocacy" in the classroom, see Louis Menand, "The Limits of Academic Freedom," in Menand (ed.), *Future of Academic Freedom*, pp. 14–17.

54. For details about the "wedge" techniques aimed at giving academic legitimacy to creationism, see Barbara Forrest and Paul R. Gross, *Creationism's Trojan Horse: The Wedge of Intelligent Design* (Oxford: Oxford University Press, 2004). A synopsis of the book is Barbara Forrest and Glenn Branch, "Wedging Creationism into the Academy," *Academe* 91.1 (2005), pp. 37–41.

55. Peter Slevin, "Battle on Teaching Evolution Sharpens," *Washington Post*, March 14, 2005.

56. Especially useful here is the essay by David Hollinger, "What Does It Mean to Be 'Balanced' in Academia?" paper given at the annual meeting of the American Historical Association, January 9, 2005. This paper was first presented to the conference out of which this volume has come. Using a number of striking and witty examples, Hollinger shows the absurdity of accusations made against the academy by right-wing groups. "We must remember," he argues, "that any particular disciplinary community exists within what we might see as a series of concentric circles of accountability in an informal but vitally important structure of cognitive authority.... The farther you get from the technical particulars of the field, the less authority you have to decide what should be going on, but in a democratic society there is some authority distributed all the way out."

57. A judicious and persuasive account of the politics of this field is Zachary Lockman, *Contending Visions of the Middle East: The History and Politics of Orientalism* (Cambridge: Cambridge University Press, 2004). See especially the chapter "After Orientalism" for a comprehensive analysis of the political motivations behind the campaigns to dominate and police knowledge about the Middle East.

58. In the 1950s, for example, some foundations were used to launder money from intelligence agencies to universities, to minimize the degree to which the academy was perceived to be willing servant of the nation-state. For this and other details about area studies, see Bruce Cumings, "Boundary Displacement: Area Studies and International Studies During and After the Cold War," *Bulletin of Concerned Asian Scholars* 29.1 (1997).

59. Lie, "Moral Ambiguity."

60. The key articles in the campaign against the Ford Foundation appeared in an investigative series, "Funding Hate," published in *Jewish Telegraphic Agency*. Edwin Black wrote the articles. See http://www.featuregroup.com/fgarchive/jta.org/ for more details. See also Daniel Golden, "Colleges Object to New Wording in Ford Grants," *Wall Street Journal*, May 4, 2004. In addition to instituting the new language, Ford funded a major new initiative to combat anti-Semitism, with a focus on Europe.

61. They are Harvard, Yale, Princeton, Cornell, Columbia, Stanford, the University of Pennsylvania, Massachusetts Institute of Technology, and the Uni-

versity of Chicago. All but Stanford relented after the initial round of changes, which declared respect for individual academic freedom and focused instead on "official speech" by colleges and universities. This is a dangerous development, as it aggravates the tension between faculties and administrations over issues of governance. Now administrations have even more cause to discipline professors and students for their research and speech when it comes to hot-button issues, which was one of the central aims of the groups that pressured the foundations in the first place.

62. ACLU press release, October 19, 2004, http://www.aclu.org/news/newsprint.CFM?ID=16838c=206.

63. See, for example, Gary Rhoades, "Capitalism, Academic Style, and Shared Governance," *Academe* 91.3 (2005), pp. 38–42.

64. See, for example (in chronological order): David F. Noble, *America by Design: Science, Technology, and the Rise of Corporate Capitalism* (Oxford: Oxford University Press, 1977); Rebecca S. Lowen, *Creating the Cold War University: The Transformation of Stanford* (Berkeley: University of California Press, 1997); Christopher Simpson, *Universities and Empire: Money and Politics in the Social Sciences During the Cold War* (New York: New Press, 1998); Derek Bok, *Universities in the Marketplace: The Commercialization of Higher Education* (Princeton, NJ: Princeton University Press, 2003); Eric Gould, *The University in a Corporate Culture* (New Haven, CT: Yale University Press, 2003); Christopher Newfield, *Ivy and Industry: Business and the Making of the American University, 1880–1980* (Durham, NC: Duke University Press, 2003); Roger L. Geiger, *Knowledge and Money: Research Universities and the Paradox of the Marketplace* (Stanford, CA: Stanford University Press, 2004); Sheila Slaughter and Gary Rhoades, *Academic Capitalism and the New Economy: Markets, State, and Higher Education* (Baltimore: Johns Hopkins University Press, 2004); Jennifer Washburn, *University, Inc.: The Corporate Corruption of American Higher Education* (New York: Basic Books, 2005). Historians of higher education cannot help but notice that we are rushing forward into the late nineteenth century, which was characterized by naked corporate control of universities, a wide gap in access to knowledge between the haves and have-nots, and the narrowing boundaries of permissible speech. See Richard Hofstadter and Walter Metzger, *The Development of Academic Freedom in the United States* (New York: Columbia University Press, 1955), pp. 413–20. Of course, the context has changed. The legacy of advances in academic freedom since then cannot be ignored. At the same time, corporate control of boards of trustees seems less threatening than the transformation of the university into a corporation in structure and ethos.

65. I see the following tragic story as a symbolic warning about the intellectual and spiritual emptiness of unchecked privatization of knowledge. On Octo-

ber 22, 1996, Kathleen Chang, a classically trained ballet dancer and activist who haunted the streets of Philadelphia, performing one-person plays and making speeches about justice, liberty, and the need to protect the environment, walked onto her favorite campus grounds, the lawn near the Van Pelt Library of the University of Pennsylvania, as she often did in a vain attempt to attract students' attention. This time, she stood just a few feet behind the peace-sign sculpture, doused herself with gasoline, then lit a match. For a few days, a modest pile of flowers marked the spot where she burned to death. http://www.ainfos.ca/A-Infos96/7/0173.html.

66. Frank Newman, Lara Couturier, and Jamie Scurry, *The Future of Higher Education: Rhetoric, Reality, and the Risks of the Market* (San Francisco: Jossey-Bass, 2004), pp. 213–19.

67. State universities, which account for almost three-quarters of all college enrollment, have been especially hard hit. Contrary to conventional wisdom, public funding has actually increased, but it is not keeping pace with private funding. See Newman, Couturier, and Scurry, *Future of Higher Education*, p. 41. Also, open competition for government funding based on peer review is giving way to noncompetitive legislative funding priorities generated by lobbying and political influence instead of scientific merit. Consequently, the amount of money that universities spend on professional lobbying in Washington, D.C., nearly tripled in just five years (1998–2003), from $23 million to $62 million. See Alan B. Krueger, "The Farm-Subsidy Model of Financing Academia," *New York Times*, May 26, 2005. The process of politicizing and commercializing funding will take on new meaning if the U.S. delegation to the World Trade Organization has its way. The delegation has proposed including all higher education in the global free market. See Newman, Couturier, and Scurry, *Future of Higher Education*, p. 26.

68. The Bayh-Dole Act of 1980 was a turning point in corporate investment in and control of university science research (Washburn, *University, Inc.*, pp. 59–72). Corporate sponsorship of research jumped from $850 million in 1985 to $4.25 billion in 1995. Not surprisingly, a slew of scandals followed corporate censorship of and meddling in scientific research at the expense of truth and the public interest. See Newman, Couturier, and Scurry, *Future of Higher Education*, pp. 61–63.

69. David L. Kirp, *Shakespeare, Einstein, and the Bottom Line: The Marketing of Higher Education* (Cambridge, MA: Harvard University Press, 2003), pp. 259–60. For a full account of the Novartis affair, see ch. 1 of Washburn, *University, Inc.* In April, 2005, Ignacio Chapela, a microbial biology professor, filed a lawsuit against the University of California, claiming that he was refused tenure in 2003 for political reasons stemming from his vocal opposition to the Novartis

deal. On May 23, 2005, the university announced that he had been granted tenure.

70. Some universities, such as Harvard, are trying hard to admit more students from working-class families, but the dynamic of privatization is benefiting elite students with access to first-rate public or private schools, almost all of which are located in well-to-do neighborhoods. See Newman, Couturier, and Scurry, *Future of Higher Education*, p. 11. Also see Robert H. Frank, "The Intense Competition for Top Students Is Threatening Financial Aid Based on Need," *New York Times*, April 14, 2005.

71. See Newman, Couturier, and Scurry, *Future of Higher Education*, pp. 66–67.

72. Cornelia Dean, "Evolution Takes a Back Seat in U.S. Classes," *New York Times*, February 1, 2005.

73. Ben Feller, "First Amendment No Big Deal, Students Say," Associated Press, February 1, 2005. The study involved over 100,000 students, 8,000 teachers, and over 500 administrators in both public and private high schools. The study was funded by the John S. and James L. Knight Foundation and conducted by the University of Connecticut.

74. Joan W. Scott, "Academic Freedom as an Ethical Practice," in Menand (ed.), *Future of Academic Freedom*, p. 177.

75. *Ibid.*, p. 174.

76. Edward W. Said, "Identity, Authority, and Freedom: The Potentate and the Traveler," in Menand (ed.), *Future of Academic Freedom*, p. 228.

77. *Ibid.*, p. 227.

PART ONE: CONTENDING VISIONS

The Structure of

Academic Freedom

Robert Post

Reminiscing on his sixty-fifth birthday, Sidney Hook recalled that when he began his college career in fall 1919, "it would be no exaggeration to say that the belief in academic freedom was regarded as faintly subversive even in many academic circles."[1] As a graduate student at Columbia University, Hook remembered that President Nicholas Murray Butler exercised power "almost as unlimited as that of an absolute monarch."[2] Hook no doubt recollected Butler's notorious cancellation of the academic freedom of the entire Columbia faculty for the duration of the First World War:

> So long as national policies were in debate, we gave complete freedom, as is our wont, and as becomes a university.... So soon, however, as the nation spoke by the Congress and by the President, declaring that it would volunteer as one man for the protection and defense of civil liberty and self-government, conditions sharply changed. What had been tolerated before becomes intolerable now. What had been wrongheadedness was now sedition. What had been folly was now treason.... This is the University's last and only warning to any among us, if such there be, who are not with whole heart and mind and strength committed to fight with us to make the world safe for democracy.[3]

Academic freedom was subversive because it challenged the authority of university administrators unilaterally to control the research and publication of faculty. It protected scholars from the repercussions of criticizing sacred national pieties, like "the protection and defense of civil liberty and self-government" that were the putative goals of our entrance into the First World War.[4]

Today, as the country prosecutes yet another war, we have no difficulty appreciating the importance of academic freedom as a shield against the retribution typically inflicted on those perceived to be disloyal.[5] But we do not so easily remember the intellectual framework that defenders of academic freedom were forced to construct in order to invent this shield.

We have forgotten that, in essence, academic freedom sought to redefine the employment relationship between professors and universities. In 1919, "the generally accepted default rule in the United States" was employment-at-will,[6] which meant that employers could "discharge or retain" employees "for good cause, for no cause or even for cause morally wrong, without thereby being guilty of a legal wrong."[7] As employees, professors were subject to this "arbitrary power of dismissal."[8] Nicholas Murray Butler's pronouncement was for this reason well within the authority that any American employer felt entitled to exert over his employees. The primary challenge of academic freedom was to justify limitations on this broad authority.[9] Today, even though employment-at-will "remains, weakened but alive, in every United States jurisdiction,"[10] we can scarcely recall that the ideal of academic freedom was formulated precisely to transform basic American understandings of the employment relationship between faculty and their university or college.[11]

This amnesia is unfortunate, for it has facilitated the rise of an entirely different conception of academic freedom. In the past half-century, America has developed a culture of rights,[12] and we have accordingly come to conceive of the structure of academic freedom in terms of "rights of free expression, freedom of inquiry, freedom of association, and freedom of publication."[13] We now tend to conceptualize academic freedom on the model of individual First Amendment rights possessed by all "citizens in a free society."[14] The difficulty is that this reconceptualization of academic freedom can neither explain the basic structure of faculty obligations and responsibilities within universities, nor provide an especially trenchant defense of the distinctive freedoms necessary for the scholarly profession.

It is time, therefore, to return to first principles. In this chapter, I shall discuss the origins of academic freedom in the United States, in the hope that this act of historical recuperation will uncover an intellectual framework that will both illuminate the actual practices of American universities and offer effective resources for protecting scholarly independence in this time of national crisis. I turn to historical materials not out of any sense of fealty to the past, but rather because, in my view, the analysis developed by those who first created American academic freedom still provides the sturdiest and most robust defense available for the protection of modern faculty.

Academic Freedom, the University, and the Profession

The American ideal of academic freedom derived from the *Lehrfreiheit* of the great German universities,[15] where it was unambiguously rooted in a vision of the scholarly vocation that demanded "a wide latitude of utterance" within the university, but that was suspicious of "participation in partisan politics" because it was thought to spoil "habits of scholarship."[16] American scholars produced their own version of *Lehrfreiheit*, one that reflected both the influence of "a stronger social and constitutional commitment to the idea of freedom of speech" and a more pragmatic commitment to the social utility of professional scholarship.[17] But these shifts in emphasis should not obscure the essential fact that the American vision of academic freedom derived almost entirely from a particular account of the vocation of scholarship.[18]

Of course, academic freedom and constitutional rights of freedom of expression can in certain circumstances overlap and converge, but the confusions that result from conflating one with the other are deep and multiple. Every citizen holds First Amendment rights, which must therefore be defined to express values that are relevant to each and every citizen, such as the importance of democratic participation or individual autonomy. Only faculty, by contrast, possess academic freedom,[19] which implies that academic freedom must derive from values that attach to the distinct professional role of the scholar. First Amendment rights, moreover, apply only against the state. Academic freedom, by contrast, applies to institutions of higher learning, whether public or private. If academic freedom were to be understood on the model of First Amendment rights, it would be accorded to all employees of colleges and universities, not just to faculty, and it would attach to public institutions like the University of California or the University of Michigan, but not to private universities like Stanford or Harvard.

The deepest point of contrast between academic freedom and

the constitutional rights of "citizens in a free society," however, is more subtle and difficult to grasp. Americans now instinctively conceive of all protections of liberty on the paradigm of individual rights, by which I mean that the rights are not merely held and asserted by individual persons but also, and more importantly, that the rights are designed to protect interests that are defined by the perspective and horizon of individual persons.[20] First Amendment rights are commonly conceived of as individual rights of this kind.[21] Understood as this kind of an individual right, academic freedom would protect the liberty of individual faculty to research and publish free from the constraints of institutional regulation, whether that regulation is imposed by the state, university presidents, or faculty peers.

In point of fact, however, academic freedom in the United States does not function in this way. It may be asserted in particular cases by individual faculty, but it does not protect interests that are defined by reference to the perspectives and horizons of individual professors. Rights of academic freedom are instead designed to facilitate the professional self-regulation of the professoriat, so that academic freedom safeguards interests that are constituted by the perspective and horizon of the corporate body of the faculty. The function of academic freedom is not to liberate individual professors from all forms of institutional regulation, but to ensure that faculty within the university are free to engage in the professionally competent forms of inquiry and teaching that are necessary for the realization of the social purposes of the university. In this sense, "academic freedom is a *professional* freedom."[22] The logic and structure of academic freedom, as it actually exists in the United States today, will remain inexplicable so long as it is viewed through the lens of individual rights.

The first systematic and arguably the greatest articulation of the logic and structure of academic freedom in America was the "1915 Declaration of Principles on Academic Freedom and Academic Tenure," published by the newly formed American Association of University Professors (AAUP). The academic freedom we now enjoy derives directly from the vision of the "Declaration." It is important to be clear, therefore, about the profound ways in which the "Declaration" repudiates a framework of individual rights and instead locates academic freedom in an account of the distinctive social functions of universities and scholars.

The "Declaration" was chiefly drafted by the economist Edwin R.A. Seligman and the philosopher Arthur O. Lovejoy, both of whom were intimately acquainted with and appalled by the application to the professoriat of the American doctrine of employment-at-will.[23] Both had been involved in the notorious dismissal of the economist Edward A. Ross in 1900. Advocating for free silver and against the importation of cheap Asian labor, Ross had so profoundly distressed the co-founder and proprietor of Stanford University, Mrs. Leland Stanford, that she had written to David Starr Jordan, president of the university: "I must confess I am weary of Professor Ross, and I think he ought not to be retained at Stanford University.... I trust that before the close of this semester Professor Ross will have received notice that he will not be re-engaged for the new year."[24] Jordan obeyed his instructions. Lovejoy was so outraged that he resigned his position at Stanford; Seligman was so offended that he instigated a pathbreaking investigation of the incident by the American Economic Association.

At the very time when they were drafting the 1915 report, both Seligman and Lovejoy were also involved in the AAUP's investigation of the notorious dismissal of an assistant professor, Scott Nearing, by the Trustees of the University of Pennsylvania, "because it is understood that the Trustees did not approve of some of the doctrines he taught."[25] The Trustees gave no explanation for Nearing's peremptory removal;[26] as the New York Times opined in response to the resulting furor, "The Trustees are not obliged to give reasons for dismissal."[27] When the University of Pennsylvania trustee George Wharton Pepper was asked to explain Nearing's firing, he replied: "If I was dissatisfied with my secretary for anything he had done, some people might be in favor of my calling him in here and to sit down and talk it over. Others might think it wiser to dismiss him without assigning any cause. But in any case I would be within my rights in terminating his employment."[28]

The lesson was not lost on the American professoriat. Trustees "have legal authority to employ and dismiss whomsoever they wish in the service of their institution — the President, the professors, administrative officers, janitors, and day laborers. And no one of these, it is well to note, has any more constitutional security of tenure than another. They can discharge a janitor who complains that his wages are low, or an instructor who makes the fact known to his classes."[29] This allocation of authority was justified, the *New York Times* explained, because

> Men who through toil and ability have got together money enough
> to endow universities or professors' chairs, do not generally have it
> in mind that their money should be spent for the dissemination of
> the dogmas of Socialism or in teaching ingenuous youth how to live
> without work. Yet when Trustees conscientiously endeavor to carry
> out the purposes of the founder by taking proper measures to prevent that misuse of the endowment, we always hear a loud howl
> about academic freedom.
>
> We see no reason why the upholders of academic freedom in that
> sense should not establish a university of their own. Let them provide the funds, erect the buildings, lay out the campus, and then
> make a requisition on the padded cells of Bedlam for their teaching
> staff. Nobody would interfere with the full freedom of the professors, they could teach Socialism and shiftlessness until Doomsday
> without restraint.[30]

The first and foremost task of those who sought to protect academic freedom was to alter this idea that a university professor was
an employee serving at the mere sufferance of his employer — a
notion that, as John Dewey wrote the *New York Times*, was "based
upon the conception of the relation of a factory employer to his
employe."[31] The radical nature of academic freedom cannot now
be grasped unless we first recover an appreciation of how academic freedom would seem "peculiar chiefly in that the teacher is in
his economic status a salaried employee, and that the freedom
claimed for him implies a denial of the right of those who provide
or administer the funds from which he is paid, to control the content of his teaching. The principle of academic freedom is thus,
from a purely economic point of view, a paradoxical one; it asserts
that those who buy a certain service may not ... prescribe the
nature of the service to be rendered."[32]

The "1915 Declaration" confronts this paradox head-on. It
attacks the "conception of a university as an ordinary business
venture, and of academic teaching as a purely private employment."[33] Faculty, it asserts, "are the appointees, but not in any
proper sense the employees," of universities.[34]

[O]nce appointed, the scholar has professional functions to perform in which the appointing authorities have neither competency nor moral right to intervene. The responsibility of the university teacher is primarily to the public itself, and to his judgment of his own profession; and, while, with respect to certain external conditions of his vocation, he accepts a responsibility to the authorities of the institution in which he serves, in the essentials of his professional activity his duty is to the wider public to which the institution itself is morally amenable. So far as the university teacher's independence of thought and utterance is concerned — though not in other regards — the relationship of professor to trustees may be compared to that between judges of the federal courts and the executive who appoints them. University teachers should be understood to be, with respect to the conclusions reached and expressed by them, no more subject to the control of the trustees, than are the judges subject to the control of the president, with respect to their decisions; while of course, for the same reason, trustees are no more to be held responsible for, or to be presumed to agree with, the opinions or utterances of professors, than the president can be assumed to approve of the legal reasonings of the courts.[35]

The core principle of academic freedom may be found in this remarkable passage, which sounds not in the language of individual rights, but in that of social function. "The dispute between the upstart profession and entrenched regental authority . . . was seen, correctly, as a confrontation over the status of the faculty within the institution" of the university.[36]

The "1915 Declaration" justifies the transformation of faculty from employees into appointees on the basis of two key conceptual premises. The first concerns the purpose of the university as an institution; the second concerns the professionalism of faculty. The "purposes for which universities exist," the declaration asserts, "are three in number: (a) to promote inquiry and advance the sum of human knowledge; (b) to provide general instruction to the students; and (c) to develop experts for various branches of the public service."[37]

The "Declaration" interprets the first of these purposes as implying a theory of knowledge that directly sustains the idea of academic freedom. "[T]he first condition of progress," the declaration declares, "is complete and unlimited freedom to pursue inquiry and publish its results. Such freedom is the breath in the nostrils of all scientific activity."[38] It follows that "the university teacher's independence of thought and utterance"[39] is required by the basic purpose of the university. As Lovejoy later succinctly put it, the university's

> function of seeking new truths will sometimes mean ... the under-
> mining of widely or generally accepted beliefs. It is rendered impos-
> sible if the work of the investigator is shackled by the requirement
> that his conclusions shall never seriously deviate either from gener-
> ally accepted beliefs or from those accepted by the persons, private
> or official, through whom society provides the means for the main-
> tenance of universities.... Academic freedom is, then, a prerequisite
> condition to the proper prosecution, in an organized and adequately
> endowed manner, of scientific inquiry.[40]

The "Declaration" acknowledges that institutions of higher education exist that call themselves "universities" but that are actually dedicated to propagating a particular vision of the truth, such as, for example, when "a wealthy manufacturer establishes a special school in a university in order to teach, among other things, the advantages of a protective tariff."[41] But the "Declaration" insists that such organizations should be branded as "essentially proprietary institutions" that do not "accept the principles of freedom of inquiry, of opinion, and of teaching; ... [T]heir purpose is not to advance knowledge by the unrestricted research and unfettered discussion of impartial investigators, but rather to subsidize the promotion of opinions held by the persons, usually not of the scholar's calling, who provide the funds for their maintenance."[42] It is "manifestly important," the "Declaration" asserts, that such institutions "not be permitted to sail under false colors," so that "any university which lays restrictions upon the intellectual freedom of its professors proclaims itself a proprietary institution, and should be so described whenever it makes a general appeal for funds; and the public should be advised that the institution has no claim whatever to general support or regard."[43]

The "Declaration" addresses university trustees who understand "the relation of trustees to professors ... to be analogous to that of a private employer to his employees; in which, therefore, trustees are not regarded as debarred by any moral restrictions, beyond their own sense of expediency, from imposing their personal opinions upon the teaching of the institution, or even from employing the power of dismissal to gratify their private antipathies or resentments."[44] Such trustees, the "Declaration" charges, do not comprehend "the full implications of the distinction between private proprietorship" and the "public trust" entailed by a proper account of the social function of the modern university.[45] They fundamentally fail to appreciate that the production of knowledge, which is the constitutive function of a true university as distinct from a private proprietorship, requires freedom of inquiry.

The second key premise of the "1915 Declaration" is that faculty should be regarded as professional experts in the production of knowledge. The mission of the university defended by the "Declaration" depends on a particular theory of knowledge that today might be controversial in some circles.[46] The "Declaration" presupposes not only that knowledge exists and can be articulated by scholars, but also that it is advanced through the free application of highly disciplined forms of inquiry, which correspond roughly to what Charles Peirce once called "the method of science," as distinct from the "method of authority."[47] The "Declaration" claims that universities can advance the sum of human knowledge only if they employ persons who are experts in scholarly methods, and only if universities liberate these experts to pursue freely the inquiries dictated by their disciplinary training. Although this claim seems most apparently defensible in the context of classical scientific inquiry, it retains its force whenever we believe that disciplinary training actually adds value to scholarship.

The implication of this perspective, however, is that the "liberty of the scholar within the university to set forth his conclusions, be they what they may, is conditioned by their being conclusions gained by a scholar's method and held in a scholar's spirit; that is to say, they must be the fruits of competent and patient and sincere inquiry."[48] The "Declaration" thus conceives of academic freedom not as an individual right to be free from constraints but instead as the freedom to pursue the "scholar's profession"[49] according to the standards of that profession. Academic freedom consists in the freedom of mind, inquiry, and expression required by proper performance of professional obligations. Because regulation may be necessary to ensure that scholars comply with the requirements of the "scholar's method," the "Declaration" explicitly repudiates the position that "academic freedom implies that individual teachers should be exempt from all restraints as to the matter or manner of their utterances, either within or without the university."[50]

This account of academic freedom explains why universities today routinely require faculty to comply with academic standards.[51] Universities award tenure to professors whose work meets these standards, and they deny tenure to professors whose work fails them. They hire and promote professors on the basis of professional evaluations that are supposed to reflect the application of professional norms. They distribute grants on a similar basis. Academic departments define the content and ordering of courses and instruction based on these same criteria. It is no exaggeration to say that universities simply could not function if they were deprived of the capacity to apply such standards.[52] In this sense, academic freedom does not now, nor has it ever, protected the autonomy of professors to pursue their own individual work, free from university restraints. Instead academic freedom is designed to create the liberty necessary to facilitate the advancement of knowledge, understood as the unimpeded application of professional norms of inquiry. This distinction is fundamental and underlies the routine and pervasive regulation of faculty speech that characterizes modern universities. Although the First Amendment may prohibit the state from penalizing the *New York Times* for misunderstanding the distinction between astronomy and astrology, no astronomy professor can insulate herself from the adverse consequences of such a mistake.[53]

The "Declaration" insists that professional standards "cannot with safety" be enforced

by bodies not composed of the academic profession.... Lay governing boards are competent to judge concerning charges of habitual neglect of assigned duties, on the part of individual teachers, and concerning charges of grave moral delinquency. But in matters of opinion, and of the utterance of opinion, such boards cannot intervene without destroying, to the extent of their intervention, the essential nature of a university — without converting it from a place dedicated to openness of mind, in which the conclusions expressed are the tested conclusion of trained scholars, into a place barred against the access of new light, and precommitted to opinions or prejudices of men who have not been set apart or expressly trained for the scholar's duties.[54]

Because faculty are "professional scholars" who have received "prolonged and specialized technical training" in the disciplinary expertise necessary to advance knowledge,[55] the "Declaration" is clear that they should be accorded the prerogative of governing themselves. In effect, therefore, the "Declaration" advances a theory of academic freedom that invokes "not the absolute freedom of utterance of the individual scholar, but the absolute freedom of thought, of inquiry, of discussion and of teaching, of the academic profession."[56]

The declaration's argument for professional self-regulation rests on two premises. The first is the privilege of expertise. Lay persons are said to lack the training and skills necessary to apply norms of professional scholarship, which can only be acquired through a rigorous apprenticeship. The second is the notion that the university's mission to advance knowledge would be impaired if research were subject to the application of standards other than those of professional scholarship. Because lay persons have not been socialized into the knowledge and practice of professional norms, they will tend to enforce standards that are extrinsic to the profession. The "Declaration" imagines such standards as dangerous, seeing them as likely to distort professional norms of inquiry in the service of popular political beliefs (in the case of public universities), private prejudices (in the case of proprietary universities), or ecclesiastical dogma (in the case of parochial universities). Lay enforcement of professional norms would thus invite regulatory interventions that might well prove incompatible with the university's basic mission.[57]

On the whole, the professoriat's claim to self-regulation has proved remarkably durable and successful. Other professionals — lawyers, doctors, even the clergy — have had to submit to increasingly pervasive forms of public regulation. But if the exceptions that prove the rule are set aside, the professional autonomy of the faculty remains a powerful and effective fact of university life. This might be because the public, although it cares very much about the actions of doctors and lawyers, is relatively indifferent to the actual practices of universities. But it might also be because the progressive vision articulated by the "1915 Declaration" remains persuasive. It might be that the public genuinely believes that universities have, on the whole, successfully fulfilled their function of producing socially valuable knowledge, and that this production would be seriously compromised were universities to truncate academic freedom. The public might also genuinely believe that this freedom is best understood as the liberty to pursue professional inquiry within a matrix of disciplinary norms defined and enforced by those who are competent to understand and apply such norms.

If this is true, then a great strength of the ideal of academic freedom propounded by the "1915 Declaration" is that it ties the protection of academic freedom to the production of a social good that the public actually requires. In the long run, public support for academic freedom will be as firm and enduring as the public need for the creation of knowledge. Such support would be undermined, however, if academic freedom were reconceptualized as an individual right authorizing faculty to research and publish as they personally see fit. This may not be immediately obvious, because we are so accustomed to thinking of individual First Amendment rights as establishing a "marketplace of ideas."[58] But there is no particular reason to believe that unrestrained speech, by itself, will produce knowledge.[59] On any plausible account, the production of knowledge requires not merely the negative liberty to speculate free from censorship, but also an affirmative commitment to the virtues of reason, fairness, and accuracy.[60] As the philosopher Bernard Williams reminds us, compliance with these virtues, enforced through social and legal means, is central whenever we witness a sustained dedication to the actual production of knowledge, such as exists in the practice of organized science.[61]

The traditional ideal of academic freedom, with its twin commitments to freedom of research and to compliance with professional norms, nicely balances these negative and affirmative dimensions. This balance would be lost if academic freedom were to be reformulated as an individual right that insulates scholars from professional regulation.[62] Understood as an individual right, academic freedom would essentially enforce the premise, explicit within First Amendment doctrine, that there is an "equality of status in the field of ideas."[63] It is clear that this premise is inconsistent with the advancement of knowledge, which requires precisely that ideas be treated unequally, that they be assessed and weighed, accepted and rejected.[64] The individual freedom that underlies the structure of First Amendment rights is for this reason ill suited to the production of knowledge. It is, in fact, far better understood as instantiating the postulate of equal intrinsic dignity that is the foundation of legitimacy in a democratic state.

Reformulated as an individual right to be free from professional regulation, academic freedom would perforce conceive of faculty liberty as an intrinsic value, rather than as instrumental for the production of knowledge. The most plausible candidate for such a value is the good of free and critical inquiry. But deep conceptual and practical difficulties immediately arise once academic freedom is justified as an effort to safeguard this value. In a democracy, each and every citizen is entitled to enjoy the liberty of free and critical inquiry; it is therefore unclear why scholars should receive special protections for this liberty, protections that other Americans do not generally possess against their private employers. If faculty claim these special protections by virtue of their rigorous professional training, it must be explained why free and critical inquiry is more valuable to those who have undergone this training than to those who have not, especially in light of the claim that academic freedom should immunize scholars from the application of the very professional norms that this training is designed to instill. And if faculty claim these special protections by virtue of their association with universities, it must be explained why scholars, as distinct from other university employees, should enjoy these special protections, and why universities, as distinct from other private institutions in a democracy, should be especially required to respect the value of free and critical inquiry.[65]

Academic freedom, if it is to do the hard work of protecting faculty from the waves of repression that periodically sweep through the American polity, must explain why scholars ought to enjoy freedoms that other members of the public do not possess. The ideal of academic freedom advanced in the "1915 Declaration" offers a compact and apparently convincing explanation of this disparity. Academic freedom is conceived of as the price the public must pay in return for the social good of advancing knowledge. If academic freedom were to be reconceived as an individual right, however, it is difficult to see how academic freedom could effectively counter public demands for restrictions on scholarly liberty. Were academic freedom primarily a protection for the value of free and critical inquiry, which is a universal value in a democracy, public control over scholars would seem neither more nor less justifiable than restraints that apply to the public generally.

The Content of Academic Freedom: Tensions and Uncertainties

The "Declaration" rejects the doctrine of employment-at-will on the basis of the twin concepts of institutional mission and professional self-regulation. The "Declaration" does not hold that professors can never be regulated, disciplined, or even fired. It holds only that employment decisions must be made in ways that are consistent with these concepts. In particular, the "Declaration" declares that these concepts require that professors be accorded "academic freedom," which it defines as consisting of three components: "freedom of inquiry and research; freedom of teaching within the university or college; and freedom of extramural utterance and action." Subsequent articulations of academic freedom have kept this tripartite division. The "1940 Statement of Principles on Academic Freedom and Tenure,"[66] in particular, provides that academic freedom consists in "full freedom in research and in the publication of the results"; "freedom in the classroom"; and freedom "from institutional censorship or discipline" for extramural expression "as citizens."[67] Each of these three aspects of academic freedom has its own ambiguities and difficulties, which I shall briefly discuss.

Freedom of Research and Publication

Freedom of research and publication is the core of academic freedom. It is the freedom that follows most directly from the social function of the university. The basic claim is that researchers cannot advance knowledge unless they are free to inquire and to speculate. They cannot advance knowledge unless they are free to share the results of their research with peers and with the general public. Today, there is general agreement on these principles.

A deep conceptual difficulty nevertheless lurks at the center of this essential aspect of academic freedom. "Independence of thought and utterance"[68] is essential to the advancement of knowledge only when it is exercised within a framework of accepted professional norms capable of distinguishing work that contributes to knowledge from work that does not. This framework connects academic freedom with the goal of disciplinary advancement. As Edward Shils has observed:

> Academic freedom certainly extended to intellectual originality. It was for the departmental colleagues of their own university and their peers outside their own university, when one of them departed from that consensus, to decide whether the individual in question was being original, or divergent within reasonable limits, or eccentric to the point of mental incapacity, or impermissibly arbitrary, indolent, or otherwise irresponsible. Sanctions for their failure to conform with accepted intellectual standards could not be denounced on the grounds that they infringed on the right of academic freedom.[69]

The difficulty is that independence of thought and utterance cannot be so easily cabined. Critical inquiry can turn on the very framework of "accepted intellectual standards" that is meant to convert academic freedom into the production of knowledge. An individual scholar can always claim that she ought to be free to exemplify new and different professional norms, and this claim can be justified on the incontestable ground that such norms are themselves forms of knowledge that must be open to critique and development.[70] We are thus led to a paradox. Professional norms are needed to constrain the exercise of academic freedom so as to connect that freedom to the production of knowledge, and yet professional norms are also themselves forms of knowledge that are best advanced when debated with the kind of dissent that requires academic freedom. Academic freedom thus appears to be simultaneously limited by and independent of professional norms.

This paradox lies coiled at the core of the traditional justification for freedom of research and inquiry. On the one hand, it is plainly unacceptable to imagine that professional norms ought to be uniquely immune from criticism and disagreement. Like all forms of knowing, academic standards can be improved by the dialogue that flows from independence of thought and utterance. The point is succinctly articulated by Joan Scott:

> Disciplinary communities...share a common commitment to the autonomous pursuit of understanding, which they both limit and make possible by articulating, contesting, and revising the rules of such

pursuits and the standards by which outcomes will be judged.... This recognition insists on a place for criticism and critical transformation at the very heart of the conception of a discipline and so guarantees the existence of that scholarly critical function that discipline is meant to legitimate and that academic freedom is designed to protect.[71]

On the other hand, it is also plainly unacceptable to believe that professors possess academic freedom to violate professional norms at will. Without institutional processes of peer review that apply "accepted intellectual standards," the very justification for freedom of research and publication is undermined, because that freedom is severed from the production of knowledge. There can be no "equality of status in the field of ideas" within universities, at least within universities as we now know them.[72]

The dilemma is not quite as sharp as it might first appear to be, because an appreciation of controversy, and hence of independence of thought and utterance, is built into the very structure of professional academic standards. Contestation drives the conversation that constitutes ordinary scholarly life. Dispute and innovation are propelled by many factors, including naturally arising differences of opinion, competition for prominence and success, the ordinary progression of generations, and, as David Hollinger has shrewdly observed, by the fact that "any particular disciplinary community exists within what we might see as a series of concentric circles of accountability in an informal but vitally important structure of authority."

> In order to maintain its standing in the learned world as a whole, a given community must keep the communities nearest to it persuaded that it is behaving responsibly, and it must also, partly through the support of these neighboring communities, diminish whatever skepticism about its operations might arise in more distant parts of the learned world, and to some extent in the society which scientists and scholars do, after all, serve.... The farther you get from the technical particulars of the field, the less authority you have to decide what should be going on.[73]

Toleration of disagreement, and thus freedom of research and publication, is in this way woven into the everyday practice of scholarship.

That said, it must also be observed that the application of professional norms involves judgment and interpretation and is therefore always contestable. It can be quite controversial whether, in any given case, professional norms ought to be interpreted in a manner that tolerates variant forms of scholarly practice. In exceptional cases we can even conceptualize such controversies as testing the very boundaries of professional standards themselves. It might be said, then, that in extreme circumstances protecting independence of thought and inquiry requires striking some balance between enforcing and suspending professional standards.

The essential point is that whether they are seen through the lens of the toleration required by professional norms or through the lens of the willing suspension of professional norms, cases at the frontier of a discipline can grow highly contentious, and they can generate sharp disputes that are not susceptible to definitive theoretical resolution. This has important consequences for the practice of academic freedom. It implies that the institutions of peer review that apply professional standards are perennially vulnerable to suspicion and distrust. They can always be charged with having become merely the self-serving guardians of entrenched forms of academic power. Unfortunately, there are all too many occasions for such charges. Controversies over professional standards are endemic to American universities. "Quantitative versus qualitative, positivist versus metahistorical, Robertsonian versus Lévi-Straussian, realist versus Leo Straussian: the academic life has always been an endless series of turf battles."[74] Especially in the years since the Vietnam War, these battles have proceeded in the general context of a growing "antinomianism" within American intellectual culture that is skeptical of authority and that distrusts those who seek to exercise power.[75]

When this antinomianism presses on exactly the most vulnerable point of scholarly self-governance, that is, the extent to which faculty ought to have academic freedom to reformulate the very professional norms by which their peers judge them, the results can be corrosive. This is, no doubt, an important reason why academic freedom has in recent decades come increasingly to be conceived of as an individual right to be asserted against all forms of university regulation, including the constraints of peer review. It is easier and more comfortable to support the conscience of the individual scholar than to support the potentially abusive authority of an established and corporate faculty that may merely be protecting its own prerogatives and prejudices.

It is worth noting, therefore, that no university currently deals with its faculty as if academic freedom were an individual right. Universities instead hire, promote, tenure and support faculty based on criteria of academic merit that purport to apply professional standards. Individual faculty have no right of immunity from such judgments, which reflect the exercise of institutional authority. To reconceive academic freedom as an individual right would require developing not merely a new justification for freedom of research and publication — a justification that would not depend on the connection between disciplinary standards and the production of knowledge — but also a new and convincing account of these pervasive structures of contemporary university governance. No solution to either challenge is currently visible on the horizon.

At least for the moment, therefore, there are good reasons to stand by the traditional account of freedom of research and publication. But our support must be disenchanted to the extent of recognizing that it may be impossible definitively to distinguish institutions of peer review that properly apply disciplinary standards from those that merely engage in professionally self-serving behavior. The most that can be done is to proceed in a way that gives institutions of peer review the best possible chance of acquiring a legitimacy that will authorize them to make the tacit judgments necessary to balance toleration with discipline or, alternatively, to bridge the tension between suspending and enforcing professional norms. Because such legitimacy must be earned in the coin of recognition, institutions of peer review must actually be perceived as making good-faith, responsible judgments.[76] As a practical matter, the most effective strategy for earning this respect will be the maintenance of a sensible and wise equilibrium between innovation and stability.

This analysis suggests that the traditional ideal of academic freedom is imperiled in at least two distinct ways. The first threat is external. The danger is that the general public will override the prerogatives of faculty self-governance as they have overridden the ambition for self-regulation of professions like law and medicine. The strongest defense against this external threat is the contention that academic freedom is necessary for the production of a socially desirable good, such as the creation of knowledge. But this defense makes visible a second, internal threat to the account of academic freedom in the "1915 Declaration." This danger is skepticism. The external defense of academic freedom will collapse if faculty themselves lose faith in the professional norms necessary to define and generate knowledge. It follows that the traditional ideal of freedom of research can be sustained only if existing institutions of peer review interpret these professional norms in a manner that maintains their internal legitimacy. This implies that the content of these norms will predictably and appropriately be influenced by judgments about the dynamic social cohesion of the profession that are necessary to sustain the authority of these norms.[77]

From this perspective, the conception of academic freedom as an individual right is potentially quite dangerous. To the extent that it differs from the traditional ideal of academic freedom, it organizes institutions of peer review and faculty self-regulation on the basis of a professed skepticism of professional norms, and this skepticism threatens to undermine whatever authority these norms might, in fact, possess. The conception of academic freedom as an individual right seems superficially attractive because it appears to promise greater security for academic dissent, but, in reality, it potentially undermines the professional norms necessary for the external defense of academic freedom. And without this defense there are forms of political power that surely stand ready to seize control of the American academic community.

Freedom of Teaching
Academic freedom in the classroom is an exceedingly complex and ill-defined topic. The freedom of the individual professor must be balanced against not only the academic freedom of the corporate body of the faculty to design and implement curricular requirements, but also against the academic freedom of students. These complex and conflicting imperatives can be clarified only if we adequately define the value to be served by freedom of teaching.

In one sense, the value served by this freedom is the same as that served by freedom of research and inquiry. Insofar as the scholar must be free to disseminate the results of her research to the general public, she must also be free to disseminate these results to her students.[78] But this definition cannot capture the full range of classroom freedom. It would imply, for example, that freedom of teaching depends on research, yet it seems clear that academic freedom in the classroom is not restricted to university faculty who have research obligations. Lecturers are not obligated or expected to conduct research, but they are nevertheless understood to enjoy academic freedom in carrying out their pedagogical responsibilities.

It might be thought that freedom of teaching could be justified on the grounds of professional expertise. University faculty are expert and professional teachers, and it might thus be claimed that lay persons lack competence to control or evaluate their teaching. But this argument would prove too much, for it would suggest that all professional teachers, from the kindergarten level up, should enjoy academic freedom, and that is certainly not the case.

The "1915 Declaration" offers yet another possible explanation of the value of academic freedom in the classroom. The purpose of university education, it states, is "not to provide … students with ready-made conclusions, but to train them to think for themselves, and to provide them access to those materials which they need if they are to think intelligently."[79] The "Declaration" argues:

> No man can be a successful teacher unless he enjoys the respect of his students, and their confidence in his intellectual integrity. It is clear, however, that this confidence will be impaired if there is suspicion on the part of the student that the teacher is not expressing himself fully or frankly. … It is not only the character of the instruction but also the character of the instructor that counts; and if the student has reason to believe that the instructor is not true to himself, the virtue of the instruction as an educative force is incalculably diminished.[80]

An implicit theory of higher education underlies these passages. In contrast to elementary and secondary schools, universities seek to instill in their students the mature independence of mind that characterizes successful adulthood. Universities cannot reach this goal merely by conveying information. Instead, university professors must model for their students the exercise of responsible, independent thought. Professors can serve this function only if they are accorded the freedom to express themselves fully and frankly in the classroom.

Different professors instill mature independence of mind in their students in different ways. Some refrain from articulating their own opinions; others set forth their own views but invite critical discussion; still others exemplify the very process of inquiry. It all depends on the "character of the instructor." It is difficult if not dangerous to attempt to lay down exact and abstract rules, because the quality of the connection that a professor is able to forge with her students depends so heavily on her style and personality. The essential point is that a professor's pedagogical approach must educate, rather than indoctrinate, students.

It is important to emphasize that the line between education and indoctrination cannot be drawn without reference to applicable professional norms. Consider, for example, a mathematics student who refuses to internalize and apply proper rules for solving differential equations. If we conclude, as we are likely to do, that such a student is not exercising a mature independence of mind but is instead displaying a stubborn refusal to learn, it is because the profession understands these aspects of mathematics to be dogmatic in character. We would apply the same analysis to the case of a medical student who refuses to reproduce the anatomical information offered him by his instructor.

Contrast these examples to an English student who refuses to agree with his professor's interpretation of *Paradise Lost*. Whether we determine that such a student is thinking for himself or that he is stubbornly refusing to learn will depend on our appraisal of the quality of the student's own countervailing interpretation of *Paradise Lost*, an appraisal that is impossible without the framework of relevant professional norms of literary criticism. This suggests that the distinction between education and indoctrination does not depend on anything so simple as whether a student is required to learn or reproduce specific information or facts or theories. The distinction follows instead from a normative account of the kind and nature of relevant professional knowledge. This strongly suggests that the distinction between education and indoctrination is largely internal to academic standards. If academic freedom were reinterpreted as an individual right that was immune from the discipline of these standards, this distinction would be left exposed and untheorized, which could radically increase the vulnerability of the profession.[81]

Freedom of Extramural Expression

The most complex and theoretically troublesome aspect of academic freedom is freedom of extramural expression. This dimension of academic freedom does not concern the freedom to communicate in ways that are connected to faculty expertise, for such communication is encompassed within freedom of research, a principle that covers both the freedom to inquire and the freedom to disseminate the results of inquiry. Instead, freedom of extramural expression refers to a professor's freedom to speak in public in her role as a citizen in ways that are unrelated to professional expertise. An example might be a professor of chemistry who elects to speak out against the war in Iraq. The issue for analysis is whether and how professors should be immune from sanction for such speech, even if it damages the university that employs them.

The issue is controversial. Since its founding, AAUP's docket of alleged violations of academic freedom has been "overwhelmingly...dominated by extramural freedom cases."[82] The conceptual difficulty posed by such cases is that, by hypothesis, they concern expression that is unrelated to faculty competence and professional expertise. It is thus deeply unclear how freedom of communication can, in such circumstances, be justified by reference to the distinct professional status of faculty.

The "1915 Declaration" is exceedingly cautious and circumspect in its explanation of the freedom of extramural expression:

> In their extramural utterances, it is obvious that academic teachers are under a peculiar obligation to avoid hasty or unverified or exaggerated statements, and to refrain from intemperate or sensational modes of expression. But subject to these restraints, it is not, in this committee's opinion, desirable that scholars should be debarred from giving expression to their judgments upon controversial questions, or that their freedom of speech, outside the university, should be limited to questions falling within their own specialties. It is clearly not proper that they should be prohibited from lending their active support to organized movements which they believe to be in the public interest. And, speaking broadly, it may be said in the words of a nonacademic body already once quoted in a publication of the Association, that "it is neither possible nor desirable to deprive a college professor of the political rights vouchsafed to every citizen."

It is, however, a question deserving of consideration by members of the Association, and by university officials, how far academic teachers, at least those dealing with political, economic, and social subjects, should be prominent in the management of our great party organizations, or should be candidates for state or national offices of a distinctly political character. It is manifestly desirable that such teachers have minds untrammeled by party loyalties, unexcited by party enthusiasms, and unbiased by personal political ambitions; and that universities should remain uninvolved in party antagonisms. On the other hand, it is equally manifest that the material available for the service of the State would be restricted in a highly undesirable way, if it were understood that no member of the academic profession should ever be called upon to assume the responsibilities of public office. This question may, in the committee's opinion, suitably be made a topic for special discussion at some future meeting of this Association, in order that a practical policy, which shall do justice to the two partially conflicting considerations that bear upon the matter, may be agreed upon.[83]

The "1940 Statement" is also carefully hedged in its description of this freedom:

College and university teachers are citizens, members of a learned profession, and officers of an education institution. When they speak or write as citizens, they should be free from institutional censorship or discipline, but their special position in the community imposes special obligations. As scholars and educational officers, they should remember that the public may judge their profession and their institution by their utterances. Hence they should at all times be accurate, should exercise appropriate restraint, should show respect for the opinions of others, and should make every effort to indicate that they are not speaking for the institution.[84]

Like the "1915 Declaration," the "1940 Statement" seems simultaneously to claim for faculty the right to speak "as citizens" and yet also to diminish that freedom by imposing on professors the "special obligations" to "be accurate" and to "exercise appropriate restraint." This ambiguity persists even in AAUP's 1964 reinterpretation of the "1940 Statement": "The controlling principle is that a faculty member's expression of opinion as a citizen cannot constitute grounds for dismissal unless it clearly demonstrates the faculty member's unfitness for the position."[85] Because universities typically seek to sanction professors for extramural expression that damages the reputation of or goodwill toward a university in its ambient community, the 1964 interpretation reaches quite far beyond the "1940 Statement." Yet even the 1964 interpretation does not accord faculty the full freedom of citizens, because professors, unlike citizens, can be sanctioned for speaking in ways that demonstrate professional incompetence.

To define the scope and nature of the freedom of extramural expression, we must first clarify its justifications and purpose. We must explain why professors should have freedom to speak publicly in ways that damage their universities, even if such speech is, by hypothesis, unprotected by freedom of research and otherwise unrelated to professional competence.[86] The difficulty of supplying such an explanation is so severe that Arthur Lovejoy, one of the primary authors of the "1915 Declaration," later recanted and argued that freedom of extramural expression should be regarded not as an aspect of academic freedom, but as a kind of general civil liberty:

> In some cases teachers have been dismissed or otherwise penalized because of their exercise, outside the university, of their ordinary political or personal freedom in a manner or for purposes objectionable to the governing authorities of their institutions. While such administrative action is contrary to the spirit of academic freedom, it is primarily a special case of the abuse of the economic relation of employer and employee for the denial of ordinary civil liberties.[87]

No less a champion of academic freedom than Harvard President Abbott Lawrence Lowell offered a similar analysis, concluding that "the right of a professor to express his views without restraint on matters lying outside the sphere of his professorship" was

> not a question of academic freedom in its true sense, but of the personal liberty of the citizen. It has nothing to do with liberty of research and instruction in the subject for which the professor occupies the chair that makes him a member of the university. The fact that a man fills a chair of astronomy, for example, confers on him no special knowledge of, and no peculiar right to speak upon, the pro-

tective tariff. His right to speak about a subject on which he is not an authority is simply the right of any other man, and the question is simply whether the university or college by employing him as a professor acquires a right to restrict his freedom as a citizen.[88]

If freedom of extramural expression reflects "the personal liberty of the citizen," however, we face discomforting implications. Most formulations of freedom of extramural expression award faculty *less* liberty than that enjoyed by ordinary citizens. But even if we were to interpret freedom of extramural expression to mean that faculty are "entitled to precisely the same freedom and [are] subject to the same responsibility as attach to all other citizens,"[89] then a major segment of university faculty would not actually enjoy freedom of extramural expression, because, as we have seen, most employees in most states are not immune from employer sanctions on the basis of their speech.[90] Employment-at-will remains the legal rule in the great majority of circumstances, which should remind us that the whole point of developing the idea of academic freedom was to explain why faculty should receive *greater* protections than those enjoyed by ordinary employees.

Of course, this analysis does not apply to faculty at public universities, such as the University of California. The First Amendment has been interpreted as limiting the ways state employers can sanction the extramural expression of their employees, and these limitations have typically been interpreted in light of judicial understandings of institutional purpose. Employees are therefore protected as long as their speech does not damage the legitimate institutional objectives of state employers.[91] For faculty at state universities, therefore, some form of freedom of extramural expression is guaranteed by the Constitution.[92] But even if this guarantee were construed as identical to the one set forth in the "1940 Statement," it would nevertheless not extend to faculty at private universities in states that support employment-at-will. Insofar as freedom of extramural expression is a right that should theoretically apply to all faculty, it cannot be justified by the civil liberties guaranteed by the First Amendment or by civil law generally.

Theoretical explanations of the freedom of extramural expression are not easy to imagine. I can think of two distinct lines of analysis. The first argues that it is impossible and dangerous artificially to mark the limits of faculty expertise, so that efforts to distinguish speech within a scholar's competence from speech outside that competence ought to be discouraged. This analysis is challenged by what appear to be clear cases, such as the illustration, posed by Lowell, of the astronomer who opines on the tariff. Such challenges can be met only if it is claimed that *nothing* is theoretically beyond the legitimate professional purview of a scholar, because the "prolonged and specialized technical training" of the professoriat instills a methodological rigor that can contribute to the search for knowledge in any and all subjects.

Although this claim may seem implausible, consider the example of Noam Chomsky. Trained only as a linguist, and hired only to teach linguistics, Chomsky nevertheless continues to author highly controversial publications about foreign policy.[93] To assert that Chomsky's freedom of research can extend only as far as the courses he happens to teach, or only as far as the training he happened to receive, would needlessly inhibit the natural expansion of his professional interests. From this perspective, we might argue that the scholarly ambition and form of Chomsky's publications justify their protection as an aspect of his freedom of research. If this argument were generalized, however, it would suggest that freedom of research and publication ought to apply to *every* communication by a scholar that evidences scholarly standards of thought.

This approach would protect roughly the same set of extramural utterances as those that are immunized by the "1940 Statement." But it would differ from the "1940 Statement" in that it would assimilate freedom of extramural expression to freedom of research and publication and hence deny that extramural expression constitutes a distinct dimension of academic freedom that privileges a scholar's role as citizen. The persuasiveness of this approach would depend heavily on the social authority carried by professional norms of inquiry and discussion. Respect for these norms would justify protecting not merely the technical disciplinary communications of faculty, but also all publications that reflect "a scholar's method and . . . a scholar's spirit; that is to say, . . . the fruits of competent and patient and sincere inquiry."[94] The question is whether this abstract and rather thin conception of academic professionalism has the strength to sustain freedom of extramural expression.

A second and different explanation for freedom of extramural expression might focus on the particular institutional circumstances of universities. Universities typically seek to suppress the speech of professors when their expression offends the deeply held beliefs of important university constituencies, such as wealthy donors in the case of private universities, or the general public, in the case of state universities. The danger that these constituencies might take offense at faculty speech perennially overhangs universities, and this threat persists whether faculty speech relates to faculty expertise, as in the case of Edward A. Ross, or whether it is seemingly unrelated to that expertise, as in the recent and controversial case of Sami Al-Arian at the University of South Florida.[95]

The most effective way that universities can insulate themselves from this threat is categorically to disclaim responsibility for the extramural expression of their faculty. Just as universities disclaim responsibility for the many conflicting contentions of the millions of books they collect in their libraries, so that no one can plausibly claim that a university supports fascism merely because its library contains a copy of *Mein Kampf*, so universities typically disclaim responsibility for the many conflicting contentions of their faculty, so that no one can plausibly claim that a university supports high tariffs merely because a professor in its economics department happens to advocate for such tariffs. The "1915 Declaration" argues that this lack of responsibility follows directly from the fact that freedom of research prohibits universities from controlling the research publications of their faculty.[96]

It is plain that universities would be placed in an extremely awkward position were they to refuse responsibility for publications of faculty that relate to professional competence, but accept such responsibility for extramural expression that is unrelated to professional competence. In such circumstances, universities would virtually invite offended constituencies to argue that faculty publications should be censored because they are insufficiently related to scholarly expertise to merit the protection of freedom of research. Universities would thus strengthen their ability to protect freedom of research if they were categorically to refuse responsibility for the publications of their faculty, regardless of the precise connection between such publications and the academic expertise for which faculty are hired or trained. The advantages of such a categorical rule prompted Abbott Lawrence

Lowell to support exactly this rationale for freedom of extramural expression:

> If a university or college censors what its professors may say, if it restrains them from uttering something that it does not approve, it thereby assumes responsibility for that which it permits them to say. This is logical and inevitable, but it is a responsibility which an institution of learning would be very unwise in assuming.... If a university is right in restraining its professors, it has a duty to do so, and it is responsible for whatever it permits. There is no middle ground. Either the university assumes full responsibility for permitting its professors to express certain opinions in public, or it assumes no responsibility whatever, and leaves them to be dealt with like other citizens by the public authorities according to the laws of the land.[97]

Freedom of extramural expression can be defended on these grounds, as good policy designed to minimize the institutional vulnerability faced by universities seeking to protect freedom of research and inquiry. Viewed in this way, however, freedom of extramural expression ceases to constitute a distinct right of academic freedom; instead, it finds its justification in counsels of institutional expedience and prudence.

Coda: The International Studies in Higher Education Act of 2003

To unpack the premises and tensions that inform the traditional ideal of academic freedom is not merely to indulge in the arcana of intellectual history. The triumph of the "1915 Declaration" has been so complete that we have grown soft and complacent.[98] We have come all too easily to assume academic freedom as our "God-given right"[99] and have become oblivious to its distinct justifications and limitations. We have lost touch with the many ways in which the academic freedom we actually enjoy is rooted in progressive-era ideas about the function of the university, the role of professional expertise and self-regulation, and the preconditions for the production of knowledge. We blithely rely on the political strength and power of these ideas, even as we edge, more or less consciously, toward conceptions of academic freedom that depend instead on the authority of individual rights. We have yet squarely to face the dangers and difficulties of building a defensible structure of academic freedom on this alternate form of authority.

These dangers and difficulties might perhaps be worth pursuing if the old ideal of academic freedom were so antiquated as to be useless in the face of contemporary debates. I shall conclude this short essay, therefore, by briefly examining how the concept of academic freedom set forth and defended in the "1915 Declaration" might illuminate the contemporary controversy that inspired this conference, the proposed International Studies in Higher Education Act of 2003 ("ISHEA") that was passed by the House on October 21, 2003.[100]

The act would amend Title VI of the Higher Education Act of 1965[101] to provide that the Secretary of Education should consider, in decisions about how to allocate Title VI funds to foreign language, area, or international studies centers at universities, "the degree to which [their] activities . . . advance national interests, generate and disseminate information, and foster debate on American foreign policy from diverse perspectives."[102] ISHEA would create an International Advisory Board to "study, monitor, apprise [sic], and evaluate" programming supported by Title VI funds and to make recommendations to the Secretary of Education and to Congress about how "to improve the programs under this title to better reflect the national needs related to the homeland security, international education, and international affairs" and how "to assure that their relative authorized activities reflect diverse perspectives and the full range of views on world regions, foreign languages, and international affairs."[103]

The purpose of the Board was made clear by Congressman Howard Berman, who stated, in support of ISHEA, that it would

> help redress a problem which is a great concern of mine, namely, the lack of balance, and indeed the anti-American bias that pervades title VI–funded Middle East studies programs in particular. To the extent that it advances the national interest to commit taxpayer funds to institutions of higher education for the purpose of fostering expertise with regard to key regions of the world — and I would emphatically affirm that it does — then surely it is troubling when evidence suggests that many of the Middle East regional studies grantees are committed to a narrow point of view at odds with our national interest, a point of view that questions the validity of advancing American ideals

of democracy and the rule of law around the world, and in the Middle East in particular.

The Advisory Board's oversight function does not impinge on the academic freedom that is and must be enjoyed by our institutions of higher education. In establishing the board, we are doing no more than exercising our responsibility to ensure that the Federal funds we authorize and appropriate are expended properly.[104]

Conceived of as an individual right to be "from" external restraints, academic freedom would seem to have little to say about ISHEA. The act does not constrain research or publication; it simply funds expression that serves the purposes of the federal government. Seen from the angle of First Amendment rights, moreover, ISHEA would also seem unobjectionable, because the First Amendment typically allows government to spend its funds in ways that promote legitimate goals, and the advancement of both "diverse perspectives" and "national interests" seem to be perfectly acceptable objectives.[105] Congressman Berman is quite right that on this account the Advisory Board "does not impinge" on academic freedom, since its function is simply "to ensure that" federal funds are "expended" for the purposes for which they have been authorized.

Seen from the perspective of the traditional ideal of academic freedom, however, matters look quite different. Academic freedom as it has descended from the "1915 Declaration" focuses not merely on freedom from external constraints, or on the limits of state power, but also on the affirmative purposes of the university. It therefore requires us to ascertain whether the terms on which a university has received conditional funds, be it from the federal government or from a private donor, are consistent with these purposes. Congressman Berman's remarks confirm that ISHEA is most naturally read as imposing a standard of "diverse perspectives" that does not reflect the professional judgment of scholars, but that instead advances a specifically political principle of neutrality. In effect, the act requires that universities, as a precondition for funding, maintain "balance" between faculty "who both support and oppose American foreign policy."[106] Understood in this way, ISHEA uses an overtly political standard to override norms of professional competence and relevance. It would thus be incompatible with academic freedom for a university to impose this standard of "diverse perspectives" on its faculty in any decisions regulating teaching or research. The same would be true, a fortiori, for the act's requirement that Title VI centers serve "national interests."

It is true, of course, that the traditional idea of academic freedom does not yield the conclusion that ISHEA is unconstitutional or illegal. It does not in any way prevent the federal government from offering funds to universities on the terms contained in the act. But it does provide rather clear guidance to universities on the distinct question of whether and how they can ethically apply the standards contained in ISHEA. It is one thing for a university to use Title VI funds to stage a politically "balanced" event featuring speakers who are for and against American policy in the Middle East. It is quite another for a university to accept Title VI funds on the condition that it use ISHEA's standards of "diverse perspectives" and "national interests" in designing its curriculum or in selecting, evaluating, or supporting its faculty. The latter would be plainly prohibited by the "1915 Declaration," because it would transform a university into a "proprietary institution" that merely promotes "opinions held by . . . persons . . . who provide the funds for [its] maintenance."

The danger of our universities' regressing to this kind of proprietary status is, paradoxically, greater now than ever before. In 1902, John Dewey warned that "the financial factor in the conduct of the modern university is continually growing in importance, and very serious problems arise in adjusting this factor to strict educational ideals. . . ."

> The danger lies in the difficulty of making money adequate as a means, and yet keeping it in its place — not permitting it to usurp any of the functions of control which belong only to educational purposes. To these, if the university be a true university, money and all things connected therewith must be subordinate. But the pressure to get the means is tending to make it an end; and this is academic materialism — the worst foe of freedom of work in its widest sense.[107]

The need for money has only grown worse, exponentially worse, since 1902.[108] And now, as state funding diminishes, universities are turning once again to the private sources of support that the "1915 Declaration" found so potentially corrupting.

We will need clear heads to find our way through the ethical dilemmas that the escalating demand for financial resources will predictably produce. The "1915 Declaration" developed the idea of academic freedom precisely in order to explain why university faculty members ought to enjoy a concededly "peculiar" and "paradoxical" immunity from the dictation of those who paid their salaries.[109] It established a framework for the analysis and defense of academic freedom that has proved remarkably durable and successful. Conceptions of individual rights, by contrast, not only are incapable of defending the university as a site for the production of knowledge, but also tend to be notoriously poor in analyzing conditions on funding, because they intrinsically privilege the autonomous capacity of persons to consent to these conditions.

As its application to the proposed International Studies in Higher Education Act of 2003 suggests, the framework of analysis constructed by the "Declaration" offers a normatively useful map to the professional dilemmas that a future of conditional funding will predictably pose to modern universities. It is a map, however, that squarely depends on traditional progressive ideas about the relationship between knowledge and an ambient framework of professional norms of inquiry. Because this map is likely to prove increasingly indispensable in the years ahead, I strongly suggest that we continue to deploy it until we are quite certain something better is in the offing, or until our skepticism of its intellectual premises is so great as to leave us no alternative but abandonment.

NOTES

1. Sidney Hook, "Past and Future: The Long View," in Hook (ed.), *In Defense of Academic Freedom* (New York: Pegasus, 1971), p. 12.

2. *Ibid.*

3. Nicholas Murray Butler, commencement day address, June 6, 1917, quoted in Richard Hofstadter and Walter P. Metzger, *The Development of Academic Freedom in the United States* (New York: Columbia University Press, 1955), p. 499. Butler made good on his threat, harassing professors who were opposed to the war. In fact, Charles Beard resigned from Columbia in disgust at Butler's efforts to force vocal opponents of the war to leave the university (*ibid.*, pp. 499–502). The incident may be profitably compared with Butler's refusal, six years later, "to interfere with Columbia University's assistant professor of Latin because the professor is a local head of the Fascisti movement" ("Butler Won't

Discipline Fascist Professor; Declares Columbia Is for Academic Freedom," *New York Times*, April 9, 1923). Butler wrote to the General Secretary of the Italian Chamber of Commerce, "An individual whose personal acts tend to bring the university into contempt and to injure its influence may properly and without any departure from the highest university ideals be asked to carry on his work elsewhere. But to attempt to discipline a university teacher for his private or political opinions would be most unbecoming" (*ibid.*).

4. In 1907, Charles W. Eliot noted that the "principal new difficulty" "in regard to academic freedom for teachers" was "the pressure in a democracy of a concentrated multitudinous public opinion. The great majority of the people in a given community may hold passionately to some dogma in religion, some economic doctrine, or some political or social opinion or practise [*sic*], and may resent strongly the expression by a public teacher of religious, economic, political, or social views unlike those held by the majority. In parts of our country at this moment liberty of thought and speech on certain topics is, to say the least, imperfect for men who do not coincide with the prevailing opinions and sentiments of the community in which they dwell." "Academic Freedom," *Science*, July 5, 1907, p. 1.

5. See, for example, Jennifer Jacobson, "The Clash Over Middle East Studies," *Chronicle of Higher Education*, February 6, 2004, p. 8.

6. Andrew P. Morriss, "Exploding Myths: An Empirical and Economic Reassessment of the Rise of Employment At-Will," *Missouri Law Review* 59.3 (1994), p. 688.

7. *Payne v. Western & At. R.R.*, 81 Tenn. (1884), pp. 518–20.

8. Eliot, "Academic Freedom," p. 3. Eliot noted that university boards could "exclude from the teachings of the university unpopular or dangerous subjects. In some states they even treat professors' positions as common political spoils; and all too frequently, both in state and endowed institutions, they fail to treat members of the teaching staff with that high consideration to which their functions entitle them."

9. "Even in the second decade of the twentieth century, powerful persons outside the universities, and within the universities — trustees, presidents, and deans, or heads of departments — still regarded their academic staffs as hired hands to be appointed and dismissed at will. Such persons were regarded as the enemies of academic freedom." Edward Shils, "Do We Still Need Academic Freedom?" *American Scholar* 62.2 (1993), p. 187.

10. Morriss, "Exploding Myths," p. 689. Employment-at-will is typically qualified by common law and statutory exceptions that are chiefly irrelevant to the values and purposes of academic freedom. In a very few states, however, employers are forbidden by statute from discharging employees because of the

exercise of constitutionally protected rights. South Carolina, for example, prohibits employers from discharging employees "because of political opinions or
the exercise of political rights and privileges guaranteed to every citizen by the
Constitution and laws of the United States or by the Constitution and laws of
this State." *South Carolina Code*, sec. 16–17–560 (2003). Connecticut prohibits
employers from discharging or disciplining employees "on account of the exercise . . . of rights guaranteed by the first amendment to the United States Constitution . . . , provided such activity does not substantially or materially interfere
with the employee's bona fide job performance or the working relationship
between the employee and the employer." *Connecticut General Statutes Annotated*,
title 31, ch. 557, pt. 2, secs. 31–51q. See also *California Labor Code* secs. 1101 and
1102 (2004), *Ali v. Los Angeles Focus Publication*, 112 Cal. App. 4th 1477 (2003);
Louisiana Revised Statutes 23:961 (2003); Louisiana Attorney General Opinion
No. 93–567 (1993). Compare *Novosel v. Nationwide Insurance Co.*, 721 F.2d 894
(3d Cir. 1983), with *Paul v. Lankenau Hospital*, 569 A.2d 346 (Pa. 1990). But these
states are exceptional. The "prevailing view" is instead that the "First Amendment cannot be the basis of a public policy exception in wrongful discharge
claims in the absence of state action." Lisa B. Bingham, "Employee Free Speech in
the Workplace: Using the First Amendment as Public Policy for Wrongful Discharge Actions," *Ohio State Law Journal* 55.2 (1994), p. 348. See, for example,
Barr v. Kelso-Burnett Co. 478 N.E.2d 1354, 1357 (Ill. 1985) (the First Amendment
"mandate[s] nothing concerning the relationship of private individuals, including
private individuals in the employer-employee relationship," so that employers
can discharge employees on the basis of speech that would be protected by the
First Amendment from direct government regulation); *Newman v. Legal Services
Corp.*, 628 F.Supp. 535 (D.D.C.1986) (no cause of action against a private
employer for discharged for exercising their constitutional rights of freedom of
speech and association); *Allen v. Safeway Stores, Inc.*, 699 P.2d 277 (Wyo.1985)
(same); *Korb v. Raytheon Corp.*, 574 N.E. 2d 370 (Mass. 1991) (although employee
"has a right to express views with which" his employer disagrees, "he has no right
to do so at" his employer's "expense"); *Shovelin v. Central New Mexico Electrical
Cooperative, Inc.*, 850 P.2d 996 (N.M. 1993) (same).

11. No doubt this loss of memory is due in part to the widespread acceptance of the institution of tenure. We would do well to recall, however, that
tenure typically rests on contractual agreements and that the idea of academic
freedom has made American universities amenable to these agreements.

12. Lawrence M. Friedman, *The Republic of Choice: Law, Authority, and Culture* (Cambridge, MA: Harvard University Press, 1990); Mary Ann Glendon,
Rights Talk: The Impoverishment of Political Discourse (New York: Free Press,
1991).

13. John R. Searle, "Two Concepts of Academic Freedom," in Edmund L. Pincoffs (ed.), *The Concept of Academic Freedom* (Austin: University of Texas Press, 1975), p. 92.

14. *Ibid.* See Shils, "Do We Still Need Academic Freedom?" p. 18. We can begin to appreciate the depth and reach of this reconceptualization of academic freedom by parsing the mission statement of the Foundation for Individual Rights in Education (FIRE), an important organization dedicated to freedom on American campuses: "The mission of FIRE is to defend and sustain individual rights at America's increasingly repressive and partisan colleges and universities. These rights include freedom of speech, legal equality, due process, religious liberty, and sanctity of conscience – the essential qualities of individual liberty and dignity. FIRE's core mission is to protect the unprotected and to educate the public and communities of concerned Americans about the threats to these rights on our campuses and about the means to preserve them." Mission statement, Foundation for Individual Rights in Education, http://www.thefire.org/mission.php.

15. The story is told in Hofstadter and Metzger, *Development of Academic Freedom*, pp. 367–412.

16. *Ibid.*, pp. 388–89. The influences of this German vision are manifest in early statements of American academic freedom. Harlan Stone, for example, when he was dean of Columbia Law School, proclaimed, "Especially do I hold to the opinion that the university professor should voluntarily renounce the rôle of the propagandist and the agitator. The university stands for scientific truth. Its attitude, if it would preserve its influence, must never be that of the partisan, but rather than of the judicially minded. The university professor in acting such a part inevitably subjects the university as well as himself to partisan attack in a controversy in which it can with propriety take no part and to which it is powerless to offer a defense." "University Influence," *Columbia University Quarterly* 20 (1918), p. 338. The original academic freedom policy of the University of California, promulgated by President Robert Gordon Sproul in 1934, also advanced a vision of professional vocation that was deeply influenced by this German idea of a "dispassionate" scholarship which, when it considered "political, social or sectarian movements," merely "dissected and examined" and left "the conclusion . . . with no tipping of the scales, to the logic of the facts." Quoted in Richard C. Atkinson, "Academic Freedom and the Research University," http:// www. ucop. edu/ucophome/coordrev/policy/Academic_Freedom_Paper.pdf, repr. in *Proceedings of the American Philosophical Society* 148.2 (2004), pp. 196–97. The University of California recently revised its academic freedom policy explicitly to reject this vision of the professoriat: "The original language of APM–010 [University of California Academic Personnel Manual, Section 10], which was drafted

in 1934, associated academic freedom with scholarship that gave 'play to intellect rather than to passion.' . . . The revised version of APM–010 holds that academic freedom depends upon the quality of scholarship, which is to be assessed by the content of scholarship, not by the motivations that led to its production. The revision of APM–010 therefore does not distinguish between 'interested' and 'disinterested' scholarship; it differentiates instead between competent and incompetent scholarship. Although competent scholarship requires an open mind, this does not mean that faculty are unprofessional if they reach definite conclusions. It means rather that faculty must always stand ready to revise their conclusions in the light of new evidence or further discussion. Although competent scholarship requires the exercise of reason, this does not mean that faculty are unprofessional if they are committed to a definite point of view. It means rather that faculty must form their point of view by applying professional standards of inquiry rather than by succumbing to external and illegitimate incentives such as monetary gain or political coercion. Competent scholarship can and frequently does communicate salient viewpoints about important and controversial questions." University of California Academic Personnel Manual, sec. 10, http://www.ucop.edu/ acadadv/acadpers/apm/apm-010.pdf. See Robert C. Post, "Academic Freedom and the 'Intifada Curriculum,'" *Academe* 89.3 (2003), p. 19 ("There is no academic norm that prohibits scholarship from communicating definite viewpoints about important and controversial questions, like democracy, human rights, or the welfare state. Faculty must be free to communicate these viewpoints in their pedagogy. Political passion is in fact the engine that drives some of the best scholarship and teaching at the University of California, and this is particularly true in the humanities and social sciences").

17. Hofstadter and Metzger, *Development of Academic Freedom*, p. 403.

18. I should make clear at the outset that in discussing academic freedom I am not focusing on the forms of "academic freedom" that the United States Supreme Court has occasionally located in the First Amendment. See, for example, *Grutter v. Bollinger*, 123 S.Ct. 2325, 2357 (2003); J. Peter Byrne, "Academic Freedom: A 'Special Concern of the First Amendment,'" *Yale Law Journal* 99 (1989), pp. 251–340; David M. Rabban, "A Functional Analysis of Individual and Institutional Academic Freedom Under the First Amendment," *Law and Contemporary Problems* 53.3 (1990), pp. 227–301. Academic freedom as a constitutional concept is a distinct, complex, and difficult subject, which I shall not address here. For my views on the subject of constitutional academic freedom, see Robert Post, "Constitutionally Interpreting the FSM Controversy," in Robert Cohen and Reginald E. Zelnik (eds.), *The Free Speech Movement: Reflections on Berkeley in the 1960s* (Berkeley: University of California Press, 2002). Academic freedom as a constitutional concept focuses on the relationship

between the university (and its component parts) and the state. It is essentially about the limits of state power. In this paper, I shall focus instead on academic freedom as an ideal that elaborates how a university should govern itself, most particularly in its relations with its faculty. (See n.19.) The canonical expression of this ideal of academic freedom is the American Association of University Professors, "1940 Statement of Principles on Academic Freedom and Tenure with 1970 Interpretive Comments," in *Policy Documents and Reports*, 9th ed. (Washington, D.C.: American Association of University Professors, 2001), p. 3. Over 180 educational organizations have endorsed this statement, and many colleges and universities have incorporated it into their faculty handbooks. It is generally regarded as the definitive account of academic freedom at American universities. On the distinction between academic freedom as a principle of constitutional law and academic freedom as a principle of university governance, see Walter P. Metzger, "Profession and Constitution: Two Definitions of Academic Freedom in America," *Texas Law Review* 66 (1988), pp. 1265–1322; David M. Rabban, "Academic Freedom," in Leonard W. Levy, Kenneth L. Karst, and Dennis J. Mahoney (ed.), *Encyclopedia of the American Constitution* (New York: Macmillan, 1986), pp. 12–13.

19. Student academic freedom, which derives from the German concept of *Lernfreiheit*, is a very different subject that in America was disassociated from *Lehrfreiheit* quite early on. See Hofstadter and Metzger, *Development of Academic Freedom*, p. 397; and Metzger, "Profession and Constitution," pp. 1270–71. For a rare articulation of student academic freedom, see American Association of University Professors, "Joint Statement on Rights and Freedoms of Students," in *Policy Documents and Reports*, p. 261.

20. On the important distinction between the nature of the interests protected by a right and the nature of the entity that holds or asserts a right, see Robert Post, "Democratic Constitutionalism and Cultural Heterogeneity," *Australian Journal of Legal Philosophy* 25 (2000), pp. 192–93.

21. I should emphasize that I do not believe that this is a comprehensive or entirely accurate account of First Amendment rights. See Robert Post, *Constitutional Domains: Democracy, Community, Management* (Cambridge, MA: Harvard University Press, 1995). But it is plain that in the popular understanding First Amendment rights are of this character. Because most members of the academic profession are not legal professionals, they conceive of rights of academic freedom according to the same individualist paradigm that they imagine is protected by the First Amendment.

22. Robert M. MacIver, *Academic Freedom in Our Time* (New York: Columbia University Press, 1955), p. 9.

23. American Association of University Professors, "1915 Declaration of

Principles on Academic Freedom and Academic Tenure," in *Policy Documents and Reports*. On its authorship, see Walter P. Metzger, "The 1940 Statement of Principles on Academic Freedom and Tenure," *Law and Contemporary Problems* 53.3 (1990), pp. 12–13.

24. Orrin Leslie Elliott, *Stanford University: The First Twenty-Five Years* (Stanford: Stanford University Press, 1937), p. 341. Eight days later, Jane Stanford wrote to Jordan again: "There is a very deep and bitter feeling of indignation throughout the community...that Stanford University is lending itself to partisanism and even to dangerous socialism.... Professor Ross cannot be trusted, and he should go.... He is a dangerous man. Dear Dr. Jordan, I am very much in earnest in this matter, and I have just reasons for feelings so" (*ibid.*, pp. 343–44). For a discussion of the case, see Thomas L. Haskell, "Justifying the Rights of Academic Freedom in the Era of 'Power/Knowledge,'" in Louis Menand (ed.), *The Future of Academic Freedom* (Chicago: University of Chicago Press, 1996), pp. 48–53; Mary O. Furner, *Advocacy and Objectivity: A Crisis in the Professionalization of American Social Science, 1865–1905* (Lexington: University Press of Kentucky, 1975), pp. 229–59; Hofstadter and Metzger, *Development of Academic Freedom*, pp. 436–45.

25. "Academic Freedom," *New York Times*, June 20, 1915. See "Report of the Committee of Inquiry on the Case of Professor Scott Nearing of the University of Pennsylvania," *Bulletin of the American Association of University Professors* 11.3 (1916), pp. 7–57.

26. "Report of the Committee of Inquiry," p. 10. Several months later, the Board offered a somewhat fuller explanation (pp. 25–28).

27. "The Philadelphia Martyr," *New York Times*, Oct. 10, 1915. "The professors and assistant professors," the *Times* sniffed, "are the chartered libertines of speech."

28. Quoted in Evans Clark, "Business Men in Control of American Colleges," *New York Times*, June 10, 1917.

29. *Ibid.*

30. "Academic Freedom," *New York Times*, June 20, 1915. For similar views, see "Academic Freedom," *New York Times*, June 7, 1901 ("The freedom of a man who spends his money for education to elect the sort of education for which he will spend it is, on the face of it, as well established a right as any that that the educators can lay claim to"), and "Academic Freedom," *New York Times*, March 4, 1903 (questioning "the assumption that the teacher has a certain inherent right to be maintained at the cost of some one else without consulting any but his own judgment as to what or how he will teach.... Very few of us can successfully insist upon keeping our independence unimpaired and being paid for it").

31. John Dewey, "Professorial Freedom," *New York Times*, Oct. 22, 1915.

32. Arthur O. Lovejoy, "Academic Freedom," in Edwin R.A. Seligman (ed.), *Encyclopaedia of the Social Sciences* (New York: Macmillan, 1930), p. 384.

33. "1915 Declaration of Principles," p. 294.

34. *Ibid.*, p. 295.

35. *Ibid.*

36. Matthew W. Finkin, "Intramural Speech, Academic Freedom, and the First Amendment," *Texas Law Review* 66 (1988), p. 1335.

37. "1915 Declaration of Principles," p. 295.

38. *Ibid.*

39. *Ibid.*, p. 294.

40. Lovejoy, "Academic Freedom," pp. 384–85.

41. "1915 Declaration of Principles," p. 293.

42. *Ibid.* John Dewey articulated this distinction as early as 1902: "[I]t is necessary to make a distinction between the university proper and those teaching bodies, called by whatever name, whose primary business is to inculcate a fixed set of ideas and facts. The former aims to discover and communicate truth and to make its recipients better judges of truth and more effective in applying it to the affairs of life. The latter have as their aim the perpetuation of a certain way of looking at things current among a given body of persons. Their purpose is to disciple rather than to discipline — not indeed at the expense of truth, but in such a way as to conserve what is already regarded as truth by some considerable body of persons." "Academic Freedom," in *The Middle Works, 1899–1924*, ed. Jo Ann Boydston, vol. 2, *1902–1903* (Carbondale: Southern Illinois Press, 1976), p. 53. Dewey conceptualized this as a distinction between an "obligation on behalf of all the truth to society at large" and an obligation "of a part of truth to a part of society" (p. 54).

43. "1915 Declaration of Principles," p. 293. As Lovejoy would later put it: "A state may, in short, have a university or do without. But it cannot have one, in the usual and proper sense, if it excludes... the method of free inquiry and free expression, which is necessary to the functioning of this type of social institution." "Academic Freedom," p. 385.

44. "1915 Declaration of Principles," pp. 293–94.

45. *Ibid.*, p. 294. In his letter to the *New York Times* protesting its support of the University of Pennsylvania's firing of Nearing ("Professorial Freedom"), Dewey objected: "You apparently take the ground that a modern university is a personally conducted institution like a factory, and that if for any reason the utterances of any teacher, within or without the university walls, are objectionable to the Trustees, there is nothing more to be said. This view virtually makes the Trustees owners of a private undertaking.... [A] discussion by The Times of whether modern universities should be conceived as privately owned and

managed institutions, or as essentially public institutions, with responsibilities to the public, would be welcome." Dewey left no doubt that, in his view, "the modern university is in every respect, save its legal management, a public institution with public responsibilities."

46. For a discussion, see Haskell, "Justifying the Rights of Academic Freedom," pp. 63–83; David M. Rabban, "Can Academic Freedom Survive Postmodernism?" *California Law Review* 86 (1998), pp. 1377–89.

47. Charles S. Peirce, "The Fixation of Belief," in *Values in a Universe of Chance: Selected Writings of Charles S. Peirce*, ed. Philip P. Wiener (Stanford: Stanford University Press, 1958), pp. 110–11. On the interrelationship between professional standards of inquiry and the production of knowledge, see Haskell, "Justifying the Rights of Academic Freedom," pp. 63–64. On the relationship between scientific methodology and claims of academic freedom, see Hofstadter and Metzger, *Development of Academic Freedom*, pp. 363–66.

48. "1915 Declaration of Principles," p. 298. On the relationship between academic freedom and a theory of knowledge, see Searle, "Two Concepts of Academic Freedom," pp. 88–89.

49. "1915 Declaration of Principles," p. 298.

50. *Ibid.*, p. 300.

51. The "traditional conception of academic freedom . . . limits the autonomy of professors by requiring adherence to professional norms." David M. Rabban, "Does Academic Freedom Limit Faculty Autonomy?" *Texas Law Review* 66 (1988), pp. 1408–1409. Lovejoy accurately caught the tension between individual freedom and professional obligations when he defined academic freedom as "the freedom of the teacher or research worker in higher institutions of learning to investigate and discuss the problems of his science and to express his conclusions, whether through publication or in the instruction of students, without interference from political or ecclesiastical authority, or from the administrative officials of the institution in which he is employed, unless his methods are found by qualified bodies of his own profession to be clearly incompetent or contrary to professional ethics." "Academic Freedom," p. 384.

52. For a particularly blunt statement of this point, see Section 5 of the Academic Personnel Manual of the University of California: "An intelligent ('planned') education economy, which formulates plans essential for the realization of the ends for which the university exists, will necessarily define and limit the activities of individuals and departments. Such definition and limitation is no infringement of academic freedom provided (a) the plan or idea is itself reasonable, i.e., if it sets forth the conditions essential for the realization of significant aims, and if (b) the plan has come into being through the democratic means of discussion and mutual give and take, within the Faculty, rather than arbitrarily

imposed from without." Another way of stating the matter would be to say that the rights of individual members of the faculty and of individual departments are never absolute but are always to be defined in terms of functions performed, which are in turn defined in terms of the ends for the sake of which the functions are carried out.

53. What "sets academic freedom apart as a distinct freedom is its vocational claim of special and limited accountability in respect to all academically related pursuits of the teacher-scholar: an accountability not to any institutional or societal standard of economic benefit, acceptable interest, right thinking, or socially constructive theory, but solely to a fiduciary standard of professional integrity.... The maintenance of academic freedom contemplates an accountability in respect to academic investigations and utterances solely in respect of their professional integrity, a matter usually determined by reference to professional ethical standards of truthful disclosure and reasonable care." William Van Alstyne, "The Specific Theory of Academic Freedom and the General Issue of Civil Liberty," in Pincoffs (ed.), *Concept of Academic Freedom*, p. 71.

54. *Ibid.* There is a close relationship between this claim and the exemplary tradition of "shared governance" that is embraced by the University of California. See Standing Orders of the Regents, including Standing Orders 105.2 and 103.9; Daniel L. Simmons, "Shared Governance in the University of California: An Overview (1995)" (manuscript, Office of the UC General Counsel); John A. Douglass, "Shared Governance at UC: An Historical Review (1995)" (manuscript, Office of the UC General Counsel).

55. "1915 Declaration of Principles," p. 294.

56. *Ibid.* Hence the conclusion of Thomas Haskell: "Historically speaking, the heart and soul of academic freedom lie not in free speech but in professional autonomy and collegial self-governance. Academic freedom came into being as a defense of the disciplinary community (or, more exactly, the university conceived as an ensemble of such communities)." Haskell, "Justifying the Rights of Academic Freedom," p. 54. There is, of course, an ambiguity at the heart of the notion of a single "academic profession," because in practice the profession always splinters into distinct disciplinary communities. This ambiguity is reflected in the persisting tension between the centrifugal force of departmental self-governance and the centripetal force of unified faculty self-governance, frequently in the form of a faculty senate.

57. "It is ... inadmissible that the power of determining when departures from the requirements of the scientific spirit and method have occurred, should be vested in bodies not composed of members of the academic profession. Such bodies necessarily lack full competency to judge of those requirements; their intervention can never be exempt from the suspicion that it is dictated by other

motives than zeal for the integrity of science.... It follows that university teachers must be prepared to assume this responsibility for themselves." "1915 Declaration of Principles," p. 298.

58. *McIntyre v. Ohio Elections Commission*, 514 U.S. 334, 342 (1995).

59. See Frederick Schauer, *Free Speech: A Philosophical Enquiry* (Cambridge, UK: Cambridge University Press, 1982), pp. 15–34.

60. See Robert Post, "Reconciling Theory and Doctrine in First Amendment Jurisprudence," *California Law Review* 88.6 (2000), pp. 2363–66.

61. See Bernard Williams, *Truth and Truthfulness: An Essay in Genealogy* (Princeton, NJ: Princeton University Press, 2002), pp. 213–19.

62. See Shils, "Do We Still Need Academic Freedom?" p. 188: "Academic freedom ... is no longer thought [to have] any close relationship to the search for or the affirmation of truths discovered by study and reflection. It has become part of the more general right of the freedom of expression. Expression is not confined to the expression of reasoned and logically and empirically supported statements; it now pretty much extends to the expression of any desire, any sentiment, any impulse."

63. Alexander Meiklejohn, *Political Freedom: The Constitutional Powers of the People* (New York: Harper, 1960), p. 27. See Laurence Tribe, *American Constitutional Law*, 2nd ed. (Mineola, NY: Foundation Press, 1988), pp. 940–41 ("the presumption of the equality of ideas is a corollary of the basic requirement that the government may not aim at the communicative impact of expressive conduct").

64. Post, "Reconciling Theory and Doctrine in First Amendment Jurisprudence"; Robert Post, "Equality and Autonomy in First Amendment Jurisprudence," *Michigan Law Review* 95 (1997), pp. 1517–41.

65. It might be said that in a democracy all private organizations ought to respect free and critical inquiry to the maximum extent compatible with the achievement of organizational objectives. See Robert Post, "Between Governance and Management: The History and Theory of the Public Forum," *UCLA Law Review* 34 (1987), pp. 1713–1835. But on this account the objectives of higher education must be specified. If these objectives are said to include the production of knowledge, academic freedom will assume the roughly the same contours as those advanced in the "1915 Declaration of Principles." But if, as is sometimes maintained, these objectives are instead said to include the exemplification of the democratic value of free and critical inquiry, academic freedom would appear to be rendered quite vulnerable. It does not take a deep social theorist to see that if universities claim to be contributing nothing more to the public good than embodying freedoms that all in a democratic society ought theoretically to enjoy, they would rapidly attract public resentment and jealousy,

rather than support. It would be neither effective nor persuasive for scholars to demand the special privileges of academic freedom on the grounds that they happen to be lucky enough to be employed by institutions that exemplify freedoms that all ought, in the abstract, to possess. Members of a public willing to repress themselves could hardly be above the temptation to inflict similar repression on scholars who claim no function beyond shining forth the virtues of unregulated freedom, if only to remove such painful symbols of what members of the public have themselves lost. Reduced to so fragile a state, academic freedom could scarcely offer the protections that faculty require.

66. On the "1940 Statement of Principles," see n.18.

67. "1940 Statement of Principles," pp. 3–4.

68. "1915 Declaration of Principles," p. 295.

69. See, for example, Shils, "Do We Still Need Academic Freedom?" p. 194.

70. For an example of the development of an important norm of professional conduct, see n.16.

71. Joan W. Scott, "Academic Freedom as an Ethical Practice," in Menand (ed.), *Future of Academic Freedom*, pp. 166–78.

72. As Bernard Williams writes: "The orderly management of scientific inquiry implies that the vast majority of suggestions which an uninformed person might mistake for a contribution to science will, quite properly, not be taken seriously and will not find their way to discussion or publication. Very rarely the cranky view turns out to be right, and then the scientists who ignored it are attacked for dogmatism and prejudice. But, they can rightly reply, there was no way of telling in advance that this particular cranky idea was to be taken seriously; the only alternative to their practice of prejudice would be to take seriously all such suggestions, and science would grind to a halt." *Truth and Truthfulness*, p. 217.

73. David A. Hollinger, "What Does It Mean to Be 'Balanced' in Academia?" Paper presented at the annual meeting of the American Historical Association, January 9, 2005.

74. Louis Menand, "The Limits of Academic Freedom," in Menand (ed.), *Future of Academic Freedom*, p. 10.

75. Shils, "Do We Still Need Academic Freedom?" p. 203.

76. I have elsewhere argued, for example, that trust in the legitimacy of courts is what sustains the perception of the rule of law whenever the application of legal standards demands analogous interpretive judgments. See Robert C. Post, "Foreword: Fashioning the Legal Constitution: Culture, Courts, and Law," *Harvard Law Review* 117.1 (2003), pp. 4–112.

77. Because these norms are interpretive judgments, their content and authority must ultimately derive from shared community commitments. See

Robert C. Post, "The Constitutional Concept of Public Discourse: Outrageous Opinion, Democratic Deliberation, and *Hustler Magazine v. Falwell*," *Harvard Law Review* 103.3 (1990), pp. 658–59.

78. Hence Harvard President Abbott Lawrence Lowell: "Experience has proved, and probably no one would now deny, that knowledge can advance, or at least can advance most rapidly, only by means of an unfettered search for truth on the part of those who devote their lives to seeking it in their respective fields, and by complete freedom in imparting to their pupils the truth that they have found." "Report for 1916–17," in Henry Aaron Yeomans, *Abbott Lawrence Lowell, 1856–1943* (Cambridge, MA: Harvard University Press, 1948).

79. "1915 Declaration of Principles," p. 298. The declaration did not inherit the goal of empowering students to think for themselves from the German conception of university education. German practice focused far more on "'convincing' one's students ... winning them over to the personal system and philosophical views of the professor" (Hofstadter and Metzger, *Development of Academic Freedom*, p. 400).

80. "1915 Declaration of Principles," p. 296.

81. I have in mind recent conservative assaults on university faculty for allegedly indoctrinating students. See, for example, the organization NoIndoctrination.org, whose Web site may be found at http://www.noindoctrination. org, or the proposed Academic Bill of Rights, which may be found at http:// studentsforacademicfreedom.org. Even in the context of constitutional academic freedom, an account of professional norms seems essential to distinguishing education from infringements of the constitutional rights of students. See, for example, *Axson-Flynn v. Johnson*, 356 F.3d 1277, 1290 (10th Cir. 2004) (faculty immune from suit if their assignments "reasonably related to legitimate pedagogical concerns").

82. Metzger, "Profession and Constitution," p. 1276.

83. "1915 Declaration of Principles," pp. 299–300.

84. "1940 Statement of Principles," p. 4. The drafting of the statement's protection for extramural utterance is recounted in Metzger, "The 1940 Statement of Principles," pp. 51–64.

85. "Committee A Statement on Extramural Utterances," American Association of University Professors, *Policy Documents and Reports*, p. 32. For other AAUP interpretations of freedom of extramural expression, see "1970 Interpretative Comments," no. 3, in American Association of University Professors, *Policy Documents and Reports*, p. 5; "1970 Interpretative Comments," no. 4, *ibid.*, p. 6.

86. For an excellent discussion of this question, see Van Alstyne, "Specific Theory of Academic Freedom."

87. Lovejoy, "Academic Freedom," p. 386.

88. Quoted in Yeomans, *Abbott Lawrence Lowell*, p. 310. Searle, "Two Concepts of Academic Freedom," makes a similar point.

89. American Association of University Professors, "1925 Conference Statement on Academic Freedom and Tenure," *AAUP Bulletin* 11 (1925), p. 29.

90. See n.10.

91. *Pickering v. Board of Education*, 391 U.S. 563 (1968). For a general discussion, see Post, "Between Governance and Management."

92. Rebecca Gose Lynch, "Pawns of the State or Priests of Democracy? Analyzing Professors' Academic Freedom Rights Within the State's Managerial Realm," *California Law Review* 91.4 (2003), pp. 1061–1108.

93. See, for example, Noam Chomsky, *Hegemony or Survival: America's Quest for Global Dominance* (New York: Metropolitan, 2003).

94. "1915 Declaration of Principles," p. 298.

95. Sami Al-Arian, a computer science professor, was disciplined for statements concerning terrorism in the Middle East after September 11, 2001. See Joe Humphrey, "Professors Condemn Al-Arian's Firing," *Tampa Tribune*, June 15, 2003. For the AAUP investigative report on the Al-Arian case, see *Academe* 89.3 (2003), pp. 59–73.

96. "University teachers should be understood to be, with respect to the conclusions reached and expressed by them, no more subject to the control of the trustees, than are the judges subject to the control of the president, with respect to their decisions; while of course, *for the same reason*, trustees are no more to be held responsible for, or to be presumed to agree with, the opinions or utterances of professors, than the president can be assumed to approve of the legal reasonings of the courts." "1915 Declaration of Principles," p. 295 (emphasis added).

97. Quoted in Yeomans, *Abbott Lawrence Lowell*, pp. 311–12.

98. See Shils, "Do We Still Need Academic Freedom?" pp. 196–99 and 206.

99. Jacobson, "Clash over Middle East Studies."

100. HR 3077, 108th Cong., 1st Sess. (2003). See *Congressional Record* 149 no. H9759 (Oct. 21, 2003).

101. 20 U.S.C. sec. 1001 et seq.

102. HR 3077.

103. *Ibid*. The act provides that "nothing in this title shall be construed to authorize the International Advisory Board to mandate, direct, or control an institution of higher education's specific instructional content, curriculum, or program of instruction."

104. *Congressional Record* 149, no. H9757 (Oct. 21, 2003). The politics of the act are discussed in Jacobson, "Clash over Middle East Studies"; Michelle

Goldberg, "Osama University?" *Salon.com*, Nov. 6, 2003, http://www.salon. com/news/feature/2003/11/06/middle_east/index_np.html; Todd Gitlin, "Culture War, Round 3077," *American Prospect*, Jan. 1, 2004, p. 65; Alisa Solomon, "The Ideology Police," *Village Voice*, February 25, 2004; Anders Strindberg, "The New Commissars: Congress Threatens to Cut Off Funding to Collegiate Mideast Studies Departments that Refuse to Toe the Neocon Line," *American Conservative*, February 2, 2004, http://www.amconmag. com/2_2_04/ article.html.

105. For an analysis of the constitutionality of restrictions on the funding of speech, see Robert C. Post, "Subsidized Speech," *Yale Law Journal* 106.1 (1996), pp. 151–95. For a decision likely to be dispositive, see *National Endowment for the Arts v. Finley*, 524 U.S. 569 (1998).

106. Jacobson, "Clash over Middle East Studies" (quoting Stanley Kurtz, a major proponent of the act).

107. *Ibid.*

108. David L. Kirp, *Shakespeare, Einstein, and the Bottom Line: The Marketing of Higher Education* (Cambridge, MA: Harvard University Press, 2003); Sheldon Krimsky, *Science in the Private Interest: Has the Lure of Profits Corrupted Biomedical Research?* (Lanham, MD: Rowman and Littlefield, 2003).

109. Lovejoy, "Academic Freedom," p. 384.

Academic Norms, Contemporary Challenges: A Reply to Robert Post on Academic Freedom

Judith Butler

If academic freedom is no longer to be conceived of as an individual right protected under the First Amendment but rather to be seen as a prerogative that emerges in a specific institutional context, then it makes sense to supply a full and adequate description of the institutional context in which such a freedom is said to emerge. If academic norms condition the exercise of such a freedom, that is, if only faculty members who comply with academic norms earn the right to exercise a freedom that we call "academic," then a serious consideration of those norms is required, since they constitute the basis of the freedom in question here. Although Post calls his approach historical, my contention is that he does not fully treat academic norms as historical conventions, that is, ones that emerge, transform, and sometimes disappear, become the sites for consequential epistemological debate, and are subjected to repeated scrutiny as academic fields seek to renew themselves in light of new demands on knowledge and to achieve greater accountability.

The original efforts to secure academic freedom were thus efforts to clarify and institutionalize a set of employer-employee relationships in an academic setting. More specifically, academic freedom offered a constraint on employers who might dismiss faculty members on a whim, for perceived disloyalty, or for non-academic grounds, such as political affiliations and beliefs. They were not intended to establish a freedom that some individuals were said to possess, nor were they efforts to secure a right that was said to pertain to all circumstances. Of importance to Post here is the difference between academic freedom conceived of as an individual right or prerogative and academic freedom conceived of as the sign and effect of a restructured employment relationship. The contemporary understanding of academic freedom has veered from this original one, and Post seeks to rectify this wrong turn. Within contemporary life, we tend to conceive of academic freedom in terms of First Amendment rights, which we see as pertaining to all individuals by virtue of their status as citizens. In the course of individuating and universalizing rights, this First Amendment perspective fails to consider the specific institutional conditions and constraints of academic freedom. This freedom, according to Post, is to be conceived of not as a subset or instance of freedom of speech more generally, but as a freedom that is specific to the faculty-employer relationship and constitutes a precondition for conducting academic work. In particular, scholarly independence is a prerequisite for thriving in an academic position and so ought to be conceived of as a freedom that is, strictly speaking, nonuniversalizable — a freedom, in other words, that is contingent upon an employment situation, a feature of an employment relationship, and an institutional prerogative established under specific conditions.

In order to reanimate an appropriate version of academic freedom for our times, Post returns us to the "1915 Declaration of Principles on Academic Freedom and Academic Tenure." In his view, an error has occurred in the course of developing our current conception of academic freedom as an individual right on the order of First Amendment rights, universal and binding. The way to overcome this error is to return to the original formulation, which, he argues, has an important place in present debates. His argument is persuasive, but it does not consider the problem that historical translation into the present poses for our reading of the document now. Are there no new circumstances that call for a revision of the theory?

Although Post proposes to turn us away from an individualist model of rights toward an institutional model that is pervasively social, the social field he describes is structured by a version of academic freedom that appears impervious to social change. If Post believes that the doctrine of academic freedom must change in relation to new social pressures and new institutional demands, he does not tell us so in these pages. The normative claims of this paper, of course, are that it is important to distinguish between constitutional rights of free expression and academic freedom, and that the conflation of the two has obscured our understanding of the specificity of academic freedom and thus of the specific bases that justify its defense in the present.[1] The point is not to liberate faculty members from regulatory constraints but to make sure that they are free to engage in professionally competent forms of inquiry and teaching, where these constraints are construed as "necessary for the realization of the social purposes of the university" (see p. 64).

Post not only opposes individualism here but also insists on the social nature of academic work (the faculty-employer relation), situating academic work within the larger social purpose of the university. In this sense, academic freedom is construed as a *professional* rather than an individual freedom. Post sets up a contrast between understanding academic freedom as an individual-rights discourse and understanding it as a historically established way of regulating relations of employment. It is in the context of arguing in favor of this latter view that he makes the distinction between free speech, understood as an extramural prerogative of any faculty member or, indeed, any citizen, and academic freedom, understood as an exercise of freedom constrained by professional norms. One can agree with Post, as I do, that academic freedom ought not to be regarded as an individual freedom but disagree with both his conception of professional norms and his conception of the conditions for academic judgment in the contemporary academy, conditions that, in my view, clearly exceed what the founders of the 1915 document could have anticipated. In the course of his argument, Post makes a strong claim for academic freedom as a restraint imposed on administrators that obliges them to consider only the academic accomplishments of a given faculty member in hiring, promotion, and dismissal. Under the present circumstances, I'll argue toward the end of this paper, the new restrictions on grant funding proposed by the House of Representatives, as well as those adopted by some major foundations, have a strong influence on what will and will not be considered legitimate academic work.

What Is Academic Work Now, and How Is It Judged?

Upon examination, the original formulation of academic freedom would appear to rely on a very specific historical set of presumptions about knowledge, social function, and scientific progress that have, paradoxically, been revised and refuted on various grounds and in various directions over time, perhaps even as a consequence of the "advance" of knowledge itself. The "1915 Declaration" on which Post relies, suggests that academic work has a social function but is also a public service, that it requires its own place and function within an internally differentiated society and educational institution, that it contributes to knowledge quantitatively, and to the advance of knowledge, where that advance presupposes a progressive account of history itself. Importantly, as A.O. Lovejoy points out, a faculty member is charged with performing a function and rendering a service but cannot be told precisely and exhaustively how to perform that function or render that service: academic freedom delivers a mandate without a specific set of prescriptions about how best to fulfill it. Of course, rendering a service is different from performing a function, and doubtless it would be interesting to track those discourses (social service versus social functionalism) as they evolved and converged in the 1915 document. Indeed, the legal model of "separation of powers" becomes another way to understand internally differentiated functions. As Post remarks, the "1915 Declaration" notes that the president cannot approve the legal reasoning of the courts, and this is offered as an analogy for what administrators may not do in relation to academic freedom exercised by faculty members (see p. 67).

The freedom to pursue inquiry is explicitly linked with the goal of "advanc[ing] the sum of human knowledge" and "develop[ing] experts for various branches of the public service."[2] So two other discourses enter the fray: the notion of knowledge as an augmentable quantity, and thus the quantification of knowledge based on certain notions of scientific progress pertaining to knowledge acquisition; and the development of "expert" classes that are also supposed to contribute to "public service." Of course, models of scientific progress vary, and new ways of understanding scientific progress have come to complicate various fields of science in different ways. The relevance of the model of progress that assumes a quantitative augmentation of knowledge may have some relevance to a certain kind of archival work, but it is hardly represented by any of the prevailing paradigms of knowledge in the humanities or, indeed, the social sciences. Similarly, the questions whether academic professionalism is the same as an expert class and whether the stratification of society so that authority is vested in expert classes serves the public interest in the long run have been debated.[3]

These historically contingent ways of understanding the function and service of academic faculty members and the nature and direction of knowledge may have no final bearing on the argument about academic freedom. That seems yet to be determined. But they do constitute examples of historically specific ways of conceiving of the knowledge projects of academic faculty members, that projects must be described with some degree of accuracy if we are to understand the kinds of activities that a faculty member is free to perform, and the kinds of values served by preserving academic freedom. Indeed, how we conceive of knowledge has everything to do with what we consider our professional activity to be, and to be for. If an account of knowledge and knowledge production is meant to secure that academic freedom, it should agree with the ways knowledge is pursued now. Accordingly, if the "1915 Declaration" assumes that all knowledge follows the model of a conception of scientific progress that few, if any, scientists still embrace, then a clear need emerges to establish the value of knowledge inquiry in the arts, humanities, and social sciences, in ways that describe well those practices and their values.

In Post's view, academic freedom is meant to protect faculty members from the inappropriate intervention of university administrators and governmental powers; it provides no such protection from "professional norms." Those norms are considered stable and shared. But consider the quotation below from A.O. Lovejoy. Post uses it to support only the conclusion that faculty members should *not* be constrained to hold views that conform to the stated views of the university or, indeed, to the public-policy views of a particular government. This seems right. Academic expression — as distinct from extramural expression — that constitutes a divergence from professional norms is not protected under academic freedom. Lovejoy writes that the university's "function of seeking new truths will sometimes mean ... the undermining of widely or generally accepted beliefs. It is rendered impossible if the work of the investigator is shackled by the requirement that his conclusions shall never deviate either from generally accepted beliefs or from those accepted by the persons, private or official, through whom society provides the means for the maintenance of universities" (see p. 68). Interestingly, for Post, "professional norms" designate "widely and generally accepted beliefs" and to question this assumption is dangerous to academic freedom itself. For Lovejoy, though, academic freedom fundamentally implies safeguarding views that question widely and generally accepted beliefs (this was, indeed, William James's very definition of philosophical thinking). A serious disagreement thus come to the fore: *if we are to preserve academic freedom, either professional norms are necessary restraints that we ought not to question, or professional norms have to bear internal scrutiny.* In what follows, I'll consider whether it is possible to describe the work of faculty members without taking into account the ways professional norms are very often questioned and redefined by the work itself, and second, whether it is an important value of academic life to promote academic work that redefines disciplinary boundaries and modes of inquiry that change and revise the purview and character of professional norms themselves.[4]

Post draws the conclusion from positions such as Lovejoy's that a faculty member needs to be free from constraints imposed by his employer, that is, by the university, in order to be free to exercise the "liberty necessary to facilitate the advancement of knowledge, understood as the unimpeded application of professional norms of inquiry" (see p. 70). There are, however, two different kinds of constraints, one that is administrative (educational and governmental), from which any faculty member should be free, and one that is professional; for Post, there is no warrant to depart from professional norms, since they provide the necessary constraining conditions and the standards according to which free inquiry is conducted, and establish the general framework of competence.

The profession is characterized here as a norm-bearing collective subject that acts according to an instrumentalist model in "applying" commonly accepted norms. But perhaps the profession is a community that is fundamentally a venue for debate and disputation in which norms are scrutinized, revised, invoked in evaluative judgments, reconsidered, and subjected to innovation. This community is also always debating the terms by which admission to it is decided. Indeed, theorists of education such as J.S. Mill thought that there could be no "advance" of knowledge without fundamental disagreement, which suggests that if the "profession" was charged with advancing knowledge, it also needed to safeguard dissent and debate to fulfill that charge.

Apart from conceiving of the profession as grounded in a common understanding of norms, and of norms as representing common understandings, Post's description also involves a consideration of constraints that merits scrutiny. Is this the right way to conceive of how constraints actually work in the sphere of academic life? It is true that some constraints can come from the administration, such as when the administration tries to coerce a faculty member into maintaining or suppressing certain intellectual views, depending on whether those views conform to the administration's policies or threaten to produce a public-relations problem that would offend key constituencies. There are, however, other constraints that come from the profession, and under certain institutional circumstances, the two forms of constraint can and do operate together; the administration decides, for instance, to uphold an appointment or promotion on the basis of views submitted by faculty members regarded as embodying representative professional norms. Post acknowledges as much when he refers to the force that these academic standards exercise on knowledge production.

When Post refers to limits imposed by the administration, he talks about "constraints," but when he refers to limits imposed on a faculty member by professional norms and methods, he terms them "restraints." These latter are understood as necessary bulwarks against an excessive and unbridled freedom, one associated with individualism and a wrong-headed idea of academic freedom. This will turn out to be a significant distinction, since the latitude given to the latter form of constraint turns out to be a condition of the meaningful exercise of academic freedom for Post. This will turn out to be a problem when this model is applied to the humanities in general and to interdisciplinary research in particular.

Post acknowledges that norms are put into question as matter of course by professional academic activity itself. Indeed, Post makes room for what he calls "dissent," but he cannot account for the way academic norms change over time, how innovation emerges in the making of new fields, and how the history of norms opens up through positions first deemed unacceptable and only later accepted as "paradigm shifts." It seems to me that as long as voices of dissent are only admissible if they conform to accepted professional norms, then dissent itself is limited so that it cannot take aim at those norms that are already accepted and, hence, cannot inaugurate or innovate new fields or disciplinary paradigms. To limit forms of dissent in advance to those that conform to existing norms is to safeguard those very norms against dissent, not only imposing a certain censorship on the reach of dissent, but also undermining the creative power of dissenting views to initiate new fields of knowledge and new disciplinary or cross-disciplinary paradigms.

To question existing professional norms must, then, be part of any bona fide academic inquiry, and we can certainly document with ease how the emergence of whole fields of study, including performance studies,[5] anthropology, American studies, and women's studies,[6] to name a few, followed trenchant criticisms of this kind. To question existing norms is not the same as questioning the existence of norms in general or calling for a postnormative mode of academic inquiry (which itself would be positing a norm of postnormativity and so giving the lie to its own thesis). To allow that the specific academic norms that govern particular fields have a historicity, change under pressure, are revised in response to intellectual challenges, undergo paradigm shifts, is *not the same* as disputing the relevance of professional norms, but is only to ask which norms ought to be invoked and for what reasons and to concede that debates of this kind precede any possibility of the "application" of these norms. Indeed, a critical relation to norms, as evidenced precisely by such debates, may instead be understood as essential to the dynamic and historical life of academic norms, constituting the basis of a reflexive and critical approach that disciplines must take toward their own methodologies and customary modes of inquiry if they are not to stagnate as dogma or become calcified as rote formulas.

In Post's view, either we accept common standards or we devolve into a form of individualism that leads faculty members to think they are entitled to academic positions as "rights." Post makes two points in this regard: first, he says that no individual has a right to an academic position, since those positions are given on the basis of academic merit and an academic review is necessary for hiring. This is an uncontroversial claim. I can think of no one in the academy who would refute this view and can find within my intellectual landscape no position that would question it. Second, he argues that only in "exceptional cases" are the boundaries of professional standards tested, and that to tolerate those kinds of tests, it is important to protect "independence of thought and inquiry" (see p. 77). I suggest that this invocation of tolerance misunderstands the fundamental way disciplines remain vital and become the sites of genuine innovation. The point is not, as Post suggests, that professional standards must be suspended to allow for independence of thought and then enforced to shore up the authority of the discipline as a community capable of making judgments. This view fails to acknowledge that norms are themselves in vital and constant tension with one another, that existing conflicts among norms are very often the theme and subject of academic work, and that innovation in academic life depends in part on invoking and elaborating new norms over and against established fields of knowledge. Innovation and "independence of thought" do not happen without reference to norms, but they do presume that norms can be interpreted and reformulated anew, that their history is not over, and that they are still and continuously in the process of being made.

It seems clear that Post believes that unless we can rely on common standards, the disciplines will lose the authority they require to make and enforce academic judgments, where judgments are conceived of as the application of existing and accepted norms to academic work. But here I would make two rejoinders to this point. The first has to do with "authority" in the disciplines, the second with the model of interpretation and judgment that relies on a technical conception of "applying" existing norms. As for authority, Post clearly signs on to the view that present culture is beset with "antinomianism," understood as a generalized distrust of authority. I am not equipped to judge this claim about today's culture, but if I were asked whether this putative antinomianism was at work in debates about academic freedom, I would have to say no. I understand that certain conservative thinkers believe that the world has divided perilously into those who back claims of reckless freedom and those who stand by the bulwarks of authority. And I suppose that some forms of naive leftism subscribe to this view as well. But I think that the debates in their contemporary form are more occluded than illuminated by that framework, and that we make a mistake if we concede legitimacy to that description when so many more pressing issues are upon us. It seems crucial to distinguish, for instance, between a critical inquiry in which norms are appropriately invoked in order to judge a piece of academic work, and a claim that any norm or any person wielding a norm is wrong because that constitutes an exercise of authority, and authority is intrinsically bad. The second rendition makes a serious critical debate into an adolescent complaint, and so misreads and dismisses the terms of the debate in advance.

If it were always clear in advance which community and which discipline ought to judge a piece of work, and how membership in that community was determined, then one could rely on that putative community to make a judgment, and the matter would be finished. But scholarship often finds a home in one department at one university when it would never find a home in the same department at another university. This is because there are serious and important differences about which norms the discipline should use, whether the norms should take into account interdisciplinary work, and, if so, in what way, and whether modes of judgment need to be revised by virtue of new challenges to the discipline or new ways the discipline has been configured in light of interdisciplinary work. Thus, the opposition to Post's view of professional norms would emerge not primarily from those who are said to oppose authority or nurse "skepticism" toward authority as a result of putatively generalizable antinomianism (a term that takes its meaning from church debates that are significantly different from academic debates and rest on very different historical conceptions of authority), but only from a realistic understanding that there is significant disagreement about which norms ought to be invoked, and in light of which scholarship, and that new disciplinary innovations have made these questions the norm, rather than the exception, in such deliberations.

Indeed, the questions most often posed about disciplinary judgments of academic work have to do not with the authority of those who make the judgments or of the norms by which the judgments are made, but with the legitimacy of the judgment, whether those who made it have thought critically and well about the norms that are needed to understand the work in question or are willing to take account of changes and innovations in the field.

Second, the idea of "applying" academic norms sets up those norms as if they were already formulated, already accomplished, and available now as so many instruments that a good technician could apply to the material at hand. The material has no influence on which norms might be invoked, and the technician is not exactly a good figure for the thinking and interpreting person we might want a responsible faculty member making judgments to be. I would suggest that what happens in the context of academic review and evaluation is less a process of applying existing norms than an act of interpreting and reading a set of norms as they come to bear on a given academic project. The model of applying a preestablished set of terms is one that assumes a fundamentally technical model of judgment, one in which the terms by which we judge — the standards according to which we judge — are fixed in advance, and the case before us appears as an instance to be classified or not under the general model of "complying with professional norms" that we have on hand.

Dissension as the Norm

It is doubtless true that when we are given a body of scholarly work to judge, we have to situate that work in the context of established norms. It may be equally true, however, that we learn something significant about the innovative character of that work when we see that it does not conform to existing norms. Such work, in its noncompliance, may well be rearticulating academic norms in an original way or opening up new norms, setting a model for a future tradition. When we write, for instance, that a given scholar "establishes a new level of excellence for her field," we concede that the work we are evaluating exceeds our measures for its evaluation. We also take it to be a good thing that the work exceeds those measures in that way. Similarly, when we claim, in a laudatory vein, that someone's scholarship has refashioned the field, as people have doubtless said of Clifford Geertz or Henry Louis Gates, we are saying that new standards of excellence in the field have come into being, that from this point on we will judge and see the field differently, perhaps even call it by a new name. I

gather that such innovations, which are, of course, grounds to gar-
ner the highest academic praise, are possible only because norms
themselves are social and historical; they change through time, and
their change — when it produces new configurations of knowledge and new lines of inquiry — is generally considered good,
even if (or precisely because) it is controversial. Of course, it is
also possible to point out instances in which new configurations
of existing fields are categorically refused, as surely happened
when Walter Benjamin's *habilitations* thesis was rejected by the
faculty at Frankfurt in the early 1920s. The Frankfurt faculty
could grasp his study of baroque tragic drama neither as philosophy nor as literature. And yet the book, and books like it, came to
reconfigure scholarship at the nexus of those two fields for generations of scholars. Doubtless, there are still philosophers and literary critics who might reject his thesis, but there are others who
would not only accept it but even praise it as one of the most
important studies of its kind. Similarly, James Watson, who was
credited with codiscovering the structure of DNA, had his grant
applications regularly rejected by his peers, who thought the routes
he was following were worthless and without scientific promise.
Luckily, he found some funding elsewhere; otherwise the professional norms that governed the judgments of his peers would have
impeded the advancement of human knowledge. His discovery
restructured the understanding of how chemistry and biology
ought to proceed, encouraging the use of methods not generally
accepted or seen as promising before.[7]

There are endless examples of this kind. Psychoanalysis as a
field is hardly unitary, and fundamental disagreements concerning method and interpretation abound. Whereas some would
claim that psychoanalysis has meaning only as an empirically sub-
stantiated science, others understand it as an interpretive art that
operates in a different relationship to empirical facts. Similarly, in
any group of political theorists, one will find game theorists, who
believe they have imported rigor, clarity, and predictability into
the field, and others who claim that reflections on justice and
equality cannot be substantively served by such methods. All
these people are compelled to sit in judgment of one another,
even though they do not operate with the same set of professional
norms. They might recognize the historical range of plausible and
conflictual positions that operate now, countenance the internal

dissension of norms, and be willing to accord merit to scholarship whose presuppositions they do not share, or dispute that merit, though not because the presuppositions do not conform to their sense of how the discipline should proceed.

The evaluation of any given body of academic work is at once an evaluation of the relationship to the existing field of norms that the academic work implies. Sometimes the work becomes an example of existing norms, but sometimes it seeks to revise them. This latter aim is not an exception but is now, in the interpretive sciences generally, a norm. I gather that this is not a norm that can be applied to an instance but an insight to the effect that every work implies a position on what the disciplinary norms should be. Some of those challenges might be regarded as "too much," but at times, others are heralded as significant breakthroughs. And what is "too much" at one time may become a disciplinary paradigm at another.

Similarly, historians regularly argue about the status of narrative and interpretation. If histories must be told, and if they must use narrative structure in the telling, how are such narrative structures different from literary narratives, if they are? I gather that the views in the profession now range from the claim that recounting a history is not the same as telling a story or rendering a narrative, to the claim that it does involve narrative device, to the argument that the truth-claims of a historical narrative are not so different from those of a literary one, and that those of a literary one have their own historical dimensions, for instance, the predominance of 'realist tropes' in historiography. A similar debate happens in philosophy. A Nietzsche scholar might argue that a fable or parable has philosophical significance, and a philosopher of language and logic might respond that a fable or parable has philosophical significance only if it can be effectively transposed into propositional and argumentative form. Whole departments divide on this issue. A job candidate in history or philosophy is invariably greeted by this disagreement when she presents her work for consideration. The department, when it splits, disagrees not only on the desirability of the candidacy, but also on the very method and norm by which the work ought to be evaluated — indeed, on *the very conception of professional norms that the work implies*. Some claim that any position that argues *z* is disqualified as good history or philosophy, whereas others laud the argument as a sign of innovation and originality.

The problem in such disagreements is *not* that there are *no* professional norms or that someone gets up at a meeting and claims that norms do not exist. In fact, the disagreement is a consequence of conflicting norms' existing emphatically at once; norms are multiple and in contestation with one another. There is no implicit consensus presupposed by the very existence of a norm, although norms are, by definition, social and hence shared to some degree. Instead of understanding there to be a single norm that corresponds to a given discipline or field, we must, in contemporary circumstances, identify major points of contention, rifts, debate, and dissonance. When academic work is reviewed, so are professional norms; not only does the work imply a relationship to those norms, but those norms are also often redefined in light of the work itself. Indeed, such scenes of evaluation constitute the successive moments in the history of a set of norms; they establish norms as *historically changeable and socially negotiated.* As a result, in the debates over which norms ought to be invoked to evaluate a given body of scholarship, those norms are themselves assessed and renewed, and sometimes rearticulated and changed. This is not far from what Dewey imagined as a pragmatic account of judgment.

That such standards and norms are historically changeable and socially negotiated does not mean that we cannot use them. On the contrary, that very changeability and internal dissension implies that we must judge — and we do — and that we constantly have to give reasons for invoking and commending the version of academic norms that we choose. Note, however, that judgment here is not a technical exercise of applying a preestablished norm, since part of any evaluative procedure is to decide not only which set of norms to use, which set is implied by the work in question, but also how the work acts on the norm itself. Precisely because there is no preestablished agreement in the humanities, at least, on a single norm to be used to judge the quality of work, we must give reasons for the choices we make, and they must be persuasive. If norms were uncontested and taken for granted, there would be no significant disagreement of this kind, and it would be unthinkable that a certain kind of academic work would require reconsidering the parameters of a field, the legitimacy of its methods, and the possibility of accommodating or foreclosing innovation.

In this sense, I differ from Post's description of what we do when we make evaluations of this kind. When technical models provide the norm for thinking about such evaluative judgments, a ready-made norm is applied to an instance, and the instance is deemed to fit the norm or not. Surely life would be easier if this were how we engaged in these evaluative activities. In the humanities, the language of "applying" norms is regularly eschewed, and for good reason. When we read a work for evaluative purposes, we try, among other things, to ascertain its argument, its method or mode of proceeding, the context of scholarship in which it is operating, whether it takes account of that scholarship and the material on hand, whether it makes a significant contribution to the field, whether it is well wrought as a piece of writing and argumentation. We make arguments for or against the work based on our interpretation of what the text is doing. But the judgment is bound up not only with our interpretation — and our capacity to make our interpretation persuasive — but also with *an interpretation of the professional norm itself.* In other words, the norm is not received as a given, or available to us as a tool, but rather invoked and interpreted anew in light of the scholarship that we are to evaluate. Similarly, the scholarship we are evaluating is also establishing an interpretive relationship to a set of complex and internally conflictual set of norms. A literary scholar might think that to be too formalist will prove unacceptable by contemporary standards of evaluation; another may feel that to be too Marxist will prove similarly inappropriate. On occasion, a judicious reviewer will say, "Although I do not adhere to the formalist principles at work in this scholarship, I recognize that this scholar has done an excellent job of offering a formalist analysis in accord with the standards that pertain to that kind of scholarly work." But more often we hear "This is no longer acceptable as a way of proceeding" or "No credible scholar works this way anymore," to which there are rejoinders such as "But surely they do," and examples are given, and debate ensues.

It seems to me that ethics comes to bear precisely here, that is, in the disposition we adopt in relation to what has become, within the contemporary field of knowledge, an inevitable set of debates and contests over what constitutes good work in the humanities. The question is whether, at such moments, we can recognize good work that adheres to modes of inquiry and methods that we do not share. Judicious people are capable of such recognition when it is deserved, whereas others will seek to legislate a norm and thus to discredit modes of inquiry that fail to comply with their conception of the field. In a world in which common standards cannot be assumed, in which what has become most common is the predicament of finding that norms are open to interpretation, the ethical problem is not how best to apply a pregiven norm (fabricating its stability in the moment of its use) but how to be open to a clash of norms while making the best possible judgment in the fray (that is, without overruling the contestatory character of the field of norms at the time).

Post obliquely refers to such a problem in his discussion of teaching Milton's *Paradise Lost*. Post mentions the case of a student who refuses to agree with a professor's interpretation of the text. That refusal can be understood as stubbornness or as independence of mind, but, Post argues, how we answer that question depends on "an appraisal that is impossible without the application of relevant professional norms of literary criticism" (see p. 81). This instrumental approach to "norm application" does not exactly describe what goes on, however, since a teacher may well retaliate against disloyalty, citing professional norms or, indeed, the professor's own standing. A judicious professor, however, would still see the field of norms as internally diverse, since surely there are professionally acceptable readings of *Paradise Lost* that are radically at odds with one another (which would not be the same for mathematical formulas). What makes a given interpretation legitimate includes the possibility of arguing on the basis of textual evidence for it, against another interpretation (which, in this case, may be the one to which the professor holds), and of showing the explanatory power of the new interpretation in light of the text and other, prior readings of it. Indeed, a professor of English longs for a new interpretation of *Paradise Lost*, and a good faculty member will welcome and reward a well-grounded interpretation that defeats his or her own. If we think that all literary scholars will agree on what "well grounded" is, though, we are mistaken. A student can be faulted for adhering too closely to the text by, for instance, those who take a more sociological approach to literature, or for paying the "wrong" sort of attention to a text by, for instance, those who think one should read for historical resonances rather than for the logical operation of figures. Our ability to identify and evaluate students who dis-agree with us, as well as the way we proceed depends on our recognition of a range of interpretative possibilities that consti-tute the fields in which we work and that exceed our own. With-out this humility, which is conditioned by an insight into the instability and internal variance of professional norms, our capac-ity to judge will be seriously impaired; we will find ourselves either legislating one norm and effacing the diversity of the field, or taking up an embattled position within the range of norms and politicizing to an unacceptable degree the concept of legitimate student work.

It seems important to note, based on the foregoing discussion, that Post's argument presumes two polarized views that do not encompass the whole range of views on how best to conceptual-ize academic freedom. In his exposition, there are those who understand academic freedom as an individual right, modeled on First Amendment rights and oppose regulations or constraints on the expression of one's views, and those who, like him, hold that institutionally defined and secured academic norms are the neces-sary preconditions for the exercise of academic freedom as the professional prerogative of faculty members. I agree that this shift should be made, that it makes better sense to understand schol-arly work in all its dimensions as fundamentally conditioned by social and institutional structures and norms. If we refuse, how-ever, to see that norms not only have a history that is still being made but, in fact, must have one, that norms are revisable through time and in response to changing currents of thought and inquiry, then we treat institutional norms as if they were already fully accomplished. The historical dimension of Post's analysis, there-fore, is unnecessarily limited. Norms are in the process of being produced, and sometimes judgment is the very site where norms are renewed, revised, and invented. Indeed, without their contes-tatory character, norms would be essentially dead, frozen in time, and so too, sadly, would be the vocation of knowledge itself.

Finally, then, let us consider Post's view on whether academic freedom can and should extend to extramural expression, that is, political speech that may well be unrelated to faculty competence and expertise, as determined by professional norms. It seems important to remember here that Post began his argument by claiming that professional norms were necessary to secure the institutional conditions for the exercise of academic freedom, and that this exercise was important for the public good, where the public good included a notion of the advancement and augmentation of knowledge. The professional status of faculty members thus secured claims made on behalf of academic freedom, but that professional status depended on a larger conception of "advancing the sum of human knowledge," for the good of society. He cites the "1915 Declaration" to this effect: "It is clearly not proper that [faculty members] should be prohibited from lending their active support to organized movements which they believe to be in the public interest" (see p. 82). The public interest and the good of society thus provide the basis on which both academic freedom and extramural expression are legitimated. The public interest justifies professional norms that in turn justify the exercise of academic freedom. And the public interest is also served by extramural expression. As a result, although extramural expression might not be exactly the same as academic expression, it would seem that they are nevertheless joined as two different ways the public interest is served. In fact, it may be that two different kinds of public interest are served, if academic work seeks to augment knowledge, and extramural expression adds substantively to the "free marketplace of ideas" that is considered foundational to any democracy.

Are these two different contributions always rigorously separable? I gather that matters become controversial precisely when it is not possible to distinguish clearly between expression that is protected as academic freedom and expression that qualifies as extramural expression. It is easy enough to use the example of the astronomer who takes a public view on taxation, since the example delineates the difference between professional and extramural in a clear way. But if a historian of classical Greece starts to write on popular culture and reviews Michael Moore in a public venue, or a Straussian political philosopher starts to write in the *Weekly Standard*, relating his political philosophy to contemporary foreign policy, the lines become somewhat blurred. If the professional profile of the scholar is changing — and we can think of many such instances — then new kinds of publications and teaching become relevant to that profile. A professor of health medicine may join or take a stand on the organization Doctors Without Borders, or an anthropologist who works in Kenya and Sudan may write essays on the genocide in Sudan and criticize his own country's policy for its implications there, or a professor of constitutional law may write briefs regarding the legality of the war tribunals established for detainees at Camp Delta in Guantanamo Bay. These are plausible developments in an academic life, and some of those publications may well be submitted for review on the occasions of tenure and promotion. At this point, reviewers would be hard pressed to distinguish between academic and extramural. They would doubtless be compelled to regard all submitted materials as academic expression by virtue of their having been submitted at all.

As a result, whether a given publication or presentation is considered extramural or academic can be a complex matter, especially if what starts out as extramural activity within a given vocation turns out to constitute a separate area of professional competence over time (the case of Noam Chomsky is a good one). Of course, there are times when a faculty member may want to claim that certain views — and activities — ought not to be considered in the evaluation of his or her work, and that they should be set aside as not pertinent to the academic profile under review (I myself keep certain publications off my professional record for this reason). If the faculty member submits those views, which may include publications, as part of the academic record, then those works are open to evaluation by academic standards. But if those views are brought in ex post facto by reviewers, then surely there are rights at issue, rights that are not necessarily purely individual but that pertain to there being just and transparent procedures for the submission and evaluation of work and the promotion of faculty members.

One question that can emerge in the course of an academic review is whether a given piece of work counts as academic or extramural expression (by the way, "extramural activities" constitute a category of accomplishment in promotion and review at the University of California and are thus not immune from review on these occasions). Because a faculty member is also a citizen and is protected by rights pertaining to citizenship, including the First Amendment, it is important that faculty members be protected in their exercise of academic freedom, but also that administrators not trespass outside academic territory to impose constraints on free speech more generally.

Post's view is that it is expedient and prudent for universities to disclaim responsibility for extramural expression, and he underscores that extramural expression is not a right of academic freedom (although he concedes that there are some aspects of academic freedom that cover extramural expression). This seems true enough, but the argument fails to take into account precisely the protections that faculty members require as citizens, so that administrators and governmental authorities do not overstep their regulatory purview. Post's analysis takes the point of view of a university that seeks to protect itself from damage or the perception of damage, so he advises that administrations disclaim responsibility for extramural political speech to protect their public-relations interests. It seems to me, however, that administrations have to serve not only their own public-relations interests but also the public interest more generally; they must safeguard intellectual life and preserve the university campus as a site for the consideration of a host of potentially conflicting positions, and this means refusing to act in ways that disrupt the exercise of First Amendment rights, that is, the right to freedom of extramural speech outside the classroom, on campus, or elsewhere in public. In this way, the university administration has a role in making sure that governments do not intrude on this sphere of free speech. Post notes that he is not focusing on free speech as a constitutional concept in his essay, but he would do well to clarify the relationship between the constitutional and the nonconstitutional meaning of academic freedom to provide a fuller picture of the complex relations between academic and extramural expression. Surely rights of academic freedom are at issue for a faculty member who seeks to establish a clear distinction between extramural and academic expression, if the inappropriate consideration of extramural expression constitutes a violation of proper governance. And for those faculty members for whom the academic and the extramural are not fully distinguishable from each other, it seems crucial that both protocols governing academic freedom and those pertaining to the First Amendment be brought into play, if only to differentiate the academic from the extramural.

Post seems concerned to make sure that individuals do not get to say anything they like in the name of freedom and claim that it ought to have academic standing. This is understandable. He is also concerned that no faculty member feel constrained to express only those views that conform to the stated policies of the university. This seems right as well. For Post, professional norms, conjured as secure and uniform, are meant to condition legitimate exercises of academic freedom, and administrative and governmental authorities should be constrained from intervening in this domain. What goes missing here is a consideration of how universities should consider the domains of public expression that blur the distinction between academic and extramural, to make sure that universities are not trespassing on the domain of free speech in their evaluations of academic conduct and expression. As we all know, a faculty member can be punished for political views in the name of "professional norms," and his or her extramural expression can be brought to bear on the consideration of academic expression through subterfuge. In his haste to oppose a version of academic freedom that assigns rights to individuals on the basis of an uncritical individualism, Post does not pursue the point that even a version of academic freedom based on institutionally secured prerogatives — which he favors — can furnish a set of rights that do not subscribe to an ontology of individualism. Rights discourses are not the only ones to presuppose individualism, and they are, in this instance, surely compatible with the shift to considering the institutional conditions and constraints on academic freedom that he favors.

If we assume that professional norms never abrogate academic freedom, and that dissent and debate over what those norms should be *undermine* academic freedom, we end up subscribing to a mode of intellectual conservatism that erroneously describes the contemporary state of disciplinary and interdisciplinary academic work. By identifying the threat to academic freedom with unbridled individualism, on the one hand, and retributive administrative and governmental powers, on the other, Post ends up with a form of political liberalism that is coupled with a profoundly conservative intellectual resistance to interdisciplinarity and disciplinary innovation. If we fail to consider the ways external constraints structure and enforce professional norms, we also miss out on being able to describe and counter forms of censorship that are at once subtle and forceful.

In his consideration of the revision to Title VI, the act that reauthorized the Higher Education Act and that, in its current form, monitors programs that receive area-studies funding, especially

Middle East studies programs, Post returns to his earlier formulation of the paradoxical character of academic freedom. No individual is entitled to a place in a university, but once an individual becomes a faculty member, after an appropriate vote and review, that individual becomes entitled to exercise academic freedom within the framework of professional norms. Importantly, professional norms operate as constraints within which academic freedom can be conceptualized. This means that academic freedom cannot be a full freedom *from* constraint without dissolving the conditions of its own possibility. As faculty members, we are constrained to be free, and in the exercise of our freedom, we continue to operate within the constraints that made our freedom possible in the first place. Constraint is academic freedom's presupposed condition, but also its abiding condition, one that makes its continuing exercise possible. But are these constraints always the same, and are they debatable and revisable?

Here Post subscribes to a conception of freedom that is positive and nonprivative in relation to professional norms, but negative and privative when it comes to administrative and state regulation. As faculty members, we are never free from professional norms, yet we must always be free from administrative or state constraints on the expression of our political views. Professional norms, however restrictive, are enabling, but university and state restrictions on scholarship based on its political content undermine the freedoms that professional norms are meant to secure. This position has the virtue of logical clarity, but it does not include a consideration of the historical character of the norms that are supposed to secure both our freedom and our professionalism. If the historical changes and innovations in those norms may, or rather must, take place through contestation, and the norms must become sites of conflict and argument, and if norms change to accommodate and promote new kinds of scholarship — and the production of new forms of knowledge — then it would seem that we need an account of the history of norms. Even if we agree that academic freedom is not — or cannot be — the right to be free from all norms, there remains the crucial task of judging which norms work today and which do not. That involves us in domains of interpretation from which we can never get free; indeed, we are *constrained to interpret* if we are to fulfill our function as academics. This is why we do not, cannot, employ norms as if they were tools in a box. They are, more broadly, the evolving social conventions by which we think and act, ones that demand a critical relation to their history and to their future.

New Challenges for Academic Freedom and Extramural Speech

The claim that professional norms are, as a matter of fact, "restraints," not administrative and political interventions, minimizes the implicit and consequential ways public policy has shaped and continues to shape the professional norms that govern specific fields of inquiry. We have seen how McCarthyism did this for the American philosophical establishment,[8] and we are seeing it now in the effort to censor certain perspectives in Middle East studies. We might respond that this makes it all the more necessary to strengthen the distinction between them. It may be possible to track instances in which the federal government withholds funds from a program because of its perceived alliance with views deemed damaging to U.S. interests, and to claim, as Post surely says we ought to do, that scholarly views should not be corrupted by those who fund them. It is, however, more difficult to trace the forms of constraint that govern hiring and tenure of faculty members in certain fields with certain perspectives, when political oversight remains an explicit or implicit feature of government and administrative intervention. In these instances, the state and the university articulate what come to be regarded as "professional norms" that decide in advance who may and may not exercise the right of academic freedom, and the distinction between the professional and administrative spheres that Post has worked so hard to secure threatens to give way.

The view of academic freedom on which Post relies presumes that appropriately educated people retain the power to determine autonomously what prevailing academic norms will be. But we can see that norms have origins other than the well-meaning and well-educated judgments of professionals. Academic norms are wrought not only from cognitive judgments but also from a confluence of historically evolved and changeable institutional and discursive practices. Indeed, if governmental authorities stipulate what topics may be funded, they contribute to a public discourse that shifts the common understanding of the line that divides legitimate from illegitimate academic inquiry. Indeed, as I will show toward the end of my essay, private funding institutions are now adopting and extending this public discourse on appropriate venues for scholarship, thus showing state discourse's tributary effects on the formulation of academic norms. These public and private agencies thus take part in establishing and circulating norms that govern acceptable scholarship, and these norms in turn have an effect not only on what kind of scholarship will be made available for review in cases of promotion and tenure, but also on what kinds of judgments will be leveled against the scholarship.

At this writing, the International Studies in Higher Education Act, HR 3077, has already passed the House of Representatives and is pending before the U.S. Senate in a revised form. Although the committee that the act sets up to review recipients of area studies federal grants is termed "advisory," it has the power "to study, monitor, apprise [sic] and evaluate a sample of activities supported under [Title IV]." Indeed, it turns out that the range of activities it is entitled to sample and monitor is relatively unrestricted, so that any activities related to the area that the grant recipient studies, including political associations, could be monitored by this committee. Organizations such as the American Council on Education and the National Humanities Alliance have objected to what they see as an intrusion into research activities, curriculum planning and implementation, and unspecified activities of the faculty. It is unclear whether this advisory committee, which is clearly supervisory, will have access to government agencies to collect information on individual grantees, and whether it will be able to make use of the new surveillance powers secured under the revised USA Patriot Act. Indeed, it would seem that Title VI implicitly cites or rests on the USA Patriot Act, insofar as it seeks to monitor grant recipients to make sure that they are not forming alliances with perceived enemies and that federal money is not going to those who might threaten the nation's security through their political actions or associations.

It is ironic that area studies was developed by the State Department, and that the current critique of area studies within the academy is that it too readily accepts the geographical map that the government produced as part of its Cold War agenda. This is, first of all, a prime instance of government interventions establishing disciplinary parameters and, by extension, professional norms of evaluation. Apparently, this governmental creation now threatens to defeat its maker. The fear is that someone who studies an area may well "go over" in a fascinated ethnographic immersion or may use the grant to establish contacts that would be regarded as inimical to U.S. state interests. Area studies is considered a potential threat to security, and this threat is countered by the production of a new authority whose legal powers remain vaguely circumscribed. If, under the new Patriot Act provisions, it is no longer necessary to go through a court to obtain authorization to collect information on what individuals read and with whom they associate, the advisory board for Title VI recipients may have similar powers, especially if it can give evidence to the functionary in charge that a threat to national security is at issue.

What happens to academic freedom in this climate, when the "threat to national security" can easily be invoked to brand whole fields of knowledge and modes of inquiry? The implicit dimension of censorship is not to be underestimated, given the stigma attached to engaging in any activity that can be construed, even if by the most paranoid, as a threat to national security. Edward Said was mentioned as an exemplary "danger" more often than any other scholar in the House discussions of HR 3077. How many of us would be more than pleased to advise graduate students who compared, intellectually and politically, with his range and brilliance?

When we consider the new restraints imposed on grant recipients by the Ford and Rockefeller foundations, we can see once again how disciplinary boundaries are being promulgated through restrictions on political expression and activity. The point here is not just that a person may not get funding for a project if he or she adheres to certain views or engages in certain activities, but also that certain views are no longer considered "fundable" and so are regarded as socially illegitimate. This can only have a deleterious effect on freedom of speech in the academy, since foundation guidelines are part of the discursive field in which professional norms are created, changed, augmented, and restricted.

Indeed, it seems to me that the new challenges to academic freedom cannot be easily referred to a community of like-minded professionals, not only because such communities are often defined by disagreement about which academic norms ought to be brought to bear on a given case, but also because academic norms are in the process of being wrought by public policy and private institutional stipulations that bear on what kinds of scholarly inquiries are considered legitimate and what kinds of extramural activities disqualify faculty members from funding for research.

On October 19, 2004, the American Civil Liberties Union (ACLU) declined $1.15 million in grants from the Ford and Rockefeller foundations, claiming that the foundations' new restrictions on the political activities of grant recipients were a threat to existing civil liberties. Earlier, the Ford Foundation had voluntarily adopted language that would exclude certain grants from consideration based on the political content of scholarly research projects as well as the extramural political activities of applicants. It is important to recognize that whereas HR 3077 is a proposed *government* policy, the new language regarding grant restrictions adopted by the Ford and Rockefeller foundations is private and not mandated by law. As a result, we are witnessing private funding institutions limit the field of applications by imposing restrictions that parallel those recently imposed on recipients of federal grants; whereas the federal government seeks to monitor the activities of researchers in area studies, the foundations do not make clear how it will ascertain whether applicants have ever participated or now participate in the proscribed activities. Ford, despite being a private institution, elected to conform to proposed Title VI restrictions under other kinds of pressures, and in doing so illustrated the effect that governmental regulation of legitimate scholarship can have on private considerations of the same. The Ford Foundation apparently formulated its new restrictions in response to the charge that it had funded some Palestinian groups that attended the United Nations' 2001 World Conference Against Racism, Racial Discrimination, Xenophobia, and Related Intolerance, held in Durban, South Africa.[9] As a result, the Ford Foundation now states, as part of its criteria for grant allocation, that grant recipients may not engage in any activity that "promotes violence, terrorism, bigotry, or the destruction of any state." The Rockefeller Foundation adopted slightly different language, stating that recipients of its funds may not "directly or indirectly engage in, promote, or support other organizations or individuals who engage in or promote terrorist activity."

At least two features must be noted about these new restrictions. The first has to do with the ambiguity of the terms themselves and the overreaching interpretations to which they could give rise. The second is whether this policy is enforceable and what means these foundations would use to enforce it. Will these organizations now engage in information gathering about the political activities of grant recipients, or rely on federal agencies to do so? Let's consider the problem with the wording itself and then turn to the ethical and potentially legal issues that follow from the question of enforceability.

Although it surely seems reasonable that the Ford Foundation does not want its funds to be used to support bigotry, violence, or terrorism, it is unclear what those terms mean and whose definitions will prevail when judgments have to be made. The question of whether a given research project involves a normative claim about whether an existing state should continue in its present form raises yet another set of issues that I will consider below. The term "bigotry," as the ACLU ably pointed out, can and does refer to discriminatory attitudes, statements, and actions, but it is also sometimes invoked inappropriately to quell open disagreement on policy issues. For instance, there are those who say that any criticism of Israel is anti-Semitic, relying on the premise that anti-Semitism is an unacceptable form of bigotry, to conclude that any criticism of Israel or the structure of that state is an unacceptable form of bigotry. Whereas the second premise is indisputably true, it is far from clear that the first is. Indeed, one might wish for a separate state for the Jews on the basis of Jewish values, as did, for instance, Martin Buber and Judah L. Magnes, who attempted to establish a binational state before 1948. At what point does a dissenting opinion on the state of Israel, its current boundaries, its constitutional basis, its military and economic policy toward the Palestinians become equated with bigotry? Surely, organizations in contemporary Israel such as Ta'ayush constitute an effort to provide a cultural and political alternative to Zionism or renew an earlier version of it, just as organizations such as Brit Tzedek v'Shalom (the Jewish Alliance for Justice and Peace) and Tikkun represents Jews who, within a Jewish framework, object to the Israeli state at various levels. Barring a thoughtful analysis of this issue that would yield a well-considered set of criteria for deciding what is bigotry, the claim, accepted by some, that criticism of the state of Israel is tantamount to bigotry might well hold sway and preclude consideration of research projects on binationalism,

on Buber, on the array of Palestinian proposals for self-government or cooperative power-sharing — indeed, even on the prehis-
tory of the state of Israel. If the Ford Foundation were to accept
this view, then it would have to decide whether all or just some
criticisms were tantamount to bigotry. Could it, for instance, be
unbigoted to criticize Israel for the separation wall, the check-
point policies, the settlements, the killing of Palestinian children
and other innocent civilians, the occupation and its effects on
medical care and educational access for Palestinians, the discrimination against Mizrahi Jews as well as Palestinians in Israel and
the Occupied Territories? Could one level such criticisms, within
research projects or extramurally, and still be eligible for a Ford
Foundation grant? Which of these critical perspectives would be
considered worthy of debate within scholarship and public life,
either pursued as part of a research program or espoused extramurally as part of a political viewpoint? Which of these views would
be included in a roster of views that deserve at least a hearing in
the public sphere, and which of these, if any, would constitute evidence of bigotry and so lie outside the bounds of legitimate research
or public debate? How would one adjudicate the claim that some
or all of these points of view constituted bigotry or discrimination?

Frequently, members of the International Solidarity Movement (ISM), a group that includes individuals with a wide range
of opinion, are stopped at the Israeli border on their way to offer
assistance to impoverished, isolated communities in the West
Bank, and are not permitted to enter Israel. Such actions are taken
against Jewish and non-Jewish members of the ISM. The grounds
for barring these individuals from entry into Israel were that they
posed "a danger to the state," a claim that suggests that their
actions would imperil national security or be complicit with terrorist activities. If those who seek to assist Palestinian organizations, some of which are infrastructurally related to Hamas, are
considered "terrorists" or "terrorist sympathizers," then it might
follow that any grant recipient who engages in activities with the
ISM or in support of its actions could be construed as "terrorist"
or "bigoted." If protesting the separation wall and taking medicine to Palestinians isolated from adequate medical care under the
conditions of occupation constitute potential dangers to the state,
and if such a judgment were accepted by the Ford or Rockefeller
Foundation, then it would follow that political participation in an

organization like the ISM or others like it — which is commonly protected by rights of free speech and free association — would be enough to disqualify an applicant or to warrant the termination of a grant.

Even if the terms "bigotry," "violence," and "terror" were used unambiguously, that is, invoked in ways that were not intended to quell political expression, and elaborated according to refined criteria of application, the formulation of the final restriction stipulated by Ford — the one that currently maintains that grant recipients may not engage in any activity that calls for "the destruction of any state" — is untenable on other grounds. Let us imagine a grant recipient who, either as part of his or her research or in political activity apart from that research, maintains the view that only through regime change will the right of free expression ever become universally guaranteed in Iran. If by "regime change" that person means that one state is to be supplanted by another state, then that person is effectively calling for the destruction of one form of the state in the hope of bringing about a new and more democratic form of that state. What if, under apartheid in South Africa, a grant recipient either in the context of research or in extramural activity, had called for the replacement of the South African constitution by one in which equal rights of political participation were guaranteed to all citizens regardless of race? That person would be calling for the destruction of one state, hoping that another, more radically egalitarian state would be established in its place. Similarly, if someone were to argue for a binational state where Israel and the Palestinian territories now exist and were to assert, either in research or in extramural expression, that the one-state solution had advantages over either the two-state solution or continued occupation, that person would be arguing for a new form of statehood for those lands. Indeed, some now claim that a person with such views is effectively calling for the "destruction" of the nation of Israel. A one-state solution would, at the very least, destroy the current law governing rights of citizenship and political participation in Israel, and it would also destroy the most recently established borders. This ambiguity plagues public discussion on the Middle East, since even proponents of political and nonviolent solutions who suggest that the conditions of citizenship in Israel are not legitimate and ought to be reformulated to include Palestinians are accused of destroying the state of Israel. These positions are regularly confused with ones that call for violent attacks on Israeli property and people.

Should the Ford Foundation conclude that anyone who makes an argument in favor of binationalism (as Edward Said did in the *New York Times*, as Tony Judt did in *The New York Review of Books*, as Neve Gordon does in his writings from Israel in *The Nation*) is effectively calling for the destruction of an existing state, and that this should therefore disqualify the person from receiving grants? Imagine how this would have worked if it had been applied before 1989, to foreign-policy scholars who called for the establishment of a democratic state to replace the Soviet Union or East Germany? How would the third Ford restriction now apply to individuals who make arguments concerning the future of a democratic state in North Korea? If all of these people are arguing that an existing state should be discontinued in its current form, then they would be arguing for the "destruction" of that state in some sense. As we can see from the example of those who call for an alteration in the definition of Israeli citizenship, the accusation that a grant applicant seeks the destruction of a state does not, in its current usage, restrict itself to those who call for a *violent* destruction; it includes those who may well be calling for a more egalitarian and inclusive democratic government. Indeed, if one were to argue, regarding Israel, that rights of citizenship and full political participation ought to be granted to all individuals who are currently citizens, live under conditions of occupation, or have clear entitlements to the land, and if one were to base such a view on classical liberal principles that bar race and ethnicity, for instance, from being prerequisites of citizenship, such a view would widely be regarded as "destroying" the state of Israel, where the existing state is understood to depend on principles of Jewish sovereignty. Regardless of one's view on this difficult and recurring issue, it would seem that these various possibilities (including the ones laid out in the Middle East peace plan known as the road map and the Geneva Accords), should be included as arguable opinions within the sphere of public debate. For a major granting organization to disqualify any applicant who plans to research these alternatives or who is actively engaged in political organizations seeking to find resolution for these issues is effectively to say that only one point of view on this question is legitimate: the one that claims that any effort to rethink the bases of citizenship and political participation in Israel is tantamount to the destruction of that state. As in the above examples, it may be possible to make a normative argument regarding a new state-formation that would involve supplanting the current state with one that promises to realize more fully democratic ideals. Such a viewpoint might be misguided, but to prevent it from being articulated at all by any potential recipient of a grant from these foundations would constitute a form of serious censorship and a dogmatic allegiance to the political status quo.

It might be useful to consider the kinds of works that would be excluded from consideration under the new restrictions imposed by Ford and Rockefeller. Surely, Frantz Fanon would not have been funded, and neither would Georges Sorel; Desmond Tutu and Nelson Mandela at earlier stages in their careers would not have been funded, and probably Mandela's views on Palestine would also now lie outside the fold. I wonder about the revolutionary thinkers from the eighteenth century who called for the destruction of one sort of state, and about foreign-policy scholars who call for military intervention (state violence) to implement certain humanitarian goals. Could Locke get funding after calling for the end of the divine right of kings? What about Montesquieu and his work on the new state constitutions in the United States? Would funding arguments such as Philip Rieff's or Michael Ignatieff's in favor of limited uses of violence also prove problematic? What about a tract on nonviolence that admits that under certain conditions violence might be needed to effect democratic change? Is that no longer a position we should even consider teaching in our courses on violence and politics, even if we address it only to understand why historical change has sometimes happened as it has, to critically assess its allure, its consequences?

Because the term "terrorist" is bandied about so readily, it is important to maintain a critical understanding of its usage and not to assume that a common meaning can or should be presumed. When the Rockefeller Foundation, for instance, claims that recipients of its grants and fellowships may not "directly or indirectly engage in, promote, or support other organizations or individuals who engage in or promote terrorist activity," it neglects to define "terrorist" and thus fails to give any guidance on what constitutes a legitimate use of the term. The label "terrorist" works to describe those who harbor or enact violent designs against a state, but it is also used to tarnish or brand certain kinds of opposition movements, to create conditions of fear, to instill suspicion about the political motives of certain movements, and to use stigmas as a way of quelling speech. In the age where you're "either with us or against us," it stands to reason that any form of critical dissent from the current "war on terror" (a war that is now focused on Iraqi insurgents unaffiliated with any of the scenes of terrorism that originally motivated the war effort), could be construed as sympathizing with terrorists or as simply terrorist. Given that the term has been and continues to be used so variously in the popular media and in mainstream political discourse, it follows that thoughtful efforts to pry apart these various discursive uses and subject the term to critical inquiry could be construed as complicit with terror itself. Grant recipients attuned to the workings of language will now be compelled to delete any references to a critical perspective on terrorism from grant applications, but they may also be dissuaded from even applying, because they have held and propounded dissenting views or participated in political activities counter to the continuing "war on terror."

It is important to remember that private foundations are not obligated to protect free speech in the way that public institutions surely are. But the guidelines that private institutions adopt enter public discourse and help form a popular consensus on what constitutes acceptable political expression and activity. When asked why the Ford Foundation would adopt the restrictions that the ACLU opposes, Susan Berresford, the president of the foundation, sought to differentiate between the aims of the two organizations: "We accept and respect that we have a different mission from the ACLU, even while we share the same basic values," she wrote. "We are proud to support the ACLU's defense of free speech. We do not, however, believe that a private donor like Ford should support all speech itself (such as speech that promotes bigotry or violence)."[10]

Interestingly, Berresford includes in these remarks only two of the four grounds for denying applicants grants and mentions bigotry and violence only in parentheses. Those two grounds sound reasonable enough, even though there is no indication here or elsewhere how those terms will be interpreted or applied. Significantly, in her public comments, Berresford omits the two more

controversial criteria for exclusion: "terrorism" and "promot[ing]
. . . the destruction of any existing state." Perhaps we can read in
her elision an implicit recognition that these are the weakest and
most confused criteria. These restrictions accept a popular term
that is used, on the one hand, interchangeably and without reflective analysis to describe Chechen insurgents — both violent and
nonviolent — Palestinians of all kinds, Arabs of all kinds, Hamas,
the Palestinian Authority, Al Aksa Martyrs Brigades, the Taliban,
the Baathists, and al-Qaeda, and, on the other, as a threatening
appellation that will eventually describe anyone who does not
accept the usage as it is currently ratified and circulated and comes
perilously close to proscribing public efforts at critical thinking.
One might argue that we have not yet arrived at a point where
public thinkers who seek to refine and parse the various uses of
the term "terrorist" are branded terrorist based on the critical
efforts they pursue. But if highly regarded funding agencies ratify
the uncritical use of the term and agree to paralyze public debate
on the possible forms that a democratic polity might take, in the
Middle East or elsewhere, then they make a considerable and
decidedly negative contribution to public discourse. Because of
these new restrictions, clear-minded political reflection on vexed
political issues — something badly needed by this faltering democracy — is all the more circumscribed and thwarted, and the Ford
and Rockefeller foundations badly shirk their responsibility to
maintain and defend free expression, including critical and dissenting views, in the domain of public discourse.

For the Ford Foundation to exclude from consideration those
who claim that more democratic states might yet be in the offing
is for it to claim, implicitly, that existing states are legitimate
because they exist, and that we may hope for nothing better, no
greater equality and no more substantive democracies than the
ones we already have and know. Such a clamp on our normative
aspirations for political life seems to be nowhere sanctioned by
the stated missions of these foundations. Surely, eligible recipients
who want to imagine a better world should not be excluded from
consideration for hoping as they do, and for giving expression to
that hope during a time when expressing oneself has become a
perilous exercise.

Summary

The new restrictions on funding by both governmental and private agencies are worrisome not only in their own right but also in that they illustrate that academic norms are being rearticulated and established by such agencies, and that once these agencies and their conceptions of legitimate and illegitimate scholarship begin to circulate in the academy, this will doubtless affect the kinds of scholarly inquiries that we consider appropriate and worthy. Moreover, these funding organizations establish a link between extramural political expression and academic scholarship such that a research proposal that in no way touches on forbidden political issues can still be refused, because of the applicant's extramural expression. This also sets a problematic precedent that would break down the conventional barriers between extramural and academic speech in ways that would have to be contested and stanched in the name of academic freedom. In both cases, though, academic norms are impinged upon by culture, public and private institutions, and their own dissonant histories. The argument against preemptive censorship and in favor of open critical inquiry must recognize that academics live and breathe in the world, and that their ability to write and think depends on the success of multi-institutional struggles with complex histories. In this sense, academic freedom is not a personal right — Post is clearly correct here. But the institutional matrix that allows us to continue to think, and to think critically, is larger than the department or the personnel committee: it extends to the entire realm of open, critical public speech; it participates in a history of norms that cannot be reduced to a decisionism (the view that norms are deliberately installed through individual decisions rather than the result of complex social processes governed by conventions); and it provides a conflicting set of norms as background for the judgments we can and must make. The evaluative scene in which we make judgments is impinged upon not only by the history of the norms that are invoked to make the judgment, but also by norms for academic work that are produced by state agencies, private institutions, journalistic commentary, and emerging hegemonic understandings of legitimacy. If, given the pace and force with which hegemonic understandings of "legitimate" scholarship form, there is no *sensus communis* on such issues, this is not at all bad. That there is conflict at the heart of judgment is precisely what keeps it from becoming rigidified as dogma. One must, as it were, make the case for the norms that one is using, and this means that one must be prepared to give reasons for their legitimacy. In this way, one would have to be in a position not just to employ such norms but also critically to interrogate their legitimacy; that is, one must be open to understanding how political exigencies compel us to adopt certain norms as if they were freely chosen. Consensus on which norms to adopt is formed as a result of a hegemonic articulation that forecloses critical reflection on its own formation. If agreement on norms could be simply presumed, then the practice of legitimation would be superfluous, and the institutional conditions for critical dissent would also be eliminated. Such conclusions are precisely the ones that academic freedom now urgently need to avert, oppose, and forestall, and the ones against which new principles of free and critical inquiry need to be asserted most rigorously.

In "On Liberty," John Stuart Mill refers to the "rags and remnants of persecution," the more subtle ways of discrediting perspectives and shutting down the domain of thought itself that have taken the place of overt coercion. "Mankind," he writes, "can hardly be too often reminded, that there was once a man named Socrates, between whom and the legal authorities and public opinion of his time there took place a memorable collision."[11] Let's remember as well that this collision was with not only the state and, to a certain extent, public opinion, but also with the professional norms of the time that dictated how and in what form thinking was permitted to occur.

NOTES

1. Post himself has written on the constitutional meaning of academic freedom, and he notes that this essay concerns a different feature of the doctrine, one that pertains exclusively to governance of faculty members.

2. American Association of University Professors, "1915 Declaration of Principles on Academic Freedom and Academic Tenure," in *Policy Documents and Reports*, 9th ed. (Washington, D.C.: American Association of University Professors, 2001), p. 295.

3. Alvin W. Gouldner, *The Future of Intellectuals and the Rise of the New Class* (Scranton, PA: HarperCollins, 1979); Erik Olin Wright, *Classes* (London: Verso, 1985); Timothy Mitchell, *Rule of Experts: Egypt, Techno-Politics, Modernity* (Berkeley: University of California Press, 2002).

4. Here it should be clear that I am in substantial agreement with Joan W. Scott's position in "Academic Freedom as an Ethical Practice," in Louis Menand (ed.), *The Future of Academic Freedom* (Chicago: University of Chicago Press, 1996).

5. See Shannon Jackson, *Professing Performance: Theatre in the Academy from Philology to Performativity* (Cambridge, UK: Cambridge University Press, 2004).

6. See Robyn Wiegman (ed.), *Women's Studies on Its Own: A Next Wave Reader in Institutional Change* (Durham, NC: Duke University Press, 2002).

7. James D. Watson, *The Double Helix: A Personal Account of the Discovery of the Structure of DNA* (New York: Touchstone, 1996), pp. 92–109 and 149–52.

8. See John McCumber, *Time in the Ditch: American Philosophy and the McCarthy Era* (Evanston, IL: Northwestern University Press, 2001).

9. For some of many attacks on the Ford Foundation for ostensibly supporting "Palestinian causes," see Edwin Black, "Funding Hate" Series, *JTA: Global News Service of the Jewish People*, October 16, 2003: "Anti-Israel Activists at Durban Were Funded by Ford Foundation," http://www.jta.org/page_view_story.asp?intarticleid=13328&intcategoryid=6; "How Aware is Ford Foundation of Way Its Funds Are Being Used? http://www.jta.org/page_view_story.asp?intarticleid=13331&intcategoryid=6; "Transparency a Concerns as Millions Go to Mideast," http://www.jta.org/page_view_story.asp?intarticleid=13332&intcategoryid=6; "Audit of Palestinian Group Suggests Lax Funding Controls," http://www.jta.org/page_view_story.asp?intarticleid=13333&intcategoryid=6.

10. http://www.fordfound.org/news/views_news_detail_cfm?news_index=147.

11. John Stuart Mill, "On Liberty," in *Utilitarianism*, ed. Mary Warnock (New York: World Publishing Co., 1971), p. 150.

Why Academic Freedom?

The Theoretical and

Constitutional Context

Philippa Strum

> The First Amendment . . . presupposes that right
> conclusions are more likely to be gathered out of a
> multitude of tongues, than through any kind of
> authoritative selection. To many this is, and always
> will be, folly; but we have staked upon it our all.
> — Judge Learned Hand, *United States v.*
> *Associated Press*, 52 F. Supp. 362, 372 (1943)

As the academy contemplates the state of academic freedom after
September 11, 2001, it might do well to remember that the history
of academic freedom in American constitutional law is relatively
short. The legal boundaries of academic freedom are in fact still
somewhat unclear, and the extent to which courts will be protective of academic freedom claims post-9/11 is similarly uncertain.
In an attempt to summarize the theoretical and legal underpin-
nings of the right, this essay addresses the following questions:

1. How did the idea of academic freedom develop in the
United States?
2. What is the current judicial rationale for the constitutional
protection of academic freedom? How and on what basis does it
differentiate the speech of scholars from that of other Americans?
3. Is academic freedom an institutional right, an individual
right, or both?
4. Does academic freedom apply to students as well as faculty
members?

5. Do faculty members at private institutions have the same legally protected academic freedom as those at public institutions?

6. Is there a rationale — theoretical, constitutional, or both — for extending academic freedom to scholars working outside the academy?

7. Might academic freedom be threatened by the current dependence of institutions on funding from foundations?

History and Theoretical Context

When Harvard was created in 1636, it was the first college in what would become the United States, and its origins had nothing to do with academic freedom. Like almost all such institutions established in the seventeenth and eighteenth centuries, Harvard was founded by a religious group. The function of each college was to train its students in the beliefs of the respective founding religion.[1] There was no reason to enshrine a search for truth in the colleges; the truth — God's will — was already known.

The secularization of many American institutions of higher learning in the nineteenth and the early twentieth century, and the emergence of the modern research university in the decades following the Civil War, did not immediately produce a widely accepted concept of academic freedom.[2] There was, in fact, no authoritative statement of the rationale for academic freedom in this country until 1915, when John Dewey and other academics became concerned about the intrusion of boards of trustees into academic personnel decisions. They founded the American Association of University Professors (AAUP) and, within a few months, adopted a "Declaration of Principles" that identified three elements of academic freedom: "freedom of inquiry and research; freedom of teaching within the university or college; and freedom of extramural utterance and action."[3] While all three are important, the third element raises a somewhat different question; the discussion below therefore focuses on the first two.

Dewey and his colleagues considered academic freedom necessary if impartial scholars were to discover objective truths about the world — truths that the AAUP declaration stated could be identified in the areas of natural science, social science, philosophy, and religion. If the scholars were to fulfill their mission, which the declaration's authors believed was to serve society, then the freedom to inquire and publish without concern about external pressures was crucial. At the same time, the AAUP recognized that the right to pursue research while remaining independent of society and its accepted truths, whether religious or secular, brought with it responsibilities. These the declaration labeled the professors' "correlative obligations" to present all views of their subjects in the classroom, thereby training students to think for themselves.

In 1940, the AAUP and the Association of American Colleges and Universities fleshed out the justification for academic freedom in their "Statement of Principles on Academic Freedom and Tenure," which has become the profession's fundamental statement of its rights and responsibilities. It has been endorsed by over one hundred eighty scholarly and professional organizations and incorporated into hundreds of college and university faculty handbooks.[4] The key provisions, which follow the "1915 Declaration" in addressing the categories of research, teaching, and speech outside the university, include, first, the assertion that "The teacher is entitled to full freedom in research and in the publication of the results, subject to the adequate performance of his other academic duties." The second tenet is, "The teacher is entitled to freedom in the classroom in discussing his subject, but he should be careful not to introduce into his teaching controversial matter which has no relation to his subject."[5]

Two points should be made about these AAUP documents. First, when the "1915 Declaration" was adopted, the threat to academic freedom came primarily from university administrators and boards of trustees made up largely of lay persons. The question that concerned its authors, and the academic community in general, was less what the relationship between the academy and government should be than who within the university community should control the scholarly endeavor. The year 1940, when the "Statement of Principles" was written, was not at all coincidentally the year in which Congress passed the Smith Act.[6] The act, generated by the anti-Communist hysteria that would culminate more than a decade later in the McCarthy period, reflected the government's interest in rooting out supposed subversives, investigating behavior in all walks of life, including the academy, and imposing loyalty oaths. By the 1940s, academics were less concerned about internal academic power than they were about intrusions by the state. Nevertheless, as has been the case at least since the end of the Second World War, the objective that underlies today's professional assertions of academic freedom is protection of the scholar-teacher's intellectual endeavors from interference by either university administrators and trustees or the state or both. As discussed below, protection of the university as an institution from the state has become an additional objective — arguably the objective that is taken most seriously by the nation's courts.

A second point is that the 1915 and the 1940 statements both rest on the assumption that truths exist and can be unearthed by impartial scholars. That premise has come under attack by scholars who challenge the discriminatory and exclusionary nature of past "truths" and by others who are skeptical about the very idea of objective truth. The dispute results in an epistemological problem with which numerous scholars are wrestling, with various degrees of success.[7] If the justification for academic freedom is not the discovery of truth, what is it? The answer may be that academic freedom protects the commitment to the *pursuit* of truth, undertaken with the recognition that the truth to be found is at best partial and inevitably subject to the filtering sensibilities of the scholar, and that the search itself will enrich society in two ways. The first societal benefit is the concrete knowledge to be gained, although whether that concrete knowledge will be found only by natural scientists and not by social scientists and scholars of the humanities, and whether many "truths" even of the natural sciences are likely to remain unchallenged, are subjects for another discussion. The second benefit lies in the way the search furthers the continuing process of open inquiry that must take place within a democratic society. The search itself teaches that all ideas are open to challenge, and that progress, that elusive goal, can be achieved only through free inquiry. Free inquiry is as vital to society at large as it is to the academy, and one of the justifications for the expenditure of societal resources on colleges and universities is that they will produce leaders trained to think.

The Constitutional Context

It is, in fact, this pragmatic approach to academic freedom, rather than the epistemological one suggested by the early AAUP documents, that has been adopted by the American courts. In 1957, a majority of the Supreme Court suggested for the first time that there might be a constitutionally protected right to academic freedom.[8] *Sweezy v. New Hampshire* involved an investigation by the New Hampshire Attorney General into both a lecture given by the University of New Hampshire professor Paul M. Sweezy and Sweezy's political associations. Sweezy refused to answer questions about those subjects, invoking his First Amendment right to free speech. Chief Justice Earl Warren's opinion for the Court, upholding Sweezy's right not to reply, focused on the social utility of academic freedom.

> The essentiality of freedom in the community of American universities is almost self-evident. No one should underestimate the vital role in a democracy that is played by those who guide and train our youth. To impose any strait jacket upon the intellectual leaders in our colleges and universities would imperil the future of our Nation. No field of education is so thoroughly comprehended by man that new discoveries cannot yet be made. Particularly is that true in the social sciences, where few, if any, principles are accepted as absolutes. Scholarship cannot flourish in an atmosphere of suspicion and distrust. Teachers and students must always remain free to inquire, to study and to evaluate, to gain new maturity and understanding; otherwise our civilization will stagnate and die.[9]

Referring to "highly sensitive" First Amendment areas such as "freedom of speech or press, freedom of political association, and freedom of communication of ideas, particularly in the academic community," Warren added, "We believe that there unquestionably was an invasion of petitioner's liberties in the areas of academic freedom and political expression."[10] The Court thereby indicated that the right to academic freedom is placed somewhere in the First Amendment. Why the clause that says simply that "Congress shall make no law ... abridging the freedom of speech" should be interpreted to give academics more protection than other members of the society remained unclear (this point will be discussed further below). The Court did not elaborate, and in fact, the stated basis for the Court's overturning of Sweezy's conviction for contempt was not that professors' speech deserved special safeguards but that the mandate given to the Attorney General by the state legislature was broader than necessary.[11]

Justice Felix Frankfurter, however, wrote a concurrence that is frequently cited today as the foundation for the constitutional recognition of academic freedom in this country.

> For society's good ... inquiries into these problems [those studied by the social sciences], speculations about them, stimulation in others of reflection upon them, must be left as unfettered as possible.... This means the exclusion of governmental intervention in the intellectual life of a university.[12]

Frankfurter went on to speak of "the dependence of a free society on free universities" and then quoted from a statement by South African professors that said, in part, "It is the business of a university to provide that atmosphere which is most conducive to speculation, experiment and creation. It is an atmosphere in which there prevail 'the four essential freedoms' of a university — to determine for itself on academic grounds who may teach, what may be taught, how it shall be taught, and who may be admitted to study."[13] In other words, Frankfurter suggested that academic freedom deserves special protection not because of the benefit to the individual faculty member but because critical inquiry benefits the society at large. This concern for society is in keeping with the generally accepted pragmatic rationale for the free speech clause, which is that a democratic polity can survive only if its members have access to the ideas they need in order to make informed decisions about policy.[14] It is in keeping with that rationale that the press, which provides the citizenry with information, is given particular protection by the First Amendment. Frankfurter extended the rationale and the protection to the intellectual endeavors of the academy.[15]

One aspect of Frankfurter's opinion signals a problem that American law has not yet solved. By invoking a university's freedom to decide who shall teach what and how, he seemed to be referring to academic freedom as an institutional right. At the same time, by citing "inquiries" in the social sciences, he appeared to include the rights of individual scholars as well, since research is, of course, carried out by individuals, whether they do so within the framework of an institution or not. This duality appears in a number of Supreme Court decisions. In *Keyishian v. Board of Regents*, decided in 1967, for example, the Court struck down a New York loyalty oath as applied to teachers at the State University of New York. Justice William Brennan declared for the 5–4 majority,

> Our Nation is deeply committed to safeguarding academic freedom, which is of transcendent value to all of us and not merely to the teachers concerned. That freedom is therefore a special concern of the First Amendment, which does not tolerate laws that cast a pall of orthodoxy over the classroom.... The classroom is peculiarly the "marketplace of ideas." The Nation's future depends upon leaders trained through wide exposure to that robust exchange of ideas which discovers truth "out of a multitude of tongues, [rather] than through any kind of authoritative selection."[16]

The oath was overturned on grounds of vagueness and overbreadth, but the academic-freedom rationale was made even clearer by Brennan's inclusion of the paragraph of Justice Warren's opinion in *Sweezy v. New Hampshire* that is quoted above (see p. 147).[17] It is a pragmatic rationale, based on the need to provide the nation with competent, thoughtful future leaders.

The Court's view of the classroom as an integral part of the "marketplace of ideas" lay behind its decision in *Healy v. James* (1972), which stemmed from the refusal of Central Connecticut State College to recognize the group Students for a Democratic Society (SDS) as a legitimate campus student organization and extend to it the benefits provided to other student groups.[18] "The college classroom with its surrounding environs is peculiarly the 'marketplace of ideas,'" wrote Justice Louis Powell, "and we break no new constitutional ground in reaffirming this Nation's dedication to safeguarding academic freedom." Powell cited *Keyishian* and *Sweezy*, and as seven of the other eight justices signed on to the language of his opinion, academic freedom as a constitutional right appeared to be firmly grounded in American law.[19]

In light of the earlier decisions involving academic freedom, however, it was not clear what the nature of that academic freedom was or whose academic freedom had been upheld. As one commentator has noted, "Federal courts often use, but do not explain, the term 'academic freedom.'"[20] In *Healy*, the Court was concerned not with faculty freedom, or institutional freedom, but with students' freedom. In fact, in this case, the students' freedom was in conflict with the asserted freedom of the institution to decide that SDS was antithetical to its aims and therefore had no place on a college campus.

The conflict points to an inherent paradox in the current constitutional jurisprudence of academic freedom. It is obviously impossible to protect the kind of academic freedom celebrated by the Supreme Court without referring to the people mentioned in the two AAUP statements, as the "1940 Statement" does in its provisions "*Teachers* are entitled to full freedom in research" and "*Teachers* are entitled to freedom in the classroom."[21] Yet, as the Supreme Court noted in *University of Michigan v. Ewing* (1985), in which a former student challenged his dismissal from the University of Michigan Medical School, judicial decisions in the area of academic freedom have focused on "the prerogatives of state and local educational *institutions* and our responsibility to safeguard their academic freedom."[22] Justice John Paul Stevens spoke in *Ewing* of courts' inability "to evaluate the substance of the multitude of academic decisions that are made daily by *faculty members* of public educational institutions," thereby suggesting that academic freedom inheres in faculty members. He pointed to institutional academic freedom, however, by adding, in a footnote, "Academic freedom thrives not only on the independent and uninhibited exchange of ideas among teachers and students but also, and somewhat inconsistently, on autonomous decision-making by the academy itself."[23]

Notice that Justice Stevens cited the "exchange of ideas among teachers and students." If, as the Court suggested in *Keyishian*, academic freedom helps produce the nation's future leaders through the free exchange of ideas, then logically all the participants in that exchange — that is, both teachers and students — must be the possessors of the right to academic freedom.

Exactly how students fit into the constitutional theory of academic freedom, however, is unclear. It is not surprising that the 1915 and 1940 foundational statements about academic freedom, written as they were by the AAUP, focused on the rights of faculty members rather than those of students. The "1915 Declaration," in fact, states that it is not concerned with the rights of students.[24] The reason, as the document makes explicit, is that the danger to which the new organization was responding was attacks on professorial rights. The purpose of the "1940 Statement" is apparent in its title, "Statement of Principles on Academic Freedom *and*

Tenure."[25] While it mentions the right of the student "to freedom in learning," it does so only in passing, as the purpose of the document was to safeguard the tenure — and through it, the freedom of thought — of faculty members with unpopular ideas.[26] Small wonder, then, that if the Supreme Court justices seek guidance in these documents about the way students' academic freedom fits into the overall scheme, they are bound to be disappointed.

The Court has not filled the gap. In *Tinker v. Des Moines*, the 1969 case in which the Court upheld the right of public junior and senior high-school students to wear black armbands as a protest against the war in Vietnam, the Court specifically ruled that students do not shed their First Amendment speech rights "at the schoolhouse gate" and that those rights are particularly important "in light of the special characteristics of the school environment."[27] The Court did not, however, use the phrase "academic freedom," no doubt in part because the case involved students substantially younger (sixteen, fifteen, and thirteen years old at the time of their protest) than those usually found in universities.[28]

The confusion about to whom or what academic freedom applies was compounded by *California v. Bakke* (1978). Although *Bakke* is more commonly known as an affirmative-action case, it has implications for the law of academic freedom as well. In upholding the right of a university to choose its students in part on the basis of diversity, Justice Powell's opinion for the Court stated, "Academic freedom, though not a specifically enumerated constitutional right, long has been viewed as a special concern of the First Amendment. The freedom of a university to make its own judgments as to education includes the selection of its student body." Powell then quoted the "four essential freedoms of a university" set out by Justice Frankfurter in his *Sweezy* concurrence[29] — all of which suggest that academic freedom belongs to the university as such. The Court's decision in *Grutter v. Bollinger*, its most recent affirmative-action case, was based on equal-protection law rather than on considerations of academic freedom. Justice Sandra Day O'Connor nonetheless noted in her opinion for the Court that Justice Powell's opinion in *Bakke*, which she cited approvingly, was based on "the academic freedom that 'long has been viewed as a special concern of the First Amendment'" and on "our cases recognizing a constitutional dimension, grounded in the First Amendment of educational autonomy." She added,

"We have long recognized that, given the important purpose of public education and the expansive freedoms of speech and thought associated with the university environment, universities occupy a special niche in our constitutional tradition."[30] As in *Bakke*, her reference was to institutional autonomy.

The questions of whether academic freedom is a legally recognized right of the individual scholar rather than of the faculty or the institution as a whole, and the extent to which academic freedom is also a right of students, still remain largely unanswered. Academic freedom as defined by the academic profession appears to be a right of individual teachers against both the university as a corporate entity and the state, but as defined in the courts of the United States it frequently appears as an institutional right — one that presumably can be exercised against the individual faculty member. At the same time, however, the Supreme Court has repeatedly upheld the academic freedom of individual professors, in cases such as *Sweezy* and *Keyishian*. As J. Peter Byrne has commented, "The institutional right seems to give a university the authority to hire and fire without government interference those very individuals apparently granted a personal right to write and teach without institutional hindrance."[31] What does seem clear, however, is that just as *Bakke* recognized the utility of diversity among students, so the concept of academic freedom is in effect the recognition that there is an important societal utility in the diversity of ideas. Democracy in society is in many ways dependent on the freedom of teaching and critical inquiry. As the Supreme Court has sometimes acknowledged, the willingness to examine all ideas for their potential truth is as central to uncovering ideas that will serve the citizenry as it is to producing informed citizens who will choose among them.

Academic Freedom as an Individual Right

At this point, it is necessary to step back and consider the assumptions that are behind Justice Frankfurter's foundational language and that underlie both the theory and the current law of academic freedom.

The invocation of any constitutionally protected right necessarily implies that this right has a basis in a specific constitutional provision, whether — as in the guarantee of the right to a jury of one's peers — the language of the Constitution is explicit about the right or whether — as in the right to privacy — the right is implicit in one or more clauses. As we have seen, while the words "academic freedom" do not appear in the Constitution, the First Amendment's speech clause is invoked in discussions on academic freedom, so that clause merits closer attention here.

While the clause says, "Congress shall make no law . . . abridging the freedom of speech, or of the press," the Supreme Court held in 1925 that the provision applied to acts of state governments as well as of the federal government.[32] In effect, that altered the clause to read, "Congress and the states shall make no law . . ." Furthermore, since in practice the limitation is interpreted to apply to executive and judicial branches as well as legislatures, the current meaning of the clause actually is "The federal and state governments shall make no law . . ." Notice that only governmental bodies, not private entities, are forbidden to abridge speech. Public colleges and universities are governmental bodies, so the First Amendment clearly applies to them. Private colleges and universities, however, are run by nongovernmental entities, and the First Amendment does not prohibit a private employer, including a private college or university, from abridging the speech of its employees. That means that if the First Amendment is the sole basis for academic freedom, it would appear to apply only to faculty members at public institutions. One may ask why, if academic freedom is so important to society, it does not apply to private colleges and universities, and we will return to that point.

But that is not the only source of confusion. As is the case with most constitutional provisions, the precise application of the speech clause is unclear. If it means simply that all people in the United States have a right to speech protected from governmental interference, what is the source of the claim, referred to earlier, that academics have a greater right to protected speech than everyone else? Or that faculty members at public universities have a more significant speech right than, for example, the university's custodial or secretarial staff?

As Frankfurter's opinion and other Supreme Court decisions make clear, the answer that illuminates Court doctrine in this area lies in the rationale for the speech clause rather than in the words themselves. The Court has acknowledged that the free flow of ideas is crucial to a democracy: without access to all ideas, the electorate cannot decide which ideas are good and which are bad, or which candidates and which actual or proposed governmental policies individual voters should support or oppose. In other words, the reason for the inclusion of the First Amendment in the Constitution and the underlying rationale for Court decisions is pragmatic: democracy cannot survive without an informed electorate.[33] This is why the press (and, by extension, other, modern forms of media), which provides the citizenry with information, is given particular protection by the First Amendment.

The amendment was adopted at a time when the average citizen had no access to higher education — when, in fact, there were relatively few institutions of higher education in this country and, as noted earlier, most of them were private and sectarian.[34] While the problem of academic freedom at the college level could not, therefore, have been foremost in the minds of the people who wrote and ratified the First Amendment, the Court has recognized that a substantial part of today's electorate receives not only a body of knowledge but also an approach to evaluating information during its college years.[35] Its decisions indicate that the free flow of ideas, which initially were protected primarily in the public square, must now be protected in the college classroom as well — or, at least, in the classrooms provided by public institutions. That is the basis for protecting the speech right of faculty members *as teachers*.

Faculty members' right to free speech *as researchers* is another matter. One may argue that teachers in institutions of higher education need the benefits of research in order to educate their students properly. That does not automatically mean that they must be free to do their own research rather than to draw upon the research of others. Some colleges in the United States expect their faculty members to devote themselves primarily or entirely to teaching and place little or no emphasis on the production of original research. The argument that the only good teachers are those engaged in research is difficult to sustain as an absolute in our society, where the teacher of a senior in high school is expected not to do research but to devote himself or herself solely to teaching, whereas the teacher of that student as a college freshman is usually required to be a researcher as well. The tie between knowledge and good teaching is obvious; the need for the teacher to be the producer of original knowledge is less so.

Similarly, some faculty members in our leading institutions of higher education are only required to do research and have no teaching responsibilities at all.[36] Since they do not teach, should they be denied academic freedom? The answer, logically, is yes, if the teaching function is the only reason for academic freedom. Equally logically, therefore, there must be more to academic freedom than that.

Both the AAUP declarations and the Supreme Court decisions, in fact, suggest that academic freedom stems from more than the teaching function and that a scholar has an obligation that goes beyond the classroom. "The responsibility of the university teacher," according to the "1915 Declaration," "is primarily to the public itself.... In the essentials of his professional activity his duty is to the wider public."[37] "We ask, then, for the maintenance of academic freedom and of the civil liberties of scholars," according to the AAUP's "Academic Freedom and Tenure in the Quest for National Security," "not as a special right, but as a means whereby we may make our appointed contribution to the life of the commonwealth."[38] Justice Frankfurter argued in *Sweezy* that "society's good" required research in the social sciences.[39] The pragmatic rationale for academic freedom lies not merely in the training of society's youth by the professoriat — remember that when the "1915 Declaration" was written, only a small fraction of the nation's student-age population was in colleges and universities — but, equally, in the search for knowledge that is independent of the teaching function.[40]

The search for knowledge, particularly in the humanities and the social sciences, is usually not a collective endeavor. It is carried out by individuals. The concept of "academic freedom" — rather than, for example, a concept of "scholarly freedom" — exists because the economic reality is that most researchers, particularly in the humanities and the social sciences, hold jobs in academia. Their research is largely unpaid. However much they may enjoy the give-and-take of the classroom, most of them teach because that is how they make their living. In the United States, therefore, we have not professional associations of independent scholars but associations of scholars who are employed by colleges and universities, and it is these scholars who have framed the idea of scholarly freedom as connected to the academy. The result is twofold: we sometimes forget that rights inhere in individuals,

not collectives, and we ignore the academic-freedom claims of independent scholars.

The Declaration of Independence, which articulates the rights
rationale, and the Bill of Rights, which enumerates some of the
rights, are couched in the language of individual rather than group
rights. According to the declaration, it is "all men," rather than
"all groups," who "are created equal" in their possession of rights.
As Jefferson argued, individuals organize governmental entities in
order to protect their rights, but they do not cede possession of
their rights either to the group or to the government. "Inalienable
rights" are precisely those liberties that the individual retains in
the face of the collective. To the extent that group rights are recognized at all in this society, they are the corollary of individual
rights. The First Amendment, for example, guarantees individuals
the right to association. As a result, the Supreme Court has held
that groups to which those individuals belong cannot be required
to turn their membership lists over to the government — not to
protect any right of the group as such, but to protect the right of
the individual to join a group.[41] What may appear to be a group
right to racial or gender equality actually is a derivative of the
right of each individual to be treated equally by government and
many private entities regardless of race or gender.[42] Similarly,
institutions of higher education can claim a right to academic
freedom, but only as a corollary of the right of individual faculty
members to be free from government interference in the classroom and in their research. If this were not the case, individual
faculty members denied tenure or promotion would not be able
to sue either the faculty members who voted against them or the
university officials who finalized the decision.[43]

Academic freedom, then, is a right of individuals.[44] And if
there are two bases for the existence of an academic freedom that
goes beyond the speech right held by all individuals — the societal
needs for faculty members to teach their students properly and
for scholars to engage in the process of seeking truth — then individuals who engage in research but who do not teach are logically
entitled to the same "academic" freedom, even though they are
not employed by the academy.

As we have seen, most of the people who spend their professional lives engaged in the search for knowledge are gathered in
the academy, so colleges and universities must be protected. The

researchers and teachers — the producers and conveyers of ideas that are so important to society — must therefore be given greater protection for their utterances than is the right both of most other people outside the academy and of people such as secretaries and janitors within academia.[45] That is why most of the nation's private colleges and universities, not subject to the legal constraints of the First Amendment, nonetheless choose to follow the AAUP documents or variations of them.[46] They recognize that the need for academic freedom would exist even in the absence of the First Amendment, for the good of the society that colleges and universities seek to serve.

But it is equally true that not all scholars work in the academy. The academy might well ask whether the independent scholar has an equal right to what we call "academic" freedom. In the case of independent scholars, the freedom clearly could not be that of tenure or the right not to be fired by the academy. Might it be, instead, the right to demand the support of the profession and the academic world generally if the scholar comes under attack for his or her ideas? One might postulate that the test of the independent scholar, as opposed to anyone else without an academic position, is similar to the test of the scholar in the academy: a willingness to submit his or her results to the judgment of professional peers and the granting by the profession of credibility to those ideas. That is not a perfect test by which to differentiate a scholar from other members of society, as scholars whose ideas run counter to the prevailing orthodoxy in a discipline may be scorned, but it may be as good a test as exists. If an independent scholar's work is printed in scholarly journals or by scholarly publishers, if the scholar is invited to participate in presentations at scholarly conferences, then must not that work be considered as valuable to the society at large as the work of another scholar who happens to be employed by a university, and must not its author have a valid claim on the support of all other scholars for the protection of the right to present her or his ideas? If an important component of the rationale for academic freedom is society's need for scholars' ideas, and the understanding that, in protecting the articulation of unpopular ideas, society is simultaneously protecting its access to all ideas, is it not then logical that the right to a special kind of societal protection belongs to scholars outside the academy?[47]

Whatever one thinks about the place of the independent scholar, however, an examination of the philosophy underlying academic freedom demonstrates that the right must be seen as an individual one. The scholarly community's failure to articulate the right to academic freedom as individual, with the institutional right understood as a necessary derivative of the individual right, has left the Supreme Court and the law of academic freedom, as currently defined, in the position of not being certain whether academic freedom belongs to the faculty or to the university.

The Foundations, the Universities, and Academic Freedom

One pressing issue that has emerged in the post-9/11 period is that of financial constraints on academic freedom. Most American universities and colleges that emphasize research depend on grants from private foundations, whether these grants are given to individual faculty members or to the institutions themselves. The potential impact of that dependence on academic freedom was highlighted after a number of resolutions equating Zionism with racism were introduced at the United Nations' 2001 World Conference Against Racism, Racial Discrimination, Xenophobia and Related Intolerance, held in Durban, South Africa, in 2001. A subsequent series of articles by the Jewish Telegraphic Agency said that some of the Palestinian groups behind the resolutions had received funding from the Ford Foundation.[48] Members of Congress expressed concern, and Ford, acknowledging to Representative Jerrold Nadler that its grantees "may have taken part in unacceptable behavior in Durban," withdrew its funding from the Palestinian Society for the Protection of Human Rights.[49] Ford also added the following language to its grant agreements: "By countersigning this grant letter, you agree that your organization will not promote or engage in violence, terrorism, bigotry or the destruction of any State, nor will it make subgrants to any entity that engages in these activities."[50] Following suit, the Rockefeller Foundation adopted similar language.[51]

The provosts of Harvard, Yale, Princeton, Cornell, Columbia, Stanford, the University of Pennsylvania, Massachusetts Institute of Technology, and the University of Chicago quickly signed a letter of protest addressed to the Ford and Rockefeller foundations, arguing that the language would stifle legitimate academic activities.[52] The universities, of course, indicated their opposition to terrorism and bigotry but also expressed concern that, for example, the words "promote" (in the Ford and Rockefeller language) and "support" (Rockefeller) were undefined. According to the provost of the University of Chicago, the language could be interpreted to ban such activities as campus Palestinian film festivals or students' displays of pictures of Palestinian refugee camps.[53] "Whatever university administrators may think of the merits of the political views expressed" in such activities, the letter argued, "these fall under the protection of freedom of academic speech."[54]

While extracurricular activities are threatened by the new language, the potential effect on classrooms and research is even greater and far more serious. Does a philosophy professor who assigns the works of anarchists or of Karl Marx thereby "promote" terrorism? Does a history professor who lectures about the teachings of the Ku Klux Klan or other white supremacists promote bigotry? Is a professor of African American studies who analyzes the work of Malcolm X in an article promoting bigotry? Is a professor of political thought who parses the words of Osama Bin Laden in a scholarly article supporting terrorism? The examples can easily be multiplied.

The MacArthur Foundation, the Charles Stewart Mott Foundation, and the Bill and Melinda Gates Foundation went even further, requiring recipients to certify that they would make sure none of the grant money went to individuals or organizations on government-maintained lists of terrorists. The MacArthur language was as follows:

> Your organization hereby represents and warrants that Foundation grant funds will be used in compliance with all applicable anti-terrorist financing and asset control laws, regulations, rules and executive orders, including, but not limited to, the USA Patriot Act of 2001. In this regard, your organization agrees to take all reasonable steps to ensure that no person or entity expected to receive funds in connection with this grant is named on any list of suspected terrorists or blocked individuals maintained by the U.S. government, including but not limited to (a) the Annex to Executive Order No. 13224 (2001) (Executive Order Blocking Property and Prohibiting Transactions with Persons Who Commit, Threaten to Commit, or

Support Terrorism), or (b) the List of Specially Designated Nationals and Blocked Persons maintained by the Office of Foreign Assets Control of the U.S. Department of the Treasury.[55]

The language was inserted in grant letters after the treasury department suggested it as a voluntary "best practice" for U.S.-based charities that fund foreign organizations.[56]

That meant recipient colleges and universities were required to check all their employees or other individuals likely to benefit from a grant against the lists, which are notoriously unreliable. Many individuals' names, particularly those in languages other than English, are similar to one another, and there is inadequate identifying information of other kinds; names in languages other than English are frequently misspelled; and there is no indication of what evidence has resulted in an individual's inclusion on the list. There is also no readily available mechanism by which someone on one of the lists can challenge his or her inclusion.

This was made strikingly clear when Senator Edward Kennedy disclosed that he had been blocked from boarding American airplanes five times in one month because his name is similar to that of someone on the Transportation Security Administration's "no-fly" list, which is similar to the lists mentioned in the foundations' language. Repeated phone calls by his staff were insufficient to effect his removal from the list, which finally occurred only when the secretary of the Department of Homeland Security intervened.[57] The less well-connected scholar whose name appears on such a list would be prevented from participating in foundation-funded research or other activities. Turning colleges and universities into political monitors is a poor way to maintain the freedom of thought that is a hallmark not only of academic freedom but also of American democracy.

A number of the foundations came to that realization as a result of the protests by universities and by such nongovernmental organizations as the American Civil Liberties Union (ACLU). The MacArthur Foundation agreed to omit the list-checking requirement for domestic (but not foreign) organizations.[58] The Gates Foundation similarly differentiated domestic from foreign organizations and told domestic groups that the language requiring grantees to take "reasonable precautions to ensure that none of the grant funds will be used in support of or to promote violence, terrorist activity or related training" did not refer, in the words of General Counsel Connie R. Collingsworth, "to any particular standard, but rather relies on the judgment of the grantee, based upon the particular facts and circumstances, to take the actions they deem appropriate to avoid the potential diversion of grant funds."[59] The Ford and Rockefeller foundations maintained their original language but sent a number of universities and organizations side agreements clarifying what the language meant. Ford, for example, told the universities, "We do not want or intend to interfere with discussions in classrooms, faculty publications, student remarks in chat rooms, or other communications that express the views of the individual(s) and not the institution. Our grant letter relates only to the official speech and conduct of the university and to speech or conduct that the university explicitly endorses."[60] As a result, most major universities decided to accept funds from Ford and Rockefeller. The ACLU did not. Stating that it was "a sad day when two of this country's most beloved and respected foundations feel they are operating in such a climate of fear and intimidation that they are compelled to require thousands of recipients to accept vague grant language which could have a chilling effect on civil liberties," it rejected a $1 million grant from the Ford Foundation and a $150,000 grant from Rockefeller.[61]

There is no question that under current law, private foundations have the right to give or not give money to whomever they choose, and there are few thoughtful scholars who would seek to alter that situation. According to the Foundation Center, however, the Ford Foundation alone provides American colleges and universities with some $145 million a year, and in 2002, institutions of higher education received $7.27 billion from private foundations.[62] Most of that sum is provided for institutional or program support rather than individual grants, which means not only academic programs and research centers but also museums and theaters.[63] A scholar whose name mistakenly appears on a government list of suspected terrorists could not work for a foundation-supported department or on a foundation-supported research project, as the university in question would be forced to judge each scholar on the basis of political acceptability rather than academic credentials. Given the enormous financial influence of foundations on higher education, the potential impact on academic freedom of the conditions tied to their funding decisions is a matter of substantial concern. So is the fact that the impetus for the restrictions appears to be governmental pressure.[64]

Academic Freedom After 9/11

In examining academic freedom in the post-9/11 period, therefore, we must be mindful of the following facts.

First, while the Supreme Court has recognized the right to academic freedom as an important part of the First Amendment,[65] it is unclear precisely what freedom individual faculty members possess in the absence of support from their institutions, as well as against their institutions. A recent federal court of appeals decision, although one that hopefully will not be followed by many other courts, held that "any right of 'academic freedom' . . . inheres in the University, not in individual professors."[66]

Second, the courts have based the constitutional right of academic freedom on the First Amendment's guarantee of freedom of speech. The First Amendment, however, applies only to the state, which in this context means that it protects only the academic freedom of faculty members — and perhaps students — at public colleges and universities. The willingness of private colleges and universities to bind themselves by codes based on AAUP principles does not mean that faculty members in those institutions have the same legal recourse as their colleagues in public institutions should their academic freedom be violated by their institutions.

Third, many of the leading constitutional academic-freedom cases have emerged from and have been decided during periods of high societal tension. *Sweezy* and *Keyishian* came out of the McCarthy era; *Healy* and *Tinker* were products of the war in Vietnam. It seems only reasonable to expect that the meaning and parameters of academic freedom will be subject to close court scrutiny as this nation pursues the war on terrorism. This in turn suggests that there is an opportunity for scholars to reexamine and further their thinking about the meaning and parameters of academic freedom.

As discussed above, the Supreme Court has adopted a pragmatic rationale in upholding the right to academic freedom: academic freedom benefits society. The danger in that doctrine is that at any given moment, society can decide that a greater benefit, such as security, must take precedence over academic freedom.

An answer to such an assertion is suggested by a 2003 report by the AAUP Special Committee on Academic Freedom and National Security in a Time of Crisis. "Freedom of inquiry and the open exchange of ideas," the committee wrote, "are crucial to the nation's security.... The nation's security and, ultimately, its well-being are damaged by practices that discourage or impair freedom."[67] In a time of crisis — not only a crisis of security but the invariable crisis of liberty that stems from the way this nation responds to crises of security — it is vital for us to remind ourselves and the nonacademic world that this country is devoted to securing liberty. We can be simultaneously safe and free; we can have both security and freedom; but we cannot survive as a *democratic* nation in the absence of liberty. Academic freedom is a crucial part of that liberty.

NOTES

While the sole responsibility for this essay rests with the author, thanks are owed to Jill Norgren for her careful reading of two drafts, and to David Rabban, Ralph Norgren, Timothy Stroup, and Susan Nugent for their thoughtful comments on various drafts.

1. Of the nine colleges founded before the American Revolution, eight were the product of religious groups and were charged with training clergy. Harvard was Puritan; King's College (later Columbia) and William and Mary, Anglican; Dartmouth and Yale, Congregationalist; the College of New Jersey (later Princeton), Presbyterian; the College of Rhode Island (later Brown), Baptist; Queen's College (later Rutgers), Dutch Reformed. The College of Philadelphia (later the University of Pennsylvania) was nonsectarian. Arthur M. Cohen, *The Shaping of American Higher Education: Emergence and Growth of the Contemporary System* (San Francisco: Jossey-Bass, 1998), pp. 17–18; John S. Brubacher and Willis Rudy, *Higher Education in Transition: A History of American Colleges and Universities, 1636–1968* (New York: Harper and Row, 1968), pp. 7–8.

2. Walter P. Metzger, *Academic Freedom in the Age of the University* (New York: Columbia University Press, 1961), pp. v–vi and 42–44.

3. American Association of University Professors, "1915 *Declaration of Principles*" repr. in Louis Joughin (ed.), *Academic Freedom and Tenure: A Handbook of the American Association of University Professors* (University of Wisconsin Press, 1969), pp. 157–58; also available at http://www.campus-watch.org/article/id/566.

4. Donna R. Euben, "Academic Freedom of Individual Professors and

Higher Education Institutions: The Current Legal Landscape (May 2002)," http://www.aaup.org/Com-a/aeuben.htm.

5. "1940 Statement of Principles on Academic Freedom and Tenure," reprinted in Joughin, *Academic Freedom and Tenure*, pp. 34–38; also available at http://www.aaup.org/statements/Redbook/1940stat.htm. The third tenet is "When [a professor] speaks or writes as a citizen, he should be free from institutional censorship or discipline, but his special position in the community imposes special obligations. . . . he should at all times be accurate, should exercise appropriate restraint, should show respect for the opinions of others, and should make every effort to indicate that he is not an institutional spokesman." The versions adopted in 1989 and 1990 removed the gender-specific language.

6. The Alien Registration Act of 1940 (usually called the Smith Act after Representative Howard W. Smith of Virginia, the author of the antisedition section) made it a criminal offense, *inter alia*, "(1) to knowingly or willfully advocate, abet, advise, or teach the duty, necessity, desirability, or propriety of overthrowing or destroying any government in the United States by force or violence, or by the assassination of any officer of any such government; (2) with the intent to cause the overthrow or destruction of any government in the United States, to print, publish, edit, issue, circulate, sell, distribute, or publicly display any written or printed matter advocating, advising, or teaching the duty, necessity, desirability, or propriety of overthrowing or destroying any government in the United States by force or violence; (3) to organize or help to organize any society, group, or assembly of persons who teach, advocate, or encourage the overthrow or destruction of any government in the United States by force or violence; or to be or become a member of, or affiliate with, any such society, group, or assembly of persons, knowing the purposes thereof." Ch. 439, 54 Stat. 670, 18 U.S.C. Sec. 2385.

7. See, for example, the various essays in Louis Menand (ed.), *The Future of Academic Freedom* (Chicago: University of Chicago Press, 1996). An earlier and influential essay is Herbert Marcuse, "Repressive Tolerance," in Robert Paul Wolff, Barrington Moore Jr., and Herbert Marcuse, *A Critique of Pure Tolerance* (Boston: Beacon Press, 1969), pp. 80–117.

8. Justice William O. Douglas referred to "academic freedom" in *Adler v. Board of Education*, 342 U.S. 485 (1952), p. 509, but that was in a dissenting opinion. Justice Felix Frankfurter did not use the phrase but, in effect, cited academic freedom in his concurring opinion in *Wieman v. Updegraff* (1952). In *Weiman*, faculty members at Oklahoma Agricultural and Mechanical College challenged a loyalty oath required of all state employees. The Court struck down the requirement on non-academic-freedom grounds — in this case, the due-process objection that a member of an allegedly subversive organization might

be unaware of the organization's subversive aims — but Frankfurter, concurring, implicitly invoked academic freedom. "Such unwarranted inhibition upon the free spirit of teachers," he wrote, "has an unmistakable tendency to chill that free play of the spirit which all teachers ought especially to cultivate and practice." 344 U.S. 183, p. 194.

9. *Sweezy v. New Hampshire*, 354 U.S. 234 (1957), p. 250.

10. *Ibid.*, pp. 245 and 250.

11. *Ibid.*, p. 254.

12. *Ibid.*, p. 262.

13. *Ibid.*, p. 263, citing "The Open Universities in South Africa (A statement of a conference of senior scholars from the University of Cape Town and the University of the Witwatersrand, including A. v. d. S. Centlivres and Richard Feetham, as Chancellors of the respective universities.)" (Johannesburg: Witwatersrand University Press, 1957), pp. 10–12.

14. While theorists have presented other rationales for first speech, such as that free speech is crucial to individual self-fulfillment, the Supreme Court has consistently preferred the pragmatic rationale. See, for example, *Whitney v. California*, 274 U.S. 357 (1927), pp. 375–76 (Brandeis, J., concurring); *Abrams v. U.S.*, 250 U.S. 616 (1919), pp. 630–31 (Holmes, J., dissenting); academic freedom cases cited in this essay.

15. Ironically, Frankfurter dissented in 1960 when the Court voided an Arkansas statute compelling teachers to list every organization to which they had belonged during the last five years. Although the Court did not use the phrase "academic freedom" in its decision and held only that the statute suffered from overbreadth, Frankfurter's dissent for himself and three other justices made clear that he considered the ruling to be based on an asserted right of academic freedom. *Shelton v. Tucker*, 364 U.S. 479, 495 (1960). The plaintiffs were both college professors and high-school teachers, and Frankfurter may have believed that academic freedom differed for the two groups. The question whether education in the lower schools is designed to be more of an indoctrination in societal values than that in institutes of higher education runs throughout much academic freedom litigation.

16. *Keyishian v. Board of Regents*, 385 U.S. 589 (1967), p. 603, quoting *United States v. Associated Press*, 52 F. Supp. 362, 372 (1943).

17. *Keyishian v. Board of Regents*.

18. *Healy v. James*, 408 U.S. 169 (1972).

19. *Ibid.*, pp. 180–81. For procedural reasons, having to do with the question of whether the college had a code of behavior for student groups and, if so, whether the campus SDS had declared its intention to comply with the code, the case was remanded to the lower courts.

20. Stacy E. Smith, "Who Owns Academic Freedom? The Standard for Academic Free Speech at Public Universities," *Washington and Lee Law Review* 59 (2002), p. 300 n.2.

21. Italics added.

22. *Regents of the University of Michigan v. Ewing*, 474 U.S. 214 (1985), p. 226 (1985) (italics added).

23. *Ibid.*, p. 226 and n.12 (citations omitted) (italics added).

24. "1915 Declaration," pp. 157–58.

25. Italics added.

26. "1940 Statement of Principles," p. 34.

27. *Tinker v. Des Moines Independent Community School District*, 393 U.S. 503 (1969), p. 506.

28. The phrase does appear in the title of a law review article cited in a footnote. *Ibid.*, p. 506 n.2.

29. *University of California Board of Regents v. Bakke*, 438 U.S. 265 (1978), p. 312.

30. *Grutter v. Bollinger*, 539 U.S. 306 (2003), pp. 307 and 329.

31. J. Peter Byrne, "Academic Freedom: A 'Special Concern of the First Amendment,'" *Yale Law Journal* 99 (1989), p. 257. For the confusion in Court doctrine, see also David M. Rabban, "A Functional Analysis of Individual and Institutional Academic Freedom Under the First Amendment," *Law and Contemporary Problems* 53.3 (1990), pp. 227–301.

32. *Gitlow v. New York*, 268 U.S. 652 (1925).

33. See, for example, *New York Times v. Sullivan*, 376 U.S. 254, 270 (1964); *First National Bank of Boston v. Bellotti*, 435 U.S. 765, 776–777 (1978); *Consolidated Edison v. Public Service Commission*, 447 U.S. 530, 534–35 (1980). See also Thomas M. Cooley and Walter Carrington, *A Treatise on the Constitutional Limitations which Rest upon the Legislative Powers of the States of the American Union*, 8th ed. (Boston: Little, Brown, 1927), pp. 885–86: The purpose of the speech and press clauses "has evidently been to protect parties in the free publication of matters of public concern, to secure their right to a free discussion of public events and public measures, and to enable every citizen at any time to bring the government and any person in authority to the bar of public opinion by any just criticism upon their conduct in the exercise of the authority which the people have conferred upon them.... The evils to be prevented were not the censorship of the press merely, but any action of the government by means of which it might prevent such free and general discussion of public matters as seems absolutely essential to prepare the people for an intelligent exercise of their rights as citizens."

34. As of 1789 (the year Congress adopted the Bill of Rights and sent it to the states for ratification), there were thirteen colleges and universities in the

United States; the University of Vermont was chartered in 1791. Paul West-meyer, *A History of American Higher Education* (Springfield, IL: Thomas, 1985), p. 19. There were an estimated 1,050 students enrolled in institutions of higher education in 1790, out of a total U.S. population of 3,929,214. Cohen, *Shaping of American Higher Education*, p. 51.

35. According to the Census Bureau, as of March 2002 there were 73,166,000 U.S. residents, out of an estimated total population of 288,400,000, who had attended college but not received a degree or who had earned college or graduate degrees. Table 11, "Educational Attainment of People 18 Years and Over," in U.S. Census Bureau, *Educational Attainment in the United States: March 2002: Detailed Tables* (PPL-169), available at http://www.census.gov/population/socdemo/education/ppl-169/tab11.pdf.

36. Research professors with no classroom responsibilities may of course be expected to supervise graduate students' research or perform similar teaching functions. As long as the academy appoints research professors who are not specifically expected to carry out such responsibilities, however, the idea that the right to academic freedom is derived from more than the teaching function remains.

37. "1915 Declaration of Principles," p. 163.

38. American Association of University Professors, "Academic Freedom and Tenure in the Quest for National Security: Report of a Special Committee of the American Association of University Professors" (1956), reprinted in Joughin (ed.), *Academic Freedom and Tenure*, pp. 48–49.

39. *Sweezy v. New Hampshire*, 354 U.S. 234 (1957), pp. 261–62.

40. There were roughly 404,000 Americans aged eighteen to twenty-four in colleges and universities in 1915, at a time when there were 18,844,000 Americans aged fifteen to twenty-four (out of a total U.S. population of 100,546,000). According to the Census Bureau, 3.1 percent of the population of eighteen- to twenty-four-year-olds was enrolled in institutions of higher educa-tion. U.S. Bureau of the Census, *Historical Statistics of the United States, Colonial Times to 1970, vol. 1* (Washington, D.C.: U.S. Department of Commerce, Bureau of the Census, 1975), p. 383; U.S. Census Bureau, *Statistical Abstract of the United States, 2003: The National Data Book* (Washington, D.C.: U.S. Depart-ment of Commerce, Bureau of the Census, 2003), http://www.census.gov/statab/hist/HS-03.pdf.

41. *NAACP v. Alabama ex rel. Patterson*, 357 U.S. 449 (1958); see also *Louisiana ex rel. Gremillion v. NAACP*, 366 U.S. 293 (1961).

42. See, for example, *Missouri ex rel. Gaines v. Canada*, 305 U.S. 337 (1938); *Brown v. Board of Education*, 347 U.S. 483 (1954); *Reed v. Reed*, 404 U.S. 71 (1971); *U.S. v. Virginia*, 518 U.S. 515 (1996).

43. See, for example, *University of Pennsylvania v. EEOC*, 493 U.S. 182 (1990).

44. For other statements of this point, see, for example, Elizabeth Mertz, "The Burden of Proof and Academic Freedom: Protection for Institution or Individual?" *Northwestern University Law Review* 82 (1988), pp. 492 and 518; Steven G. Poskanzer, *Higher Education Law: The Faculty* (Baltimore: John Hopkins University Press, 2002), p. 102.

45. The speech rights of other public employees are not similarly protected. See, for example, *Connick v. Myers*, 461 U.S. 138 (1980); *Waters v. Churchill*, 511 U.S. 661 (1994).

46. The contractual commitment of private colleges and universities to academic freedom may be expressed in collective bargaining agreements, letters of appointments, faculty handbooks, or institutional rules and regulations. See Jim Jackson, "Express and Implied Contractual Rights to Academic Freedom in the United States," *Hamline Law Review* 22 (1999), pp. 467–500. It should be added that in the late twentieth and the early twenty-first century most institutions of higher education were heavily dependent upon government grants and therefore were arguably bound by the First Amendment in many of their activities. For the most part, however, adoption of AAUP-type principles predated the dependence on government funds.

47. The situation is complicated further by the case of scientists who work for corporations; for example, biologists employed by pharmaceutical companies. As most pharmaceutical companies encourage the biologists they employ to publish in peer-reviewed journals, these scholars would also logically be entitled to the protection provided to independent scholars who work outside the corporate world. I am grateful to Ralph Norgren for this insight.

48. Edwin Black, "Funding Hate" Series, *JTA Global News Service of the Jewish People*, Oct. 16, 2003: "Anti-Israel Activists at Durban Were Funded by Ford Foundation," http://www.jta.org/page_view_story.asp?intarticleid=13328 & intcategoryid=6; "How Aware is Ford Foundation of Way It Funds Are Being Used?" http://www.jta.org/page_view_story.asp?intarticleid=13331&intcategoryid=6; "Transparency a Concern as Millions Go to Mideast," http://www. jta. org/page_view_story.asp?intarticleid=13332&intcategoryid=6; "Audit of Palestinian Group Suggest Lax Funding Controls," http://www.jta.org/page_view_story.asp?intarticleid=13333&intcategoryid=6.

49. Daniel Golden, "Colleges Object to New Wording in Ford Grants," *Wall Street Journal*, May 4, 2004.

50. See "Ford Foundation Reaches Agreement with Representative Jerrold Nadler and U.S. Jewish Leaders; Answers Concerns About Foundation's Work in the Palestinian Territories," Ford Foundation News, November 18, 2003,

http:// www.fordfound.org/news/view_news_detail.cfm?news_index=85; Press Release, "Nadler Receives Ford Foundation's Response; Calls Ford Actions 'Important and Concrete' and 'Highly Commendable,'" November 18, 2003, http://www.house.gov/apps/list/press/ny08_nadler/2003_11_18_ford.html; Susan V. Berresford, letter to Jerrold Nadler, November 17, 2003, http://www. fordfound. org/newsroom/docs/svb_letter.pdf.

51. The Rockefeller Foundation language is, "In accepting these funds, you certify that your organization does not directly or indirectly engage in, promote, or support other organizations or individuals who engage in or promote terrorist activity."

52. Golden, "Colleges Object to New Wording in Ford Grants"; Justin Pope, "Foundations' Limits on Grants Draw Fire from Universities," *Philadelphia Inquirer*, May 6, 2004, http://www.philly.com/mld/inquirer/news/nation/8598978.htm?lc.

53. Richard Saller, cited in Golden, "Colleges Object to New Wording in Ford Grants," and quoted in "Campus News," *University of Chicago Magazine* 96.6 (2004), http://magazine.uchicago.edu/0408/campus-news/bird.shtml.

54. Pope, "Foundations' Limits on Grants Draw Fire from Universities."

55. The Mott Foundation language: "Your organization shall not, directly or indirectly, engage in, support or promote violence or terrorist activities.... Pursuant to the provisions of Executive Order 13224 and the USA Patriot Act, the Mott Foundation requires all organizations re-granting with Mott funds to check the terrorism watch lists issued by the United States government, the European Union, and the United Nations and refrain from providing financial or material support to any listed individual or organization." The Gates Foundation language: "You acknowledge that you are familiar with the U.S. Executive Orders and laws that prohibit the provision of resources and support to individuals and organizations associated with terrorism and the terrorist related lists promulgated by the U.S. Government, the United Nations, and the European Union. You confirm that you will take reasonable precautions to ensure that none of the grant funds will be used in support of or to promote violence, terrorist activity or related training, whether directly through your own activities and programs, or indirectly through your support of, or cooperation with, other persons and organizations known to support terrorism or that are involved in money laundering activities."

56. The "U.S. Department of the Treasury Anti-Terrorist Financing Guidelines: *Voluntary* Best Practices for U.S.-Based Charities," issued in November 2002, includes the following: "The charity should conduct basic vetting of potential foreign recipient organizations as follows: ... The charity should be able to demonstrate that it verified that the foreign recipient organization does not

appear on any list of the U.S. Government, the United Nations, or the European Union identifying it as having links to terrorism or money laundering. The charity should consult the Department of the Treasury's Office of Foreign Assets Control Specially Designated Nations List, which will identify entities designated by the U.S. Government as Foreign Terrorist Organizations or as supporters of terrorism. The charity also should consult the U.S. Government's Terrorist Exclusion List maintained by the Department of Justice, the list promulgated by the United Nations pursuant to U.N. Security Council Resolutions 1267 and 1390, the list promulgated by the European Union pursuant to EU Regulation 2580, and any other official list available to the charity," http:// www.treasury.gov/press/ releases/docs/tocc.pdf. The word "Voluntary" is italicized in the title.

57. Rachel L. Swarns, "Senator? Terrorist? A Watch List Stops Kennedy at Airport," *New York Times*, August 20, 2004; Sara Kehaulani Goo, "Sen. Kennedy Flagged by No-Fly List," *Washington Post*, August 20, 2004.

58. The MacArthur Foundation's new language for U.S. organizations: "Your organization agrees that Foundation grant funds will be used in compliance with all applicable anti-terrorist financing and asset control laws, regulations, rules and executive orders, including but not limited to, the USA Patriot Act of 2001 and Executive Order No. 13224." The new language for foreign organizations: "The Foundation is required by United States law to ensure that none of its grant funds are used directly or indirectly to assist in, sponsor, or provide support for acts of terrorism or to support organizations or persons listed as terrorists on lists maintained by the United States government, the United Nations, the European Union, and other entities."

59. Josh Gerstein, "ACLU Rejects $1.1 Million from Ford, Rockefeller," *New York Sun*, October 19, 2004, http://www.nysun.com/article/3384.

60. *Ibid.*

61. Anthony Romero, ACLU executive director, quoted in Gerstein, "ACLU Rejects $1.1 Million from Ford, Rockefeller."

62. Steven Lawrence and Leslie Marino, "Update on Funding for Higher and Graduate Educational Institutions," The Foundation Center, September 2003, http://fdncenter.org/research/trends_analysis/pdf/hiedupt.pdf.

63. *Ibid.*

64. The Combined Federal Campaign (CFC), which is administered by the federal Office of Personnel Management (OPM), enables approved charitable organizations to solicit federal employees at their workplace and permits the employees to earmark contributions for specific charities directly from their paychecks. In 2004, for the first time in the history of the program, organizations wishing to participate in it were required to sign the following certification: "I certify that, as of _____(date) the organization named in this application does not

knowingly employ individuals or contribute funds to organizations found on the following terrorist related lists promulgated by the U.S. Government, the United Nations, or the European Union. Presently these lists include the Department of the Treasury's Office of Foreign Assets Control Specially Designated Nations List, the Department of Justice's Terrorist Exclusion List, and the list annexed to Executive Order 13224. Should any change of circumstances occur during the year OPM will be notified within 15 days of such change." The American Civil Liberties Union, declining to inspect the lists to see if employees' or prospective employees' names were included, withdrew from the CFC. The American Civil Liberties Union Foundation subsequently created a coalition of a wide range of nonprofit organizations (Advocacy Institute, Americans United for Separation of Church and State, Amnesty International USA, Asian American Legal Defense and Education Fund, Breast Cancer Action, Brennan Center for Justice at the New York University School of Laws, Catholic Peace Ministry, Center for Constitutional Rights, Electronic Frontier Foundation, Global Rights, Lawyers' Committee for Civil Rights Under Law, NAACP Special Contribution Fund, NAACP Legal Defense and Educational Fund, Inc., National Committee for Responsive Philanthropy, National Council of Nonprofit Associations, National Women's Law Center, National Partnership for Women and Families, Natural Resources Defense Council, OMB Watch, Our Bodies Ourselves, Pain Relief Network, People for the Ethical Treatment of Animals, Puerto Rican Legal Defense and Education Fund, Sierra Club, and Unitarian Universalist Service Committee) that sued OPM and its director for violating proper federal procedures and for promulgating a rule that deprived them of their First Amendment rights (*ACLU Foundation et al. v. OPM and Mara Patermaster*. The complaint can be read at http://www.aclu.org/Files/OpenFile.cfm?id=16983). The entire list is at http://www.aclu.org/safeandfree. CFM?ID=16241&c=206. They asked that they and other organizations be permitted to participate in CFC without signing the certification. On March 29, 2005, OPM issued a new proposed regulation that altered the certification. The proposal would substitute the following language: "I certify that the organization named in this application is in compliance with all statutes, Executive Orders, and regulations restricting or prohibiting U.S. persons from engaging in transactions and dealings with countries, entities, or individuals subject to economic sanctions administered by the U.S. Department of the Treasury's Office of Foreign Assets Control. The organization named in this application is aware that a list of countries subject to such sanctions, a list of Specially Designated Nations and Blocked Persons subject to such sanctions, and overviews and guidelines for each such sanction program can be found at http://www.treas.gov/offices/enforcement/ofac/sanctions/. If the organization named in this application becomes noncompliant at any time subsequent to completing this certification, it will notify the OPM Office of CFC Operations immediately." (*70 Federal Register* No. 59, March 29, 2005.) The proposed language appears to eliminate the list-checking requirement. The CFC's reversal of its earlier formulation and the implied acknowledgment that some post-9/11 grant language requirements might be illegal and certainly were unnecessary surely will not be ignored by foundations.

65. This essay is a somewhat cursory review of the relevant cases. A good place to begin a more thorough examination is William Van Alstyne, "Academic Freedom and the First Amendment in the Supreme Court of the United States: An Unhurried Historical Review," *Law and Contemporary Problems* 53.3 (1990), pp. 79–154.

66. *Urofsky v. Gilmore*, 216 F.3d 401 (4th Cir. 2000), at 401; *cert. denied*, 531 U.S. 1070 (2001). Six professors at Virginia state colleges and universities challenged a state law forbidding the use of state-owned computers to access information having "sexually explicit" content. The professors argued that access to some of the sites was necessary for teaching and research, including their own and students' research on "indecency" laws, gender roles and sexuality, the "fleshy school" of Victorian poets, lesbian and gay studies, and psychological research on human sexual experience. The district court granted summary judgment, striking down the statute as overly vague. On appeal, the Fourth Circuit Court of Appeals ruled that First Amendment protection applies only to citizen speech rather than to employee speech. "A determination of whether a restriction imposed on a public employee's speech is violative of the First Amendment requires 'a balance between the interests of the [employee], as a citizen, in commenting upon matters of public concern and the interest of the State, as an employer, in promoting the efficiency of the public services it performs through its employees,'" the Court wrote, quoting *Connick v. Myers*, p. 142. "This balancing involves an inquiry first into whether the speech at issue touches upon a matter of public concern, and, if so, whether the employee's interest in First Amendment expression outweighs the public employer's interest in what the employer has determined to be the appropriate operation of the workplace.... Speech involves a matter of public concern when it affects a social, political, or other interest of a community." The Court concluded that viewing sexually explicit matter at work does not constitute "a matter of public concern" and that "it cannot be doubted that in order to pursue its legitimate goals effectively, the Commonwealth must retain the ability to control the manner in which its employees discharge their duties and to direct its employees to undertake the responsibilities of their positions in a specified way." 216 F.3d 401 (4th Cir.2000), pp. 406 and 409.

67. Special Committee on Academic Freedom and National Security in a Time of Crisis, "Academic Freedom and National Security in a Time of Crisis," October 2003, http://www.aaup.org/statements/REPORTS/911report.htm.

PART TWO: PRAXIS

Trust to the Public: Academic Freedom in the Multiversity

Kathleen J. Frydl

> When the university turns away from its central pur-
> pose and makes itself an appendage of the Govern-
> ment, with expedients rather than ideas, dispensing
> conventional orthodoxy rather than new ideas, it is not
> only failing to meet its responsibilities to its students;
> it is betraying a public trust.
>
> — Senator William Fulbright*

"Ask not what freedom is," the historian Daniel T. Rodgers exhorts at the close of his book *Contested Truths*, "for if it is worth much it is never static. Ask what the word is being used to do."[1] The injunction has force even in the circumscribed and distinct field of academic freedom. What has the phrase been used to do? An instrumental analysis, especially one focused on institutions, leads to the following conclusion: whereas academic freedom was originally defined and defended in the United States as the right to conduct research autonomously — guided by disciplinary exper-tise, and without fear of being fired by a board of trustees in thrall to a particular religious or political view — it has come to mean the right to say what you want on the campus or in the classroom without fear of reprisal. The unique rationale invoked to establish the principles of academic freedom, inextricably and explicitly tied to the power and defense of expertise, has given way to an

---

* J. William Fulbright, "The War and Its Effects: The Military-Industrial-Academic Complex," in Herbert I. Schiller (ed.), *Super-State: Readings in the Military-Industrial Complex* (Urbana: University of Illinois Press, 1970), pp. 177–78.

understanding that places the concept as part of some larger First Amendment family.

I join other authors in this volume in pointing out that this weak derivative of academic freedom deviates from the concept's original articulation and may, in some crucial respects, fail to protect freedom of inquiry. Specifically, this reworked understanding does not squarely address who retains sovereignty over the direction of research — an increasingly grave omission in the modern world of higher education, where research plays an essential role. My goal in this essay is to examine changes in the understanding of academic freedom alongside changes in the form and function of higher education itself. Obviously I am suggesting that some meaningful connection exists between the two. Although it may seem axiomatic to note the importance of the dynamic institutional context within which academic freedom is articulated and exercised, the nature of the relationship and its consequences have gone without the examination both merit. Nothing about that is surprising. In the United States, the general public usually refuses to think historically about freedom and also tends not to think of higher education as a system of opportunity structure or resource allocation that performs essential service to the state. The reluctance to do the latter becomes, again, especially problematic in light of the post–Second World War university system, which awarded a college degree that became a middle-class credential and which directly provided the state with the means to produce a menacing military threat. Failing this context, academic freedom has been successfully represented, in recent times, as an individual right, and one related to expression. The institutional aspects that relate to the direction of research have largely been lost, and this is no accident. Autonomy has come to mean speech — not a preserved terrain won on the basis of guild prerogatives.

To explain why this might be so, I focus here specifically on the post–Second World War era — a time when universities began accepting tremendous amounts of money from government and commercial interests and when they began to educate an increasing number of students for a variety of purposes. Even in this truncated time frame, resistance to viewing higher education as a system has not spared it from operating as one — commercial or state interests press their needs upon it — but has made it into a unique system that lacks definition and structure. This absence of planning presents special challenges for the understanding and exercise of academic freedom. Thus far, this challenge has been principally addressed by defending academic freedom as a negative liberty, a freedom *from*. Aiming to historicize this strategy more concretely, I examine the two components of academic freedom, defined by the American Association of University Professors (AAUP) as *lehrfreiheit*, the freedom of inquiry, and *lernfreiheit*, the freedom of learning.[2] Interestingly, the latter freedom's relevance to students was ignored by the AAUP in its seminal 1915 statement of academic freedom — although, as we will note, the original German concept had at that time already found a home in the United States. The AAUP's ultimate recognition of it in 1964 came after the era of student protests had arrived, thus confirming a trend initiated by the professors themselves: academic freedom would need to be claimed by those who paid the price of defending it.

Whether they concerned *lehrfreiheit* or *lernfreiheit*, the nature of the battles waged in the name of academic freedom changed over time and in response to transformation in the institutional capacity and mission of higher education itself. In this essay, I use the University of California as a case study and ask how definitions of freedom of inquiry were adjusted in order to accommodate enormous government and private investment in the university, and how approaches to freedom of learning were changed in analogous ways in response to increased enrollment. The University of California's choice makes clear that we will be especially concerned with the problem of academic freedom at the research university in an age when research required the support of a powerful coalition of private interests or, indeed, the state. Such financial dependence was not anticipated by the original formulators of academic freedom, and thus the untidy history of the institutional independence of the research university cannot be retold in sweeping generalities or simple narrative form. I choose instead here to describe two revealing episodes: the controversy surrounding the oath disavowing any connection to communism that UC faculty members were forced to sign under threat of removal beginning in 1949, and the Free Speech Movement (FSM), the series of clashes regarding Berkeley students' rights to speak about and recruit for potentially illegal activities while on school grounds.

Both of these campaigns sought to extend the ambit and strengthen the protection of *extramural* speech, or speech outside the classroom. Interestingly, these projects were undertaken in the midst of a revolution in the *intramural* activity of the university. I mean here to relate these two movements and consider them in conjunction with each other. *Battles over speech outside the classroom must be seen as linked to postwar transformations inside it.* As Robert Post notes, the logic girding academic freedom performs least well when asked to protect extramural speech, yet it remains precisely this kind of speech that most view as "academic freedom" (see his essay in this volume). One good reason for this is that extramural speech can legitimately be presented as part of inquiry or learning, and those who would police it often aim to indirectly shape intramural activity.

Yet, however credible and costly these battles were, I think they must now be viewed as incomplete — and many academics observing post–September 11 trends would agree. This paper was occasioned by a conference that examined proposed changes in the oversight mechanisms for funding in area studies; these alterations represent a recent manifestation of an important trend: using the carrot of money (not the stick of direct control) to shape research.[3] Of specific concern to many area-studies scholars was the reauthorization of funding for the Higher Education Act of 1965 (HEA), introduced into the 108th Congress and accompanied by the House bill HR 3077. While the majority of HEA deals with student financial aid, the legislation also contains authorization of funding for international-studies centers and foreign-language training grants (Title VI), without which area-studies programs throughout the United States could not exist. HR 3077, or the International Studies in Higher Education Act of 2003, stipulated the establishment of an advisory board to oversee the administration of Title VI funding and "provide advice, counsel and recommendations to the Secretary and the Congress on international education issues for higher education."[4] The advisory board could review course materials, curricula, and faculty hires and make funding recommendations to the Secretary of Education based on this review. Two appointees of the board would be from national security agencies.

The Republican congressman Peter Hoekstra of Michigan, the sponsor of the resolution, held hearings on Title VI of the HEA; he hosted, among others, Stanley Kurtz of the Hoover Institute, who claimed that such an advisory board was now needed to eliminate the anti-American sentiment prevalent in area studies.[5] It is hard to imagine that the hearing would ever have taken place, however, without the concerted efforts of Daniel Pipes, the director of Middle East Forum and a critic of the Middle East Studies Association (MESA), who has attempted to capitalize on the attacks of September 11 to advance his charge that this area of study suffers from an anti-Israel bias. Why didn't MESA and its constituent members see September 11 coming? This failure to forecast the attack, Pipes alleges, can be attributed to excessive sympathy to Islamist movements in the Middle East.

Whether it was the duty of the field of Middle East studies to make such predictions or not (I don't recall any movement to shut down Slavic centers when they failed to predict the collapse of the Soviet Union), one could actually argue that the lone voice alerting any student of the region to the bitter anti-American sentiment brewing there was, in fact, scholarship in Middle East area studies. Despite passing the House and enjoying the support of many Senators, HR 3077 failed to make it out of the Senate this year. Nevertheless, just as it is important to recognize the politics driving the bill, it is also important to put this attempted change in its institutional context. As the historian Roger Geiger insightfully points out, the trend toward making research accountable to bodies external to the university is but one telling signpost in the privatization of higher education.[6] Proposals in Congress can be seen as part of a larger picture of privatization, although HR 3077 is made unique by extending to the social sciences mechanisms of external accountability that used to apply primarily to biomedical research and, significantly, by making the research in question accountable to the state, as opposed to a private, for-profit entity. Privatization is the most far-reaching answer to the critical challenge posed by the research university: who shall exercise sovereignty over it, and by what logic? This — and not speech outside the classroom — is the front line of academic freedom.

Academics who object to external accountability, either in part or *in toto*, must now respond by returning to a defense of the professional norms governing intramural activity; they must return to traditional notions of academic freedom. As they survey the recent past — including the development of academic freedom in the research university — they must note not only the anachronistic position of protections of extramural speech but the poor legs of *freedom from* defenses as well. Those who wish to preserve the greatest possible meaningful autonomy of inquiry must seek an alternate strategy. While there is no going back to the untroubled faith in expertise that elitist progressives held when they originally posited their vision of academic freedom, steering by the light of their star yields the best course. In particular, the academy must be conspicuously attentive to the progressive notion of the university as a public trust — an obligation to generations past, present, and future. However one construes academic freedom, assertions of *freedom from* and extramural protection will not protect the "multiversity" from the challenges it now faces.

The Multiversity

It is appropriate to begin by defining this awkward and much maligned word. The former Berkeley chancellor and UC president Clark Kerr recently passed away, and a *New York Times* obituary credited him with coining the term multiversity.[7] Kerr used the term to describe and, really, to defend the capaciousness of the postwar university — its ability to credibly furnish different visions of higher education within the same institution. This, as Kerr knew, was more than just a question of institutional capacity; it was one of guiding philosophy. He quipped that a "university anywhere can aim no higher than to be as British as possible for the sake of the undergraduates, as German as possible for the sake of the graduates and the research personnel, as American as possible for the sake of the public at large — and as confused as possible for the sake of preservation of the whole uneasy balance."[8] The multiversity artfully maintained this state of confusion and willingness to adapt, in large part by having no overriding sense of itself apart from its very adaptability. In his most succinct definition of the neologism, Kerr wrote that "what had once been a [university] community was now more like an environment."[9]

The flexibility and social responsiveness at the core of the multiversity vision held obvious attraction for those interested in expanding higher education. And expand it did. Top research universities entered contracts with government and private industry to support a broad range of research activities. Each campus found its own balance between basic and applied research, between government and private research contracts. Rather than detail the nature of and important nuances in this support, I will cite some suggestive statistics. Public funding for postsecondary education rose from $1,700 per student in 1950 to $3,800 in 1970 — slightly more than doubling in just twenty years.[10] From 1940 to 1960, federal support alone increased a hundredfold — a breathtaking expansion.[11] This spending supported affiliated research centers, projects within the university, and students who participated in programs such as the GI Bill of the Second World War.

The University of California at Berkeley stood poised to benefit from all three types of spending. Overnight the campus became a vision in ad hoc expansion and planning; it was dotted with prefabricated buildings and overrun with students. New faculty members ministered to the expansion in school enrollment and, perhaps even more important, enabled an expansion of the curriculum. Between 1940 and 1950, the University of California at Berkeley expanded its course offerings by 25 percent. Spending per student grew by 56 percent from 1946 to 1950, and then again by 45 percent in the four years following that.[12] For UC Berkeley to remove even just the federal government from campus would render its prized research unsustainable, curtail its vaunted access to all eligible Californians, and vastly diminish the range of education careers it was able to host. It would cease to be Berkeley.

The Loyalty Oath

The potential problems for academic freedom inherent in such close financial ties to the government became manifest in the midst of this state-sponsored explosion in education. In 1949, the University of California Regents asked UC professors to take a new oath of loyalty to the state, a more specific one than the previous affirmation of allegiance to the state's constitution. The revised version asked professors to declare that they had no connection to any party wishing to overthrow the government by violent means and, in the oath's final version, that they were not members of the Communist Party.

How did such an oath come about? The Californian incarnation of the House Committee on Un-American Activities kept scrupulous watch over the University of California; when UCLA students' participation in a union-organized strike in Hollywood attracted attention, the committee warned the Regents to clean house of Communist sympathizers or UC would not receive "one half of the funds requested for postwar buildings and perhaps would get nothing."[13] In an action later justified as a preemptive move, the Regents crafted their own oath of loyalty. A year of negotiation and turmoil ensued, and in 1950, thirty-one faculty members were fired for not signing the oath.

In 1951, a state appeals court reversed the regents and allowed the reinstatement of faculty members fired as a result of their refusal to sign, and in 1952, the State Supreme Court upheld the decision. The appeals court opinion scolded the regents for attempting to reduce an institution "dedicated to learning and the search for truth...to an organ for the propagation of the ephemeral political, religious, social, and economic philosophies, whatever they may be, of the majority of the Board of Regents of that moment."[14] And this was the important point: the court recognized that the government was attempting to police the politics of professors as a way to shape, and intimidate, the campus itself. In so doing, it adhered to a logic that, if accepted, extended the protections usually reserved for intramural or classroom speech to outside or extramural speech. This crucial extension hinged on protection of the freedom of inquiry — the mission of the university itself. The bridge between free inquiry and extramural speech differed from previous articulations of academic freedom in one significant respect. Whereas the protection of intramural speech derived from a defensible claim of special privilege for the professoriat based on knowledge and expertise, the protection sought for extramural speech rested more on a logic of "sameness"; that is, professors should have the same degree of liberty as anyone else. The overt and avowed attempts by McCarthyites to use extramural policing as a way to preserve or change the university's intramural activities to their liking perhaps allowed many progressives and academic defenders to stroll over this logical bridge without any problem.

Not everyone chose to cross it. The California State Supreme Court sounded a more prosaic note when it validated the appeals court's fiery decision by pointing out that UC employees could not be ordered to take an oath substantially different from that signed by other state employees. This rather meek affirmation provided an opening once again to the legislature; in 1952, it passed the so-called Levering Act, which had been endorsed by California voters and attached the basic content of the loyalty oath to the state constitution itself.

Dejected dissenters felt they had little to cheer about, even on the reinstatement of the dismissed faculty, with back pay. The preeminent historian of the affair notes with disapproval how often the UC Academic Senate seemed preoccupied with procedural as opposed to substantive issues, and characterized the whole affair as "an extraordinary study in futility."[15] Yet the high-profile incident featured important legal and professional decisions and became an important benchmark in the ongoing attempts to protect extramural speech. Some academics outside the university passed resolutions to register their unhappiness with the Regents' vote to dismiss the nonsigning faculty almost immediately.[16] Other objections soon appeared: during graduation ceremonies at the end of that same 1950–51 academic year, Yale bestowed an honorary degree to Edward Tolman, a dismissed UC faculty member and distinguished psychologist. In its citation, Yale extolled his professional achievement and also noted his contribution as "a valiant defender of the freedom of the mind."[17] The according of such honors held perhaps the most stinging rebuke for the University of California, for it contrasted the provinciality of UC with the evident freedom and cosmopolitanism of other great research universities. Tolman certainly played his role in that script well: "I am tremendously pleased," he enthused to a reporter, "that Yale, whose motto is *Lux et Veritas*, should give me a degree."[18]

More than simple gestures between rivals came from the controversy about the loyalty oath. The AAUP took action on behalf of the professoriat to defend extramural speech. In its annual meeting in Chicago in 1953, the AAUP passed a resolution against the practice of loyalty oaths; this resolution came at the height of McCarthyism. The UCLA historian John Caughey fought the imposition of loyalty oaths and later worked to produce a position paper for the AAUP objecting to the University of Washington's dismissal of Communist teachers.[19] Clearly the demagoguery of the Red Scare put the organization, and the academy, on the defensive, for both felt the need to constantly assert academics' overwhelming loyalty to the United States. Although the organization was slow to respond and was perhaps less strident than some would have liked, it did eventually censure the University of California, as well as five other universities or colleges it judged had injured academic freedom.[20] The 1953 resolution reaffirmed the importance of professional competence — a judgment made, obviously, by professional peers — but already the organization showed signs of shifting its strategy in response to the oaths and the dismissals that followed in their wake.

The logical rallying cry for defenders of extramural speech was tenure — always the bulwark of disciplinary autonomy, now increasingly seen as the protection of individual speech. Indeed, when the AAUP celebrated its fiftieth anniversary, in 1965, it produced a volume titled *Academic Freedom and Tenure*. This handbook of case procedure also included the organization's basic statements on academic freedom and relevant policy adumbrations. Not surprisingly, the organization drew heavily on its recent experience with McCarthyism. One portion reproduced the AAUP's resolution denouncing teacher's loyalty oaths (first and rather presciently passed in 1937).[21] A 1950 elaboration stated that security clearance procedures, and indeed the very question of loyalty, should arise only for those individuals who came into contact with "secret information vital to national security."[22] In conclusion, the organization pointed out the ineffectiveness of casting a wider net than necessary but chose to end on an intellectual (and not instrumental) point: The "true gravity [of loyalty oaths]," the guide read, "lies ... in their tendency to sap the strength of American education, American thought, and American institutions by requiring conformity to official orthodoxy of opinion and conduct."[23] Here the AAUP provided the link that argued on behalf of extending academic freedom, specifically tenure, to include extramural speech. The AAUP essentially asserted that requiring an oath would have a "chilling effect" on speech and thought on campus. For the association and countless others, unfettered extramural expression became linked to academic freedom. Borrowing the logic of the First Amendment to convey the enormity of the threat of McCarthyism led many in and out of academia to view academic freedom as a speech issue rather than a defense of the sovereignty of expertise.

This misimpression persists to this day. For us, it is important to appreciate that the adroit use of "speech" to protect extramural expression did not interfere with the concurrent expansion and diversification of the mission of the multiversity.[24] The growth of the University of California continued unabated, as did the expansion of physical and course capacity throughout higher education.

In 1960, 55 percent of young Californians attended college, compared to a national average of 44 percent — considerably more than attendance before the Second World War (roughly 25 percent). The famous master plan of 1960 delineated the institutional framework of California's investment in higher education, naming the UC four-year institution as the most selective in admissions (the top one-eighth of graduating high-school seniors) and the home of graduate research, the four-year California State University as moderately selective and a feeder into the UCs after two years for qualified students, and the two-year community college as the most widely available and accessible option. Thus the social contract that supported California's enormous investment was largely premised on access — an open and legible institutional system that was perceived to operate fairly and uniformly.

Students' access to these institutions was in large part financed by service to the state. Neither opening the gates of higher education to a broader swath of students nor rendering the state essential service appeared *de novo* in the postwar world. Yet the degree to which both were practiced after the war did, in fact, constitute a difference in kind — even to the extent that both trends could be nominated as characteristic features of the multiversity. We must name the elephant in the room; we must appreciate their relation to each other. The point might be best, if bluntly, made as an observation of physical plant: as schools built new dormitories to house undergraduates and graduate students, they also built or expanded graduate schools of business, law, or medicine, new labs, or specialized equipment for those labs. These building projects ought to be viewed as linked and as authorizing one another. As the extramural battles were waged, the intramural revolution went on.

The power propelling this revolution clearly rested with the state. At the same time the loyalty oath controversy unfolded, UC and other state public school administrators lost key battles to the legislature over the nature and degree of state college expansion. Again, the issue was sovereignty: Who would control the multiversity? Engineering education located the issue pointedly: the caliber of work required from both students and faculty members led the UC system to guard this education jealously, but the legislature wanted to extend engineering education to the state colleges in order to feed valued labor into the California state economy. The legislature won. As the historian John A. Douglass points out, between 1947 (when engineering entered the state college curriculum) and 1957, California's employment increased over 40 percent, and one Stanford study estimated that defense-related industry accounted for half of this incredible growth. The Soviet launch of Sputnik I and II ended the U.S.'s sense of superiority in research and caused even Californians to question their prodigious investment in education. An advisory committee appointed by the state government returned a lengthy indictment of California's public higher education that, among other things, noted the "lack of legislative influence and responsibility in guiding public education."[25] In addition to access, then, and even in addition to a commitment to quality, the unstated but important presumption of the California Master Plan was that the system of higher education would expand in ways the state found useful or necessary.

Expansion financed by increasing national wealth and propelled by population growth followed no preordained course, so it is important to note that the explosive growth in higher education was also maintained by the system's public mandate and perceived legitimacy. This mandate expanded to justify the multiversity's new costs through an increased responsiveness to students' demands, a vocationalizing of higher education and transforming it into a middle class-credential, and an increased responsiveness to state needs that drove the growth in basic and applied research and the hard and social sciences. Thanks to the multiversity's receptiveness to diffuse and rather specific forces, the intramural revolution was well under way.

Student Speech

Such expansion obviously affected students as well. Juggling more classes for more students with any degree of efficiency forced schools to resort to a greater degree of bureaucratization than ever before. The United States never embraced the free-wheeling notion of *lernfreiheit* that the concept's German progenitors supported — including, in its original articulation, even the freedom to "migrate from one German University to another" without interference from administrators.[26] Traditionally defined as "the absence of administrative coercions in the learning situation,"[27] *lernfreiheit* in practice involved students' power to roam from course to course, choosing their own classroom section and sequence of work, and the understanding that they would be graded based only on the final exam. The most frequently cited example of the importation of *lernfreiheit* before the First World War was the decision by the Harvard president Charles Eliot to introduce the elective system. While the advance of the German research academic model made possible by elective coursework is striking for a number of reasons — freedom of learning developed in the United States as a more modest version of its German referent. Nevertheless, there was some understanding of the absence of coercion from the learning situation. Before postwar overcrowding, for example, University of Chicago students could attend any section of a course; attendance was not taken and was thus obviously considered unimportant to the student's grade for the course.

After the Second World War, however, Chicago students were not only assigned to a particular class but also required to carry "class tickets" to enter a course. One editor of the student newspaper complained that such practices directly threatened freedom of learning.[28] Class tickets and the like disrupted the university's bohemian atmosphere, placing a kind of bureaucratic distance between student and school. Another kind of distance also came as a result of expanding access, though more indirectly. A student body that was more diverse and included substantial numbers of married or working-class students dampened campus enthusiasm for sophomoric practices or parietals designed for a school serving *in loco parentis*. One married couple at Oberlin College — a school with long-standing, paternalistic rules on association between the sexes — found a school official "inside their trailer 'inspecting' it shortly after the [trailer] camp opened," and "residents used the incident to establish the principle that trailers were private homes, not dormitories subject to College intrusion."[29] This challenge to social hierarchy and occasional outright militancy vitiated norms established in more cloistered and plainly adolescent days of higher education. Single veterans also did not necessarily assent to rules governing their interaction with their female peers; at Potomac State School, three hundred veteran students went on strike to object to the expulsion of Gene Cotrill, a twenty-five-year-old Navy veteran, for violating curfew with a fellow student, Dortha Christopher.[30] Encountering the occasionally sophomoric world of collegiate life, many of these same soldiers-turned-students could not be bothered to participate and occasionally found ways to bluntly register their protests. At Oberlin, one freshman tradition had new students dress in bedsheets and submit to the jeers of upperclassmen. Veterans, on the chosen day, appeared in "GI fatigue jackets," and "upperclassmen quickly got the point."[31] A campus walkway at New York University was reserved, by tradition, for juniors and seniors, and a commission of juniors "armed with wooden paddles" even policed it for freshman and sophomore trespassers. One freshman student "absent-mindedly" walked on the path, only to be greeted by the committee and its enforcement tools. Unfortunately for the juniors, the student was a veteran of a combat platoon in Africa and Italy; after a skirmish, the freshman continued on his way while the juniors lay "strewn about the violet beds."[32]

Like many students and college administrators, Clark Kerr welcomed this change in prevailing social norms. With more students came more of what was called "student services," and Kerr credited especially veterans who became students with success in agitation for residence halls, a student union, better advising, and more sports fields. Students' desire for more recognition within the university system was not limited to Berkeley. The growth of vocational advising in particular spawned an entire battery of tests and student services that converged into one administrative division known as "student personnel," and these kinds of services were referred to as the "student personnel movement." Class tickets now shared room in students' pockets with tickets for admission to big football games, slips that showed the results of vocational aptitude tests, and receipts for medical treatment.

The distance between student and administration read differently for some after a decade. Schools now regularly assigned student identification numbers to track students and their progress, eliminating any pretense of maintaining the practices of bygone college days, when a dean knew every student by first and last name. The practice of assigning student ID numbers was famously ridiculed by student protesters in the 1960s as typical of the "knowledge factory." Some FSM students in Berkeley parodied their school's standard-issue IBM identification punch cards when they designed placards that read: "I am a student. Please do not fold, spindle, or mutilate."[33] One of the most remembered moments of the entire saga came when FSM student leader Mario Savio delivered an impromptu indictment of the multiversity and its deadening effect on the organic and spontaneous life of the campus.

Those who grieved over the loss of *lernfreiheit* to the churnings of the odious machine identified a real transformation taking place on campus. As they celebrated the virtues of an older system, they also left themselves open to criticism of that system's flaws. The annoying and unimaginative organizational procedures that bedeviled students also enabled the expansion of access to the college campus. A good portion of FSM students did not share Savio's view of the university, as the historian Robert Cohen argues in his essay on the movement's participants, and reckoning with these students' experience and reasoning facilitates a penetrating reinterpretation of *lernfreiheit*. These students remarked the same distance between administration and student that their peers criticized, but they viewed it as liberating. The student Margot Adler "felt a new sense of freedom and an almost Edenic sense of bliss" at Berkeley and thus reported it "a bit hard to see myself as the soulless IBM card depicted in FMS leaflets."[34] Cohen notes, "This positive outlook on the University was typical, moreover, of a majority not only of FSMers but of the larger Berkeley student body."[35] Though some sought leverage for critique in the remnants of outmoded educational systems, most recognized the benefits of and reconciled themselves to a new one.

Yet even those who accepted the impersonal nature of the multiversity — and were not, for that matter, regular participants in social protest — felt called to action by the Free Speech Movement. "It was with regret not joy that I walked into Sproul hall," a Berkeley student wrote after being arrested for the illegal occupation of the campus administration building, surely the most climactic moment in the drama of the entire FSM — a movement anchored initially in the assertion of the students' right to recruit for civil rights campaigns on school property and, ultimately, their right to speak about what they wished on campus.[36] Though the resignation reported by this student on taking over Sproul Hall contrasts with the boisterous and defiant images normally associated with the event, it nevertheless captures the spirit of many students who felt an obligation to call the administration back to first principles — the freedom essential to free inquiry. A number of participants specifically cast their fight for extramural liberty in terms of this ennobling higher vision. Savio offered his most searing indictment of Berkeley's administration when he said, "We believe in a university of scholars and students...with inquiry as its defining characteristic and freedom as its fundamental tool." This vision reinterpreted *lernfreiheit* and gave it new relevance: "The function of the university," an arrested FSMer wrote, "is to provide an environment where students can mature intellectually, where they may seek, without hindrance, the answers to questions they feel need to be answered, where all points of view may be put forward and discussed."[37]

I quoted as the title of this essay a portion of the stirring words offered by another FSMer identified after being arrested only as student "LL": "If the university's traditional concern for political liberties is allowed to lapse into so much academic cant," this student wrote, "then its trust to the public is betrayed. And betrayed so much the worse because the academic community begins to believe that its cowardice and cant portrays real commitment. All of us forget the concept of freedom *means* something."[38] Like the faculty members in the loyalty-oath controversy, these students struggled to protect extramural speech as part of their liberty, not merely for its own sake, but as something essential to inquiry and thus part of the university mission. This astute undergraduate went further than most and named the necessary pillar to supporting academic freedom, whether inside the classroom or not: the public trust.

The Public Trust
Anchoring the university's mission in the public trust is the predicate for any discussion of academic freedom in the United States. The American Association of University Professors recognized as much in its first statement on the ideal, in 1915. As the historian Walter Metzger relates, the AAUP was guided by the much-admired example of academic freedom in the German system. Therein it found more inspiration than instruction, however, because, unlike the Germans, American professors did not work in a well-defined system protected by the state and tradition. Seeking some justification or theory that "could be used to check continual encroachments," the AAUP resolved to invoke "the will of the whole community" or, as it was sometimes (eerily) called, the

"general will."[39] The AAUP document owned the implications of this assertion; all universities, the organization argued, no matter their charter, are "public properties."[40] But, crucially, the group took care to distinguish this concept of "general will" from popular opinion. In the AAUP's conception, the professors became stewards of the public interest and could be relied on to divine and differentiate this interest from the public opinion of the moment. But how? The AAUP did not elaborate; it considered the skill obvious and embedded in its own stature and expertise. The foundational document for academic freedom in this country was explicitly elitist — and, for some, therefore open to challenge. In the age of a much more democratic multiversity, how would such elitism continue to be accepted? This dilemma Kerr captured well when he posed the question "How may an aristocracy of intellect justify itself to a democracy of all men?"[41] For Kerr, social usefulness was the answer. His and others' exaltation of utility went without the extended discussion it deserved, since social usefulness entailed an institutional responsiveness to carrots (and sometimes sticks) that begged the question of intramural autonomy.

Not that the intramural changes went without comment. A "keep the customer satisfied" approach met with condemnation mainly from those who found their stature displaced or diminished by its advance. The embattled defender of traditional liberal arts, President Robert Maynard Hutchins of the University of Chicago, articulated well the concerns of this group when he offered this bleak prognosis on post–Second World War higher education:

> Anybody who has watched the development of the American University will have no difficulty in predicting that in the next twenty-five years it will greatly expand on the side of natural science, engineering, and the applied social sciences, such as business, industrial relations, and public administration. I have the greatest respect for all these subjects.... But I would point out that, if they move in this direction, *it is improbable that they will do so because they have considered the end and concluded that what civilization needs is more natural science, engineering, and applied social science. If they move in this direction, it is likely that they will do so because powerful pressures in society push them.*[42]

In picking up this theme in his farewell address to the nation in 1961, President Eisenhower issued a pointed, if surprising, rebuke of this unthinking responsiveness to the carrot of various economic incentives — one that has perhaps been eclipsed by his warning about the military industrial complex in the same speech, but one that deserves special attention here. A "free university, historically the fountainhead of free ideas and scientific discovery, has experienced a revolution in the conduct of research," Eisenhower said. He did not wonder why — he knew. He bemoaned the fact that "partly because of the huge costs involved, a government contract becomes virtually a substitute for intellectual curiosity" and pointedly remarked, "The prospect of domination of the nation's scholars by Federal employment, project allocations, and the power of money is ever present — and is gravely to be regarded." With these words, the retiring president must have heartened those in the academy who still felt vulnerable to the buffeting political winds, and perhaps he gave pause to those administrators and academics who had celebrated their skill in obtaining government awards. Some undoubtedly wondered why the president spurned the institutional arrangements and accruing state power that his ease and charm had made more palatable, but they must have recognized at least Eisenhower's sincerity in his special attention throughout the speech to "balance" — the need to judge and weigh various concerns against each other. In this way, he presented the model of the wise administrator, much as Clark Kerr might have done. Yet, whatever the various reactions to his beneficent judgment and stark admonition, they must have been fleeting, since the very next point Eisenhower made in his speech was contradictory and, in mapping his thinking, crucial: "In holding scientific research and discovery in respect," the president warned, ". . . we must also be alert to the equal and opposite danger that public policy could itself become the captive of a scientific-technological elite."[43]

The fear that the nation's development would be directed principally by technocrats and experts was one that, as the historian Walter McDougall points out, Eisenhower shared with Mao Zedong in China and Joseph Stalin in the Soviet Union.[44] It was, indeed, the crux of modernity's dilemma — how to develop and sustain excellence in an internationally competitive setting without undermining the power of the governing regime and stability at home. How does a modern mass society create and sustain elite and highly specialized mechanisms for producing power while also creating and sustaining legitimacy for that project in the name of the masses? In the United States, a fear of experts was the far greater influence in the country's improvised response to this dilemma, and freedom — for Eisenhower, and for many Americans — came to mean the retention of political, discretionary control over institutional life. Thus while Eisenhower may have "gravely regarded" the substitution of the contract for curiosity, during his tenure the mechanism was nevertheless embraced to ensure that political priorities took precedence over technocratic ones and, too, to blunt the academy's service to the state by making it appear voluntary and, presumably, temporary.[45] Contracts expire, and no one is forced to enter into them.

In U.S. academic life as well as its context, institutional malleability assuaged concerns over the increasingly powerful state. Institutions' very responsiveness became more essential than their structure or, perhaps more accurately, the defining characteristic of their structure. The service the state needed it elicited with the carrot — never mind that the carrot was transformative or that its removal would threaten the system itself. In this light, the McCarthyite or administrative policing of extramural speech seems like one more way political norms were imposed on academic institutions, and resistance to this project may most fittingly be deemed an exercise of academic freedom or the retention of an independent preserve.

Importantly, the defenders of the university's independence do not wage their campaign in the name of "sameness" or liberty — as some of the participants in both the loyalty-oath and the free-speech movement surmised. Instead, they anchor their cause in the mission of the university itself. As José Ortega y Gasset asserted to an audience of Spanish students in 1930, "An atmosphere charged with enthusiasm, the exertion of science, is the presupposition at the base of the university's existence," and it is not hard to hear in his desperate voice the hope that the seed of native democracy would take root and that the Spanish university might embody and propel this larger project. Even if they did not constitute the bulk of undergraduate education, Ortega held, research and free inquiry were "the soul of the institution, the principle which gives it the breath of life and saves it from being an automaton."[46]

One hears echoes of this bold declaration in the words spoken by philosophy department chair Joseph Tussman to the Academic Senate of UC Berkeley during a pivotal meeting on the Free Speech Movement. It is a moment that the historian and FSM faculty participant Reginald Zelnik, in his essay on the faculty and the movement, isolated for special attention, quoting from it extensively, as I will do here. Defending a resolution that would place the faculty on the side of protesters and against the administration, Tussman told his colleagues:

> This . . . is a sensible rule, but I think we should regard it as more than just a sensible rule, as more than a way of avoiding tough administrative problems, and even as more than a rule which protects important rights. *We should regard it and support it as symbolizing a fundamental commitment of the university to its own essential nature*, for it expresses the conviction that ours is an institution whose proper mode of dealing with the mind is educational, not coercive. *We are not the secular arm.* If we have forgotten this, we should be grateful to those who are now reminding us.[47]

And here the crux of the matter becomes apparent: did legitimacy for the multiversity rest on its independence, its upholding of the public trust, its expert interpretation of the general will? No. In fact, a large part of its mandate derived from its very social utility and the institutional malleability entailed therein. While the multiversity may not have been the secular arm in the sense of blindly carrying out political demagogues' McCarthyite agenda, it was in fact the secular arm insofar as it created the technology of the superpower and supplied the skilled workers needed to run it. The analogy becomes even more distressingly apt when we realize that, like the Catholic Church wishing the death of its enemies but unable to murder them, the modern American state needed elitist and technocratic abilities but did not have the legitimacy of a strong, central state to produce and maintain them. State power came in the form of many carrots, and the compulsion of marketplace competition and of sustaining expansion once it was undertaken elicited the desired results. In asserting that the multiversity was not the secular arm, Tussman spoke of a controversy regarding extramural speech. The claim was and is not defensible when applied to intramural activity — although it must be said that the opposite declaration (the multiversity is only and comprehensively the servant of the state) is equally untenable. Where, then, is the balance?

Participation in Power

The answer to this question is not definitive or obvious, and a balanced relationship with the state will certainly not be found if we focus on academic freedom as extramural speech and interpret it as *freedom from* state interference. Intramurally, in the conduct of our research, the capaciousness of our mission, and the composition of the classroom, we are linked to the state.

Other authors in this volume discuss the theoretical and legal complexity of extending academic freedom to include extramural protection. To this I add that one should not underestimate the political complexity of defending even the central tenets of academic freedom, to wit, the autonomy of inquiry in the weak authorizing environment of an ill-defined system of higher education. The 1965 AAUP handbook on tenure and academic freedom included a preface that read, "The American scene in higher education is a vast chaos, a sort of administrative anarchy. Since there is no central law-defining authority...it has been the historic mission of the [AAUP] to fill the void."[48] Before and since, the AAUP and student protests have done important work defending independent inquiry and filling this void with a language of liberty designed to fend off outside control.

While this inherited language is well suited to repel attempts at control, its ability to deal authoritatively with the far greater challenge of outside *influence* remains doubtful. This problem is particularly acute in the wake of the government's response to the attacks of September 11. Once-chaotic government funding mechanisms that mirrored the disarray of the multiversity now appear to be organizing into regiments of purpose. For this and other reasons related to trends in the private sector that predate September 11, I believe that the language developed to counteract the stick must be built upon so that, if need be, it can effectively challenge the carrot. I believe the future of academic freedom will be not in the courts but in budgets; the measure of it not in who is fired but in who is hired; and the guarantee of it not in tenure but in the public outreach and authorization that would take place in tenure's absence.

In the current academic environment — and political moment — I do not see any possibility of further advance in the classical liberalism defined as *freedom from*. But there are other notions of freedom. Here I use Cicero's definition: freedom is also participation in power. The simplicity of this declaration belies its complexity; nothing about participating in power can be said to be obvious or automatic. How does one know if she is influencing the course of power or merely rationalizing it? Dramatic differences in the degree of independent authority can be challenging to parse in practice. Moreover, academics do not share the same orientation to the state, nor do they have the same will or capacity to challenge it — and the same observation might be made of the institutions they serve. To further compound the difficulty, only collective and organized action can realistically promise participation in power. Indeed, an entirely different essay on the theoretical and practical problems of this more republican understanding of freedom could easily be written. All the same, defenders of academic freedom can either grapple with these complexities or continue to stand powerless against forces that seek to shape them, for better or for worse.

Some challenge those forces already. Recently, the leaders of nine of the country's most prestigious research universities signed a letter to the Ford and Rockefeller foundations expressing their discontent over new language, which recipients must agree to in order to receive money, added to these foundations' grants. Specifically, as the *Wall Street Journal* reports, the Ford Foundation has added a statement that it would withdraw funding from a university if any of its "expenditures promoted 'violence, terrorism, bigotry or the destruction of any state,'" and the Rockefeller Foundation's grant language now includes the provision that "a grantee shall not 'directly or indirectly engage in, promote or support other organizations or individuals who engage in or promote terrorist activity.'"[49] As Provost Richard Saller points out in the same article, the University of Chicago's support of a student-run Palestinian film festival might be construed by some as indirectly promoting terrorism — and, I might add, those "some" could easily be the same activists who pushed the foundations for the language changes in the first place, so the provost is not engaging in mere supposition or setting up a straw man in order to make a point. In announcing their objection to the overly broad language, the universities gave what might be called the warning shot across the bow. As the *Wall Street Journal* points out, the letters "implicitly raise the prospect that the universities might cease applying for Ford and Rockefeller grants if the language isn't altered." This deliberative community action is the very definition of academic freedom. Columbia has faced accusations from its own students that teaching in its Middle East studies department suffers from an anti-Israel bias. In response, the university launched an internal review that, in the words of Provost Alan Brinkley, will "consider, among other things, how we might respond to such problems within the framework of our strong commitment to free speech."[50] It is well to note that such action might result in curbing expression; if students complain or funders of any sort can add stipulations in reference to and with respect for the mission of the university — and academics cannot reply except to meekly assert their liberty — then the course seems clear. So far, esteem for the university's mission has not emerged as the basis of any argument for those who propose to alter current funding strategies; the contempt for the academy of a Kurtz or a Pipes is plain for all to see. Those who assert that academic freedom is not at stake in these proposed or enacted alterations because, after all, no one is forced to take the money betray an institution-by-institution understanding of higher education that, if exclusively relied upon, is incredibly distorting. When higher education is considered as a system, the necessity of these funds becomes clear.

Even if one agrees that not much more ground can be gained or even defended by relying on classical liberalism or *freedom from*, this does not simplify the intellectual and political tasks at hand, nor does it absolve one of the obligations those tasks impose. Resisting the ephemeral in the name of something more transcendent — a trust among generations past, present, and future — presupposes a knowledge of value, a robust claim as guardian or steward. Such a claim could be presented in the name of tradition, a strategy adopted by continental defenders of academic freedom, or of expertise, the rationale originally used in the United States. Strains of both persist and can be combined; they are powerful ideals. Each partakes of the other — divining tradition requires some claim to expertise, and experts implicitly or explicitly refer to professions anchored by tradition — and the latter especially still holds promise. Those who repair to it must be prepared to accept the responsibility of watching over their own disciplines, for a claim to expertise without any accountability is just a slightly more elaborate rearticulation of empty liberty.

Finally, no claim to stewardship in the name of disciplinary expertise will be successful if it is not rooted in the public mandate for the university's mission. Creating or sustaining that mandate presents a challenge to the multiversity, which celebrated its chaos, its availability to students pursuing the most prosaically vocational to the most abstrusely esoteric of goals. It is a good question: How may an aristocracy of intellect justify itself to a democracy of all men? If one is skeptical of the universal appeal and utility of expertise or tradition, and wary of even the carefully balanced pluralism of Clark Kerr or, one might say, Dwight Eisenhower, then this is a question indeed. Let us note that it can be posed to a number of institutional configurations in modern society, and that academic freedom is an exaggerated representation of the struggle of modern state power — how to create it and, even trickier, how to maintain it. Who will have sovereignty over the systems that sustain power? In its current troubles, academic freedom reveals less about the threat to expression and more about the improvisational and ad hoc way the modern U.S. state has long approached this struggle. With the collapse of Cold War mobilization and the informal yet powerful drive for excellence and distinction (particularly contradistinction) that it brought, the United States must now question whether it has the institutional structure and political legitimacy to maintain the greatness it has achieved in the past. The end of this era, and the subsequent institutional restructuring, can clearly be discerned in higher education. What Roger Geiger has called "the long era of nationalization" in college and university life is demonstrably over, and the mechanisms developed during that period do not directly translate into this one.[51]

Yet the thoughtless embrace of privatization and external accountability might do more damage than good; turning everything over to the market is an easy answer to the question "What is valuable?" that may in fact throw the baby out with the bathwater. For instance, perhaps the outsourcing of military functions saves absolutely no money if considered from anything other than the most marginal or short-term viewpoint, and perhaps it produces unintended costs that cannot be borne. By the same token, perhaps the drive to make research responsive to state needs based solely on the terms of the current regime delivers spurious results and, at the same time, depletes a field or discipline of the seeds of future innovation. Indeed, there might be features of the "national system" worth salvaging even when their virtues do not compete with peer achievements in the now defunct Soviet Union or bear immediate recognition and retain instant value in a private market.

Those who seek to fundamentally alter important institutions of national life must understand that they have benefited from the system they now seek to change, and therefore their changes must speak to future generations and not simply the perceived needs of the present. If changes such as the proposed HR 3077 keep coming, and they will, academics who expect to defend values important to them simply and exclusively under the banner of freedom from state control will not have to wait long before their voices are rendered irrelevant. This rhetoric has no strength against carrots, and it is also hypocritical. The knight who flies those colors also rides a mount and uses armor indirectly or directly provided by the state, and he must be prepared to disrobe and dismount if he wishes to join this battle.

I do not view renewed attention to the defense of intramural autonomy as necessarily an evacuation of the principle of free extramural speech, nor do I see it as an internalizion of the policing power of the state. I view it as difficult. The daunting nature of the project serves as the most suggestive clue that it bears some meaningful relation to freedom.

NOTES

This article is dedicated to the memory of Reginald Zelnik, who gave much for the cause of academic freedom, and to Beshara Doumani, who has upheld the cause by putting together the conference that spawned this essay and modeling disciplinary norms in his probity and in his thoughtful and gracious engagement with me (and others). I would like to thank John Connelly and David Hollinger, both of whom read drafts of this article and provided insights and helpful comments.

1. Daniel T. Rodgers, *Contested Truths: Keywords in American Politics Since Independence* (Cambridge, MA: Harvard University Press, 1998), p. 222. On the shifting meanings and uses of freedom, see also Eric Foner, *The Story of American Freedom* (New York: Norton, 1998).

2. See www.aaup.org.

3. On the influence of money in the post–Cold War world of higher education, see especially Derek Bok, *Universities in the Marketplace: The Commercialization of Higher Education* (Princeton, NJ: Princeton University Press, 2003), and David L. Kirp, *Shakespeare, Einstein, and the Bottom Line: The Marketing of Higher Education* (Cambridge, MA: Harvard University Press, 2003).

4. Section 633, HR 3077, 108th Congress, version reported to the Senate, available at http://thomas.loc.gov/.

5. See "Statement of Stanley Kurtz," June 19, 2003, before the House Education Subcommittee on Select Education, http://www.house.gov/ed_workforce/hearings/108th/sed/titlevi61903/kurtz.htm.

6. Roger L. Geiger, "The American University at the Beginning of the Twenty-First Century: Signposts on the Path to Privatization," in Robert McC. Adams (ed.), *Trends in American and German Higher Education* (Cambridge, MA: American Academy of Arts and Sciences, 2002).

7. Grace Hechinger, "Clark Kerr, Leading Public Educator, Dies at 92," *New York Times*, December 2, 2003.

8. Clark Kerr, *The Uses of the University* (Cambridge, MA: Harvard University Press, 2001), p. 14.

9. *Ibid.*, p. 102.

10. See http://nces.ed.gov/programs/coe/2002/section6/indicator42.asp#info.

11. Kerr, *Uses of the University*, p. 40.

12. Roger L. Geiger, *Research and Relevant Knowledge: American Research Universities since World War II* (New York: Oxford University Press, 1993), p. 74.

13. As quoted in John Aubrey Douglass, *The California Idea and American Higher Education: 1850 to the 1960 Master Plan* (Stanford: Stanford University Press, 2000), p. 208.

14. *Tolman vs. Underhill*, October 17, 1952 (Sac N.6211: 3926c).

15. David P. Gardner, *The California Oath Controversy* (Berkeley: University of California Press, 1967), p. 3.

16. "Fight Teacher Ousters: Brooklyn Professors Act in California 'Loyalty' Cases," *New York Times*, November 24, 1950.

17. "Yale Honors Educator Dismissed by California over Loyalty Oath," *New York Times*, June 12, 1951. Yale motto: Light and Truth.

18. *Ibid.*

19. Ellen Schrecker, *No Ivory Tower: McCarthyism and the Universities* (New York: Oxford University Press, 1986), p. 322. As Schrecker points out, however, the AAUP sat on its official report of the California case for longer than activists at UC would have liked (pp. 323–24).

20. Schrecker, *No Ivory Tower*, p. 334.

21. Louis Joughin (ed.), *Academic Freedom and Tenure: A Handbook of the American Association of University Professors* (Madison: University of Wisconsin Press, 1967), p. 113.

22. *Ibid.*, p. 113.

23. *Ibid.*, p. 114.

24. See Schrecker, *No Ivory Tower*.

25. Douglass, *California Idea and American Higher Education*, p. 235.

26. Hermann von Helmholtz, "On Academic Freedom in German Universities," repr. in *Science and Culture: Popular and Philosophical Lectures*, ed. David Cahan (Chicago: University of Chicago Press, 1995).

27. Walter P. Metzger, "The Age of the University," in Richard Hofstadter and Walter P. Metzger, *The Development of Academic Freedom in the United States* (New York: Columbia University Press, 1955), p. 386.

28. *Chicago Maroon*, March 17, 1947, editor's note, maintaining that tickets denied "student freedom."

29. Geoffrey Blodgett, "Oberlin and the G.I. Bill: 40 Years Later," *Oberlin Alumni Magazine* 83 (1987), p. 7.

30. "Student Strikers Offered VFW Aid," *Washington Post*, March 17, 1948.

31. Blodgett, "Oberlin and the G.I. Bill," p. 8.

32. Bill Davidson, "Bill of Rights Education Draws GIs," *Yank*, February 26, 1947.

33. Quoted in Francis E. Rourke and Glenn E. Brooks, *The Managerial Revolution in Higher Education* (Baltimore: Johns Hopkins University Press, 1966), p. 18.

34. Quoted in Robert Cohen, "This Was Their Fight and They Had to Fight It: The FSM's Nonradical Rank and File," in Robert Colen and Reginald E. Zelnik (eds.), *The Free Speech Movement: Reflections on Berkeley in the 1960s* (Berkeley: University of California Press, 2002), p. 240.

35. *Ibid.*

36. Student identified as H, *ibid.*, p. 234.

37. Student identified as MM, *ibid.*, p. 242.

38. Quoted in *ibid.*, p. 242.

39. Metzger, "Age of the University," p. 399.

40. *Ibid.*

41. Kerr, *Uses of the University*, p. 91.

42. Robert Hutchins, "The Administrator," *Journal of Higher Education*, November 1946, p. 404 (emphasis mine).

43. Dwight D. Eisenhower, "Farewell Radio and Television," January 17, 1961, http://www.eisenhower.archives.gov/farewell.html.

44. Walter A. McDougall, "Technocracy and Statecraft in the Space Age—Toward the History of a Saltation," *American Historical Review* 87.4 (1982), pp. 1010–40.

45. See especially Stuart W. Leslie, *The Cold War and American Science: The Military-Industrial-Academic Complex at MIT and Stanford* (New York: Columbia University Press, 1993).

46. José Ortega y Gasset, *Mission of the University* (New Brunswick: Transaction, 1992), p. 78.

47. As quoted in Reginald E. Zelnik, "On the Side of the Angels: The Berkeley Faculty and the FSM," in Cohen and Zelnik (eds.), *Free Speech Movement*, p. 315, emphasis mine.

48. Joughin (ed.), *Academic Freedom and Tenure*, p. vi.

49. Daniel Golden, "Colleges Object to New Wording in Ford Grants," *Wall Street Journal*, May 4, 2004.

50. Adam Dickter, "Columbia Probing Mideast Studies," *Jewish Week*, April 16, 2004, http://www.thejewishweek.com/news/newscontent.php3?artid=9336.

51. Geiger, "American University," p. 47.

The Unraveling of the Devil's Bargain: The History and Politics of Language Acquisition

Amy Newhall

> I invented that god-awful title: The National Defense
> Education Act. If there are any words less compatible,
> really, intellectually, with the purposes of education —
> it's not to defend the country; it's to defend the mind
> and develop the human spirit, not to build cannons
> and battleships. It was a horrible title, but it worked.
> It worked. How could you attack it?
> — Stewart McClure, clerk of the Senate Committee
> on Labor, Education and Public Welfare, in 1958*

Language learning and academic freedom at first do not seem to have much to do with each other, but for the last forty years university language programs and their related area-studies programs have been the site of contention between the federal government and academics. Language programs are located at the junction of a number of debates over past government actions and contemporary events and politics. In the United States, most language learning occurs within universities; in order to ensure a supply of linguistically capable citizens and to meet its own staffing needs, the government is forced to work with organizations for whom the free flow of information is essential to their function. Periodic national crises both exacerbate the government's need for language expertise and heighten its desire to curb the flow of information.

*Stated by McClure in an interview conducted as part of the Oral History Project of the Senate Historical Office, available at http://www.senate.gov/artand history/history/resources/pdf/McClure4.pdf.

The most recent and utterly shocking crisis, that of 9/11, which glaringly highlighted our nation's linguistic weakness, also coincided with a profound political climate change in which the federal political agenda became defined by disparate but extremely conservative interest groups. These groups have long sought to control the flow of information and to silence criticism, and in the current climate they believe they have found in language and area-studies programs the Achilles heel of universities' autonomy.

Two questions lie at the heart of the recent controversy: Who controls how education is conducted? What purposes should education serve? In the current climate, some people regard knowledge and those who produce it in the university as mere tools to be wielded in the service of national security and defense. Others see an obvious contradiction between the right to pursue knowledge in an unfettered manner and the imperative to serve national security objectives based on politically generated conclusions. The two groups clash when the government seeks help from the very specialists who are often articulate critics of government policies. The situation is further complicated when those critical individuals or their institutions receive federal grants, particularly when there is great government demand for linguistic expertise. The history of language training programs and federal support for them offers an excellent case study for exploring questions of federal power, the control of education, the right to the unencumbered pursuit of knowledge, and academic freedom.

Understanding what people say or think opens worlds of possibilities constrained only by the intentions of the learner. Historically, the academy has trained both those who pursue language for cultural and intellectual explorations and those who seek such expertise in an information-gathering quest of a different kind, one more oriented to strategic concerns. (The former group has not necessarily always been excluded from the latter, however.) Although narrowly defined and explicitly strategic interests dominate the thinking of post-9/11 policy makers, the core arguments linking language with intelligence gathering are quite old. Ellen Laipson, the vice chair of the National Intelligence Council, summed them up before the International Security, Proliferation and Federal Services Subcommittee of the Senate Governmental Affairs Committee on September 14, 2000:

One cannot overstate the centrality of foreign language skills to the core mission of the intelligence community. Foreign languages come into play at virtually all points of the intelligence cycle, from collection to exploitation, to analysis and production. The collection of intelligence depends heavily on language, whether the information is gathered from a human source through the relationship with a field officer or gathered from a technical system.[1]

Language has now become a key component in the drive to restore, maintain, and expand the United States' power. But the government's desire for instant fluency is stymied by core weaknesses in the fragile language-acquisition infrastructure and by competition for scarce human and capital resources. The well of available linguistic talent is very shallow — and, especially in the less commonly taught languages (LCTLs), it runs dry with alarming rapidity. For example, according to a survey conducted by the Modern Language Association in 1998, "For the last 25 years the percentage of students enrolled in language courses in higher education has remained stable at about 8%. Arabic, which has been taught seriously in the academy, has a very small slice of the enrollment pie, just five tenths of one percent."[2] The small number of enrollees is reflected in the tiny number of advanced degrees awarded in important LCTLs. For example, in the years 1999, 2000, and 2001, only twelve, fifteen, and six Ph.D.s were awarded in Arabic; only twenty-seven, twenty-one, and sixteen in Chinese; and only ten, eighteen, and seventeen in Japanese.[3]

A survey conducted by the MLA in 2002 indicates the impact of a national crisis on language enrollments; the number of students in higher education studying all foreign languages has increased by 17.9 percent. Enrollment in Arabic has almost doubled, from 5,505 in 1998 to 10,596 in 2002. This looks good, but it should also be noted that only 8.7 percent of students in higher education take any foreign language at all.[4] As we will see, the U.S. is experiencing shortages of language and area experts in part because federal incentive programs encouraging their study have been sorely underfunded for decades.

Language learning and teaching in the U.S. have long been a very low priority for state and federal governments. They become a priority only when some disaster exposes our language weakness. As Senator Paul Simon wrote in an article in the *Washington Post* in 2001, "In every national crisis from the Cold War through Vietnam, Desert Storm, Bosnia and Kosovo, our nation has lamented its foreign language shortfalls. But then the crisis 'goes away,' and we return to business as usual."[5] Attention during these periods of crisis focuses on enhancing programs and encouraging language acquisition in universities, where most languages, particularly the LCTLs, are taught. (All the languages of the states associated with terrorism since 9/11 are classified as LCTLs.) Thus an intermittently recognized federal need for language specialists has motivated the continuation of the modestly funded federal programs that now provide crucial support for critical language learning in higher education.

Dependence on universities is a natural consequence of the failure of state K–12 education systems to institute adequate language training programs.[6] Ray Clifford, the former provost of the Defense Language Institute, has testified many times before Congressional commissions and other boards. On one occasion, he described the low level of interest in language learning among the general public in the early twentieth century:

> Almost 100 years ago, World War I created a distrust of things foreign, including foreign languages. In 1923, the Supreme Court actually had to overturn laws in 22 states that restricted the teaching of foreign languages. In 1940, "The National Report" on what the high schools ought to teach, found that the high schools' overly "academic" curriculum was causing too many student failures. Foreign language instruction was among the subjects recommended for elimination. Foreign languages were not only difficult, "they took so much time that new courses could not be added."[7]

Given these attitudes, it is not surprising that foreign-language training became the preserve of universities in the period leading up to the Second World War.

Backdrop for Language Buildup: the Second World War and the Rise to Dominance

The Second World War raised national consciousness about the strategic importance of language learning by exposing the lack of linguistic expertise available to the government and military at a time of extreme need. With the perception of linguistic competence as a national security issue came the mission of achieving it as a federal responsibility. After the war, as the U.S. emerged as one of the two dominant world powers, linguistic knowledge proved useful in the assessment of new clients and old adversaries. As in many other fields, the war effort helped bring about greater cooperation among the government, the military, and academia.[8] The Office of Strategic Services (OSS) recruited many anthropologists, social scientists, and linguists, sometimes without regard to their personal politics; among them could be found a few prominent Marxists.[9] They helped develop an intelligence system, the forerunner of the Central Intelligence Agency and the Defense Intelligence Agency.

After the war and under the influence of the burgeoning needs generated by the expanding Cold War, this partnership metamorphosed; although the agencies remained units of the government, some elements were transferred to universities, among them the OSS's Soviet Division, which moved to Columbia University.[10] Federal funding of these and other transplants was sometimes laundered through supporting grants from private foundations such as Ford, Carnegie, and Rockefeller because program administrators were anxious that the government not "be involved publicly in developing area studies... to allay suspicions that such programs were little more than an 'intelligence agency.'"[11] Nevertheless, during the Cold War, security and intelligence agendas were pursued on campus; these same program administrators, many of them academics, were not above blacklisting colleagues when it came to granting research funds.[12] Federal agencies also became directly involved: "The FBI routinely checked the credit cards of academics, tailed them around, monitored their lectures, questioned their colleagues and students, and sought out reliable campus informants."[13] Since 9/11, such coercive and intimidatory methods have been revived, only this time extreme conservative and special interest groups are doing the monitoring and attempting to influence the grant award process. They no longer act surreptitiously, however: the full might of the Internet now powers their efforts.[14]

The importance of language learning to wartime defense stimulated direct as well as indirect federal involvement in language training, beginning with a secret school established at the Presidio in San Francisco in November, 1941, and the Army Special Training Program, founded in 1942, which trained linguists for service in the Second World War. Federal support continued and led to the creation of a number of specialized language training programs: the Defense Language Institute Foreign Language Center (DLI),[15] the Foreign Service Institute, and the language schools of the CIA and the National Security Agency. The DLI has since become the world's largest foreign-language institute. It is run by the U.S. Army Training and Doctrine Command with the express purpose of providing "linguists fully capable of supporting U.S. interests worldwide."[16] In the immediate postwar period, however, these programs were far removed from the general public, served a restricted clientele, and had little effect on general public interest or state education policies. In 1954, a study called "The National Interest in Foreign Languages" reported that only 14.2 percent of high school students were studying foreign languages, and 56 percent of U.S. public high schools offered no foreign-language instruction at all.[17] As Kenneth Mildenberger observed, "By the mid-1950's responsible people in government were beginning to realize that university resources especially in non-Western studies were wholly inadequate to meet present and anticipate national needs. Some measure of assistance to language and area studies seemed essential."[18] The launching of Sputnik by the Soviet Union in 1957 galvanized Congress into action.

Sputnik generated a new spirit of political, military, technological, and scientific competition that in turn stimulated public federal-academic partnerships, including those concerning language training. This was an important development, for it permitted the federal government's entry into the realm of public education, heretofore strictly and jealously guarded as the prerogative of each individual state. Thus fear of the Soviets overcame a profound suspicion of federal intrusion into local and specifically educational matters. To this day, the question of the federal right to do so is still being debated, for different and shifting reasons. Sometimes the government invokes its own lack of authority to avoid responsibilities, particularly financial ones. But the success of the fear-factor strategy established a powerful precedent. A February 2005 news release from the Department of Defense refers to the shortfall of foreign-language expertise exposed by the war on terror as a "Sputnik moment."[19] In 1958, however, the strategy was seen in a different light: fear helped "focus . . . attention on the opportunity which Sputnik, this Russian satellite, gave

all of us, who were struggling, and had been for decades, to establish a program of monetary aid to public education, and private
too, in some instances."[20]

The National Defense Education Act (NDEA) was passed by
the U.S. Congress in August 1958 and signed into law by President Eisenhower on September 2, 1958. It mandated that, along
with science and mathematics, modern foreign language study
would be supported. Section 601a of the Act provided for the
establishment of centers that would teach the modern foreign
languages for which the Commissioner of Education determined
"1) that individuals trained in such languages are needed by the
Federal Government, or by business, industry, or education . . .
and 2) that adequate instruction in such language is not readily
available in the United States."[21] Teaching about the regions in
which the languages were spoken (area studies) was also permitted. "In passing the NDEA, Congress recognized that the defense
and security of the nation were inseparably bound with education."[22] Stewart McClure, the clerk of the Senate Committee on
Labor, Education and Public Welfare, who was a key figure in the
backstage maneuvering behind the legislation, provides a little
more context: "I invented that god-awful title: The National
Defense Education Act. If there are any words less compatible,
really, intellectually, with the purposes of education — it's not to
defend the country; it's to defend the mind and develop the human spirit, not to build cannons and battleships. It was a horrible
title, but it worked. It worked. How could you attack it?"[23] It is
not clear how many members of Congress knew about the preex-
isting covert connections between academia and security agencies, or if such knowledge would have influenced the framing or
wording of the act.

No matter how it was justified rhetorically, the actual purpose
of the NDEA was to improve the educational system of the United
States. The new program was administered originally by the Department of Health, Education and Welfare and subsequently,
upon its establishment, by the Department of Education. Of the
ten titles authorized by the NDEA, one, Title VI, was concerned
with language training. Title VI had two parts: "Centers and
Research and Studies" and "Language Institutes." These funded
both individuals and institutions. The rationale for this section of
the legislation was that Title VI would provide funding to meet

the "critical need" to train language teachers and area-studies specialists in "strategic areas," with an emphasis on Japanese, Chinese, Arabic, Hindi-Urdu, and Russian. Its purpose was to train citizens who would foster and advance activities deemed instrumental in preserving U.S. interests. Although the injection of federal money and interests into what was normally the states' strict preserve raised the hackles of advocates of states' rights, their concerns about autonomy were allayed by the act's careful and reassuring words: "Nothing in the Act shall be construed to authorize any agency or employee of the United States to exercise any direction, supervision, or control over the curriculum, program of instruction, administration, or personnel of any institution or school system."[24]

Since its inception in 1958, Title VI, despite slight changes in emphasis and mandate, remains the major source of funding for language and area studies for students and university programs. It has been complemented and augmented by the enormously important and influential Fulbright-Hays Act of 1961 (which originated in 1946 legislation) that added an overseas dimension to the Title VI programs.[25] Fulbright believed that "if large numbers of people know and understand the people from nations other than their own, they might develop a capacity for empathy, a distaste for killing other men, and an inclination to peace."[26] While Section 102 of the Fulbright act emphasized a wide range of educational interchange activities, "Section 102(b)(6) focused exclusively on strengthening education in the fields of foreign languages and area studies throughout the American educational system."[27] Together Title VI and Fulbright have provided the longest-standing federal commitment to language education and area studies.

For the first ten years after its authorization, Title VI support steadily increased; in 1969–70, there were 106 federally funded National Research Centers (NRCs), which received close to $6,400,000 (about $60,000 each).[28] Peer-reviewed competitions encouraged the development of language programs and concentrations of area-studies expertise. The number of faculty positions increased as the relatively small amount of federal dollars was used to leverage university funds very successfully. The number of students taking National Defense Foreign Language Scholarships and pursuing strategic or critical languages peaked in 1967 at 2,344.

The tide turned in the early 1970s, when the Nixon administration made the first of several attempts to reduce funding for Title VI and ultimately phase out the program.[29] These moves coincided with increasingly vocal opposition by academics to government policies in Vietnam.[30] Under Nixon, the purposes of the NDEA were reinterpreted to focus on a narrower range of government needs and objectives. The old federal-state jurisdictional rhetoric was revived to provide the logic for this reinterpretation. The argument now went that the only justification for Title VI was "national interest as defined by U.S. foreign policy and defense needs"; the program was designed to train specialists who could help make foreign policy decisions. The broader purposes of support for education, language training, and diffusion of knowledge about international education were now declared state responsibilities.[31] In the sensitive political climate of the time, area-studies institutions and faculty members became alarmed at the melding of university programs with policy. Budget cutbacks also figured in their concern. Even before Nixon, during the Johnson administration, a series of disturbing scandals involving CIA operations on campus and abroad had already harmed government relations with universities.[32] The scandals were bad enough to force President Johnson to ask Undersecretary of State Nicholas Katzenbach to chair a commission investigating the CIA's relations with the academy and private foundations. The commission concluded, "It should be the policy of the United States government that no federal agency shall provide any covert financial assistance or support, direct or indirect, to any of the nation's educational or private voluntary organizations."[33] The proponents of Title VI's elimination ultimately failed because of the efforts of an extraordinary coalition of academics, area-studies organizations, bureaucrats, agencies, and powerful persons in the Nixon administration itself, among them Henry Kissinger, Patrick Moynihan, Caspar Weinberger, and, as mentioned in a 1973 AAS memo signed by Robert E. Ward, "the State Department National Security Council group that was also working on our behalf."[34]

Although Title VI survived, funding for the program was sharply reduced.[35] The number of centers was cut in half, from one hundred six to fifty, but at the same time, a number of new programmatic priorities were added. Among the most important of these was the requirement to engage in outreach beyond the centers' immediate faculty and student populations. "The idea was to broaden potential constituency and to spread international education and interest in languages. There was a belief that such changes would make the program less vulnerable by broadening the constituency beyond the major research institutions."[36] The irony for Middle East–focused national resource centers was that, starting in 1980, outreach to the community provided the pretext and the means of access for highly politicized lobbying groups acting through local communities to pursue their agenda to control information within the university.[37]

In 1979, the President's Commission on Foreign Language and International Studies reported that "Americans' incompetence in Foreign Languages is nothing short of scandalous, and it is becoming worse."[38] Nonetheless, federal funding continued to be justified almost exclusively in security-related terms until 1980, when the legislative reauthorization process introduced a new emphasis that linked international education and language training with economic productivity. From then on, international economic competitiveness joined foreign policy and national security as a major rationale for federal support. The program also changed its name from the National Defense Education Act to the Higher Education Act. Title VI remained unchanged. The program did not flourish without challenge, however. Year after year during the Reagan administration, budget requests for Title VI were zero. In at least one instance, intercession by an administration official again saved the program; Caspar Weinberger, who was Secretary of Defense by this time, wrote a letter to Secretary of Education Terrel Bell calling for the continuation of Title VI.[39]

A new program introduced in the 1986 funding reauthorization addressed the underlying issue of improving language pedagogy at all levels of instruction by supporting the establishment of a small number of national language resource centers. These new centers were charged with researching, developing, and disseminating new teaching methods, materials, and technologies and establishing new performance standards and measurements. A special emphasis encouraged the development of materials to assist the teaching of the less commonly taught languages. Developing resources for K–12 language teachers also became a high priority.

Title VI support for the National Resource Centers has kept

language learning in the United States alive since 1958 — alive, but not always robust. Current funding levels for several programs remain below their high point of the late 1960s when adjusted for inflation. For example, roughly 33 percent fewer Foreign Language and Area Studies fellowships were awarded in 2004 than in 1967; 1,643 compared to 2,344. In the 2003–2005 funding cycle, federal grant support for 123 National Resource Centers totaled roughly $30,000,000 per year. On average, each center receives $250,000 annually. An additional $29,000,000 provides 1,635 fellowships to language students affiliated with those centers (each center averages about $235,000 a year in fellowship money). The sums are modest in comparison with the importance of the project's goal.

After the Soviets: Language Study in the Service of Power

After the fall of the Soviet Union, a sudden need for professionals who were linguistically competent in the national languages of new states prompted a major expansion in government support for language training and international education. The National Security Education Program (NSEP) was created by the 1991 National Security Education Act, sponsored by Senator David L. Boren. The broadly defined aim of the program is "to address the need to increase the ability of Americans to communicate and compete globally by knowing the languages and cultures of other countries," especially LCTLs.[40] Congress members harshly criticized this wording, which they felt neither described the specific national security interests the program was supposed to serve nor expressed its purpose to develop linguistically skilled future federal employees. Federal agencies required a source of, and a pipeline for, new employees, and NSEP became the designated tool to get the gusher going. While the $150 million provided by NSEP represented a huge infusion of money into foreign language and area studies, the program also brought to boil a host of long-simmering concerns over universities' connections to defense and intelligence agencies. [41]

The program's current administration is housed in the Department of Defense at the National Defense University, but its original incarnation was located in the Defense Intelligence College, under the assistant secretary of command, control, communications and intelligence. The director of the CIA sat on the program's board. In 1994, in response to criticisms, changes were made, among them moving the program out of the DIC. Program policies and direction are provided by the Secretary of Defense, in consultation with the thirteen-member National Security Education Board, chaired by the president of the National Defense University. The board is composed of six other senior federal officials, including the director of the CIA, and six senior nonfederal officials appointed by the president. The board determines the criteria for the awards and recommends critical areas that the program should address. A broadly based group of advisers supports the board.

NSEP originally had two programs, one for institutions and one for undergraduate and graduate student fellowships. Of those original programs, only the second continues, and two national nonprofit organizations now serve as the program's administrative agents, a setup that masks its security and defense connections. The grants under this program aim to raise students to a higher level of language — level 3 or more — by sending them abroad for intensive study. Students accepting NSEP fellowships incur a national-service obligation; all recipients are required to seek employment with a federal agency or office involved in national security. If, after making a good-faith effort, they cannot find federal jobs with national security responsibilities, NSEP award recipients may fulfill the requirement by working in any agency of the federal government or in the field of U.S. higher education in the area of study for which the scholarship was awarded.[42] However, in its National Defense Authorization Act for the fiscal year 2004, Congress narrowed these employment options to "the Department of Defense or other element of the intelligence community that is certified by the Secretary."[43]

Scholarly associations and individual scholars immediately raised questions about the program's location, the board's composition, the service requirement for students, and the processes for establishing funding priorities and reviewing submissions. The findings of the 1976 Church Committee Report were still fresh in the minds of many academics:

> The CIA is now using several hundred American academics who, in addition to providing leads and, on occasion, making introductions for intelligence purposes, write books and other material to be used

for propaganda purposes abroad.... These academics are located in over 100 American colleges, universities and related institutions. At the majority of institutions, no one other than the individual concerned is aware of the CIA link. At the others, at least one university official is aware of the operational use of academics on his campus. ...The CIA considers these operational relationships within the U.S. academic community as perhaps its most sensitive domestic area and has strict controls governing these operations.[44]

The possibility that undisclosed funding could undermine the credibility of research prompted the Middle East Studies Association of North America (MESA) to issue, in 1982, a resolution requiring the public acknowledgment of all sources of funding for research, publication, and other scholarly activities. But in 1985, Middle East scholars were dismayed to discover that one of their own, Nadav Safran, the director of the Center for Middle Eastern Studies at Harvard (a Title VI National Resource Center) did not publicly disclose that he had received over $100,000 of CIA money in support of a book he was writing on Saudi Arabia, and an additional $45,000 in support of an international conference on Islamic fundamentalism. Approximately one-half of the scholars scheduled to attend the conference cancelled when they learned of the CIA funding. In its book contract with Safran, the CIA reserved "the Government's right to approve any and all intended publications" and "the Government's right to deny permission to publish." [45] The scandal prompted the Middle East Studies Association to issue a formal resolution deploring Safran's violation of MESA's 1982 resolution.[46] An editorial in the Boston *Globe* summed up many people's feelings at the time:

> In totalitarian societies, scholars and intellectuals are not allowed to pursue the truth for its own sake; they are expected, and coerced, to work for the state. In an open society, scholars, teachers and intellectuals should be able to think freely — and this means being free of service to the state. The scholar who works for a government intelligence agency ceases to be an independent spirit, a true scholar.[47]

The National Security Education Program was, and still is, perceived as a new version of an old problem for academics in general, and for area studies scholars in particular.

In a joint letter to Senator Boren, the African Studies Association (ASA), the Latin American Studies Association (LASA), and MESA argued that even indirect links to U.S. national security agencies would restrict research opportunities, endanger the safety of students and scholars studying abroad, and jeopardize the cooperation and safety of colleagues in the areas involved.[48] Their members passed formal resolutions calling on NSEP administrators to ensure "that there is separation of foreign area studies scholars, students and their institutions from military and intelligence organizations and priorities."[49] Other organizations expressed the same reservations:

> The credibility of American scholars in a number of countries has been undermined by programs through which the intelligence community did co-opt scholars to contribute to intelligence collection or covert action goals. Credibility in other countries has been undermined by unfounded rumors or allegations of such cooption. Many scholars are quite fearful that their association with this program, however remote, could set back efforts to overcome this legacy.[50]

The South Asia Council of the Association for Asian Studies, the Joint Committee on South Asia of the Social Science Research Council, and the American Council of Learned Societies urged that NSEP funds be transferred from the Department of Defense to the Department of Education and called on institutions not to accept the funds. "Past experience in South Asia as well as elsewhere amply demonstrated the perils of connections, however tenuous, between scholars and U.S. national security agencies. Possible consequences range from mistrust and lack of cooperation to physical violence against U.S. scholars and their colleagues abroad."[51] Confirming these fears, the May 1992 issue of *India Currents* reported about NSEP: "Now, for the first time, the CIA will be involved directly and openly in higher education and research on campuses. The CIA will support students and scholars interested in Third World languages and cultures.... a major purpose of the bill seems to be the training and recruitment of industrial and technological spies for international convert operations."[52] In 1993, the president of the Association of Asian Studies stated:

In many of the most critical and neglected areas of Asia, access to field work and study, and productive relationships with colleagues, will be seriously curtailed by the defense-intelligence identification. In the post Cold War world, the problems posed by the linkages with the defense intelligence community will probably increase, fostered by heightened nationalism.... Many nations will be inaccessible to NSEP students and scholars, often those most important to repairing our international knowledge and competence."[53]

Indeed it has become increasingly difficult to obtain permission to study certain topics. For example, in Egypt it is now almost impossible to obtain research permits to pursue twentieth-century history, religious movements, and women's, minority, and civil-society issues.[54] The personal risk to scholars in the field is increasing; in summer 2003, an Iranian-born Persian-language lecturer at the University of California at Berkeley was detained in Iran, jailed, and abused as a spy. [55] Not all scholars see a problem with the program, however — some regard it as a "a sheep in wolf's clothing."[56] Whether wolf or sheep, NSEP has reacted to criticism by funneling its grants through uncontroversial nongovernmental administering agents. The Institute for International Education processes the undergraduate scholarship program and its awards; the Academy for Educational Development does the same for the graduate scholarships, and the National Foreign Language Center, based at the University of Maryland, administers the new National Flagship Language Initiative program (NFLI).

NSEP introduced the NFLI program in early January 2001 to address labor shortfalls.[57] Testimony before the Senate in fall 2000 detailed a drastic shortage of employees with adequate language competence in some eighty federal agencies. Budget cuts throughout the 1990s left the State Department alone with about eleven hundred vacancies by January 2001. General Accounting Office (GAO) auditors reported, on average, a 44 percent shortfall in translators and interpreters in five critical languages.[58] "Current and projected national security needs for foreign language competence, particularly among non-language professionals, require proactive involvement on the part of the Federal government, including a new form of partnership with education," the auditors reported. This was in part because "in the language arena the federal and education system's response has been inadequate and uneven."[59] The new federal-academic partnership would foster selected universities' development of powerful language training programs that would produce graduates with high levels of proficiency who would be channeled directly into federal employment.

Again the program offered a significant infusion of dollars, but there were some strings attached. Full-fledged NFLI participating universities, or Flagship Institutions, "must be ready and able to accept those students, as well as U.S. government personnel, who may not be matriculants or degree seekers."[60] According to some critics, the program links entire academic programs and universities directly to government employment. They view with alarm direct government participation in deciding who may be admitted to university programs.[61] As of August 2004, NFLI pilot programs can be found at Emory University, where the grant supports teacher training seminars and pedagogical materials development at the Consortium for Arabic Study Abroad, which has its headquarters at Emory; the University of Washington, where it supports the study of Arabic; Brigham Young University and the University of Mississippi, for Chinese; UCLA and the University of Hawaii, for Korean; and Bryn Mawr College, in conjunction with the American Councils for International Education, for Russian.[62] As of 2005, Georgetown University hosts a new NFLI for Arabic.

NSEP scholarships and programs operate in the open and in concert with participating universities. A new program called the Pat Roberts Intelligence Scholarship Program, which was announced in fall 2004 and whose application deadline is in January 2005, avoids university bureaucracy and entanglements by dealing directly with students. In return for promising to spend eighteen months working for the CIA, DIA, NSA, or Army for every year spent in school, successful undergraduate and graduate students applicants can receive a stipend of $25,000 per year for up to two years to help fund their studies. Or the stipend can be applied retroactively as reimbursement for those who decide to join one of the agencies after graduating. Another program, the Intelligence Community Scholarship Program, offered by the Director of National Intelligence, offers even greater monetary incentives to those willing to sign up for civilian careers in the intelligence community. Each year of support requires two years of service; individuals can receive the scholarship (to cover tuition fees and other authorized expenses) for up to four years, and more with a waiver. It is not clear what, if any, effect such arrangements will have the climate of individual classes or the learning environment in general.[63]

Controlling Language After 9/11

The attacks of September 11, 2001, once again focused national attention on the importance of language learning. Shortly after the attacks, the FBI director, Robert Mueller, put out an urgent call for Arabic and Farsi translators, going so far as to post a toll-free number for applicants.[64] The crisis brought new urgency to old arguments. In the aftermath of September 11, the reservations about the NSEP and NFLIP programs expressed by scholars and scholarly associations have played into hands of the neoconservatives described in the chapter in this volume by Joel Beinin. They claim that language deficiencies and the resulting failure of information were the result not of long-term federal failure but of university programs and inefficient or uncooperative university faculty members, whose loyalty and patriotism they even questioned in some cases.

Ignoring the facts, these critics claim that universities boycott NSEP; special outrage is reserved for universities that receive Title VI funds. But there is no boycott: in 2003, 30 percent of NSEP graduate fellowships were given to students at universities with Title VI–funded area-studies centers. From 2001 to 2003, Title VI centers offered 276 LCTLs; the Defense Language Institute provided 74. The DLI just received an increase in its budget of $50 million.[65] Title VI funding in 2004 remains the same.[66] Erroneous information and polemics continue to distract from and distort the discussion. Although language education is the subject, the real object of these polemics is to control the flow of information and analysis coming out of universities, particularly those with Middle East studies programs.[67]

The 2003–2004 academic year marks the latest round of reauthorization of the Higher Education Act and Title VI. While the reauthorization process has always been challenging, the events of 9/11 made this round particularly contentious. In October 2003, the House of Representatives unanimously passed HR 3077, its version of the reauthorization legislation. The bill has become highly controversial because of a new provision establishing a powerful advisory board to oversee the Title VI National Resource

Center activities. "Advisory board" is an inaccurate description, since the board has extraordinary investigative authority, its own staff, and no requirement that it report to the Secretary of Education. Despite a sentence added at the last minute prohibiting meddling with curriculum, this advisory board would set a precedent for federal intrusion into the conduct and content of higher education. The board is authorized to "study, monitor, apprise [sic] and evaluate a sample of activities supported under this title" so that it can make recommendations for improving programs and ensuring that they meet the title's purposes. This authorization would enable the board to investigate the activities of grant recipients, including those of individual faculty members.[68]

Further, the board can conduct such a probe (and perform its other functions) with apparently unlimited authority to secure "the services, personnel, information, and facilities of other Federal, State, local and private agencies with or without reimbursement."[69] Such wording calls to mind the activities of the FBI during the Cold War. The board can also "secure directly from any executive department, agency, board, commission, office, independent establishment, or instrumentality information, suggestions, estimates and statistics," and the head of each department is required to comply to the extent permitted by law. It can secure such personnel and services with no limitation except that of funding and can obtain the services of experts and consultants without regard to U.S. code requirements. Thus the board's independence and authority extend beyond those of other federal advisory boards for comparable education programs, such as the Fund for Improvement of Higher Education and the Jacob Javits Fellowship board. For example, the board is independent of the Department of Education, and its recommendations will not be subject to review by any officer of the federal government, except in the case of legislative recommendations that must first be approved by the president.[70]

One of the board's purposes is to "make recommendations that will promote the ... development of such programs at the postsecondary education level that will reflect diverse perspectives and represent the full range of views on world regions, foreign language, and international affairs."[71] This purpose, in combination with its authority to investigate, takes the board into curriculum matters and causes concern about academic freedom and, in the case of outreach, free speech.[72] Furthermore, the composition of the board is highly vulnerable to politicization. There will be seven members, two selected by the Speaker of the House based on the recommendations of the majority and minority leaders, two by the president pro tempore of the Senate, on the recommendation of the majority and minority leaders, and three by the Secretary of Education. Two of the latter must be from federal agencies with national security responsibilities, which means once again intertwining defense and intelligence imperatives with university programs. Debate on HR 3077 continued into late June 2004, by which time the Senate still had not developed its own version of the legislation. At the end of June, a House of Representatives committee leader announced that no Higher Education Act reauthorization bill would be finalized in 2004. The issues had grown too contentious. (In 2005, the bill was reintroduced with no changes as HR 509.)

Underlying HR 3077 is the assertion by critics that international-studies faculty members are un-American, unpatriotic, and subversive.

> The real purpose of the attacks on Title VI is to use the advisory board to silence dissenting opinions, holding out the threat that federal funding will be cut unless centers (particularly Middle East centers) self-censor. Martin Kramer, an author who has made a career of attacking Middle East studies, told his academic colleagues to start worrying. Invoking tactics more common to the former Soviet Union or to the former Iraqi Regime, than to a democracy, he warned professors that their websites would be "visited late at night" to police their content. "Yes, you are being watched," Kramer wrote on his website, telling faculty to "get used to it." Intimidation is the aim of these critics, not accountability.[73]

The untenured junior professor of Middle East studies who received a flier from a senior member of her department blaming Middle East scholars for 9/11 understands this message. A more senior professor at another institution also understands: "I have been repeatedly accused of being anti-Semitic because of my critique of certain aspects of Israeli policy. It seems to be part of a crude strategy to silence criticism by affixing a label that effectively demonizes the critic — and does so without having to give a reasoned response." So does the faculty member (who happens to be Christian) who has been called a "radical Muslim hag — the sort that twattles [sic] her devilish tongue, cloaked in a black sleeping bag and who is consumed with satanic fervor. . . . You are a defender of Islamic radicalism and that makes you an enemy to this nation." The rest of the message, which was also sent to the other Middle East scholars at her institution, contains an implied threat: "It is time for the FBI and Homeland Security to investigate [that institution] . . . and the professors who belong to it."[74]

Attacks on faculty members continue, and they are becoming increasingly nasty and explicitly threatening. The case of a junior faculty member in the Department of Middle East and Asian Languages and Cultures (MEALAC) at Columbia University inspired the New York chapter of the American Civil Liberties Union (the NYCLU) to write a letter defending academic freedom to the university president. Students attacked the MEALAC professor not on the substance of his arguments but on the basis of views they found offensive. A member of Congress, who is now running for mayor of New York, urged Columbia to fire the professor, and various benefactors threatened to withhold donations to the university. The NYCLU letter concluded, "The attack upon Professor Massad and others in the MEALAC Department is fundamentally about their scholarship and political expression. Thus, the criticism of these academics must be seen for what it is: an assault upon principles of academic freedom and upon political speech."[75] Shortly after this letter was written, the New York Board of Education, in response to an article in the *New York Sun* accusing another Columbia professor, Rashid Khalidi, of holding pro-Palestine views, banned him from speaking at training sessions for secondary-school teachers. (Khalidi is also the director of the Title VI–funded National Resource Center at Columbia.) The university's president, Lee Bollinger, issued a strongly worded statement about the board's action:

> When the city, acting as the state for constitutional purposes, declares that it will not permit a person to participate in a program that has been set up and established because of purported views of that person on other matters, matters of public concern, public issues, that is very clearly what is called viewpoint discrimination, and at the very least, indicates deep, deep first amendment concerns. . . .

We believe that the position of the Department of Education on this is wrong, not only as a matter of constitutional law, but as a matter of good policy and as a matter of good conduct of education.[76]

The intent of such accusations is to intimidate and ultimately to silence. As C. Wright Mills wrote in 1951, "[The] deepest problem of freedom for teachers is not the occasional ousting of a professor, but a vague general fear — sometimes called 'discretion' and 'good judgment' — which leads to self-intimidation and finally becomes so habitual that the scholar is unaware of it. The real restraints are not so much external prohibitions as manipulative control of the insurgents by the agreements of academic gentlemen."[77] But the intent is also to set up a media trail by which the guilt of area-studies experts, particularly those who study the Middle East, is assumed unquestionably. The attacks are really aimed at scuttling the reauthorization of Title VI funds, or at least diverting them to politically supportive or inert institutions.

Eliminating Title VI would not get rid of pesky professors, however, because Title VI funds do not pay for permanent faculty positions. These funds are used to support temporary appointments and vital low-enrollment courses in unusual languages — many of which are taught nowhere outside universities, neither at the Defense Language Institute nor at the Foreign Service Institute. Although fewer than 3 percent of the nation's higher-education institutions that offer modern foreign languages have Title VI NRCs, these institutions represent 23 percent of all undergraduate enrollments in the less commonly taught languages and 59 percent in the least commonly taught languages. As for graduate enrollments, Title VI NRCs account for 59 percent in the less commonly taught languages and 80 percent in the least commonly taught languages. More than 60 percent of students enrolled in what the Department of Defense deems the most critical languages can be found at Title VI NRCs. Furthermore, Title VI–Fulbright-Hays funding has supported the development of more than half of the language textbooks now in use for the least commonly taught languages.[78]

If the attack on Title VI fails, other tactics already in play may be more successful in quieting professors. The Web site Campus Watch recommends alerting university stakeholders — in other words, donors — to the presence of "fifth column" Middle East scholars or critics of Israeli policies and encouraging them to exercise their financial clout.[79] Campus Watch's Israeli counterpart, Israel Academia Monitor, is more blunt: "Are you a donor to Israeli universities?... Learn what is happening on Israeli campuses. Be informed about what is being done with your gifts and generosity."[80] Some donors reportedly threatened Columbia after reading articles about MEALAC in newspapers, causing the NYCLU to include in its letter the statement "it is entirely inappropriate for potential donors to try to use the power of the purse to dictate the content of scholarship or the composition of a university's faculty or one of its departments."[81]

The 2002 enrollment figures compiled by the MLA show a 97 percent increase in the number of students of Arabic. As mentioned before, only six Ph.D.s in Arabic were awarded in 2001. There are not enough trained teachers to meet the demand. In the past, immigrant labor made up some of the shortages in the federal workforce and in language teachers. Now restrictions on immigration instituted by the Department of Homeland Security — particularly on people from Asia and the Middle East — are intensifying the shortages. Ironically, NFLI target languages are Arabic, Mandarin, Hindi, Japanese, Korean, Persian, Russian, and Turkish — the languages whose native speakers have the most trouble getting visas. Reports to the MESA secretariat indicate that even instructors with teaching contracts have encountered difficulties: some were unable to return after visiting their home countries, and some new hires simply could not obtain visas. Federal policy is at odds with federal needs.

The post-9/11 spike in enrollments in languages such as Arabic masks the extraordinary paucity of students of the least commonly taught languages, such as Pashto, Dari, or Hindi. (The MLA survey shows a total of fourteen students in Pashto in 2002.) Students of all these languages take longer to reach mastery than students of other languages, which exacerbates the shortage. A new program, as yet only a proposal, seeks to address such shortages by developing new sources of talent. A new program, the Civilian Language Reserve Corps would tap the large numbers of recent immigrants (referred to as heritage speakers) in the U.S. First- and second-generation Americans would be encouraged to retain their language skills and use them to serve the country. (The NFLI program has also targeted heritage speakers, but only for advanced training.) The corps would create a roster of already proficient foreign-language speakers who would be eligible to serve in cycles of four years but would be assigned tours of duty (tasks) of short duration, with the possibility of extension. Service would be voluntary, and the linguist's right to return to his or her regular job would be ensured by federal law.[82] Participants would be encouraged to keep up their language skills between tours of duty. The Department of Defense, one of the proponents of the Civilian Language Reserve Corps, recently initiated a related pilot program, the Individual Ready Reserve, which encourages Iraqi Americans to join up and provide a pool of Arabic speakers.[83]

The Civilian Language Reserve Corps program has much to recommend it, not least that it finally gives official sanction to the proposition that speaking a second language is not only admirable but also desirable. However, civil libertarians might question the creation of lists of people by ethnic or linguistic grouping, even if inclusion on the list is voluntary, especially in these highly charged times when legal protections have been diluted by home-land-security provisions. The recent improper release of census information about the Arab American population to the Department of Homeland Security has reminded many that it was not so long ago that the U.S. incarcerated suddenly suspect citizens.[84] Further, the corps bears some similarity to the National Guard or the Army Reserve Corps, members of both of which have re-cently experienced unanticipated extensions of their tours of duty abroad. The rights and responsibilities of service in any new program must be clearly delineated. Finally, although this pro-gram is not directly relevant to university programs — apart from a possible eventual role for universities in offering refresher lan-guage courses — there is reason to suspect that universities could in the future be required to provide this program or ones similar to it with information about their students. Indeed, K–12 educa-tional institutions have already been required to provide lists to military recruiters under the No Child Left Behind Act, and infor-mation about foreign students in U.S. universities must now be reported to the Department of Homeland Security under the Stu-dent Exchange Visitor Information Service regulations.

At this point the Civilian Language Reserve Corps is nothing more than an idea. In the meantime, there is a huge need for high-quality training programs, teaching materials, and teachers, and for increased enrollments. According to Gail McGinn, the deputy undersecretary of defense for plans, the Department of Defense has a host of projects to address these needs: "Such pilot programs and plans will help the U.S. better position itself for future military operations. . . . This is more than just finding linguists and people with the ability to speak languages. It's a transformation in the way language is viewed in the Department of Defense — how it is valued, how it is developed and how it is employed."[85] While military interest in a project usually results in a massive infusion of funds (one institution, the Defense Language Institute, just received an extra $50 million; the total budget for all 123 Title VI NRCs was $60 million last year), is it in the nation's interest that the focus of language learning be so narrowly construed and confined within a system that does not encourage independent critical analysis? Time will tell.

The government programs put forth to address these needs, such as NSEP, NFLI, and HR 3077, have not been well received by many faculty members and universities, who regard them as Trojan horses. Should the advisory board of HR 3077 go forward, many institutions will forgo applying for funding. This would have the unfortunate effect of widening the divide between public and private institutions. For many public institutions, the prestige of Title VI makes it possible to justify paying for expensive but small language programs even when resources are scarce. LCTLs in particular would be left to private institutions with greater resources. Quite apart from the equity concerns raised by limiting most students' access to great language programs, such a narrowing of access is simply not in a democracy's best interests. It would be positively dangerous if the nation's priorities were defined by the unrestrained factionalism of outside intellectual movements rather than by the concerted deliberation of governmental arms such as the military or the foreign service. The history of federal funding for the sciences, humanities, and education shows that the best research and teaching arise in an unregulated marketplace of ideas, nourished by apolitical, arm's-length funding.

By failing to develop a coherent and consistent language program, particularly a K–12 program, the federal government has guaranteed its own vulnerability. By relentlessly and for decades underfunding incentive programs, such as language fellowships and grants, and refusing to meet its own labor need projections, it has failed its governmental responsibilities. Now, in a panic, the government frames every rationale for language learning in terms of national security — even economic competitiveness is now subsumed into this approach. This leads to such a drop in trust between the government and academia that the government is reduced to coercive means to meet its needs. In the end, a policy of coercion, rather than the previous policy of encouragement, will not attract the best practitioners to language instruction, or the best students to language learning. Nor will lavish scholarships with strings attached necessarily bring to government service the kinds of open-minded, critical, and analytical people it so desperately needs. Such scholarships may therefore undermine the very purposes for which government introduced the coercion or the incentive in the first place.

To some extent, academia has been complicit in this loss of trust, since it was content in earlier times to use these same arguments of national security to justify continued funding. Traditionally, language programs have offered a degree of protection for the area-studies component of federally supported programs, where some of the individual critics of government foreign policy can be found. Now the devil's bargain is unraveling, to the detriment of both the government's interest in excellent and productive language programs and academia's interest in funding for free- and wide-ranging research and innovation.

And helping it unravel with willful and deliberate destruction as their goal are the special-interest groups who are willing to put narrow, single-minded agendas ahead of true interest in the national well-being. At the heart of the issue is the control of information.

Before 9/11 and the Bush administration, mutual interests, and to some degree an old-fashioned recognition that there is intrinsic value in an autonomous university system, maintained a balance of power between universities and the government. That balance has been broken. While the challenges now facing academics and universities are not new, the forces issuing them have been vastly enhanced by the political wind from the fall of the Twin Towers. We truly are in the midst of a "Sputnik moment." It is time to start paying attention.

NOTES

1. Ellen Laipson, "Foreign Language Requirements in the Intelligence Community," statement to the Senate Government Affairs Committee, September 14, 2000, http://www.cia.gov/nic/testimony_foreignlanguage.html.

2. Elizabeth B. Welles, "Foreign Language Enrollments in United States Institutions of Higher Education, Fall 2002," p. 3, http://www.wisitalia.org/web/data/MLAtext.pdf.

3. Welles, "Foreign Language Enrollments," p. 6.

4. MLA news release, http://www.learnnc.org/dpi/instserv.nsf/0/c0c9adc40125c6e785256df000750764/$FILE/2002%20Enrollmentsrev.pdf.

5. Paul Simon, "Beef Up the Country's Foreign Language Skills," *Washington Post*, Oct. 23, 2001.

6. In twentieth-century U.S. universities, language study is most often linked with area studies, that is, with courses of study focusing on the social, political, and cultural contexts of language. What the U.S. calls area studies grew from the European tradition of comprehensive cultural knowledge firmly grounded in profound linguistic expertise known as Orientalism. (It is only since the postmodernist critique of the 1970s that the designation "Orientalist" has turned from an encomium into a term of obloquy by suggesting great knowledge put to the service of reprehensible political or social agendas.) Because area-studies faculty members frequently teach language, it is sometimes difficult to separate or distinguish them from faculty members who teach language only.

7. "Statement of Ray Clifford," testimony before the National Briefing on Language and National Security, National Foreign Language Center, Washington, D.C., January 16, 2002, http://www.ndu.edu/nsep/January16_Briefing.htm.

8. For a discussion of a similar intertwining of the government, the military, and the media, see the chapter in this volume by Frydl ("Trust to the Public: Academic Freedom in the Multiversity").

9. Bruce Cumings, "Boundary Displacement: Area Studies and International Studies During and After the Cold War," *Bulletin of Concerned Asian Scholars* 29.1 (1997), p. 7.

10. Cumings, "Boundary Displacement," p. 4.

11. *Ibid.*

12. *Ibid.*, p. 7 and n.34.

13. *Ibid.*, p. 5, and Sigmund Diamond, *Compromised Campus: The Collaboration of Universities with the Intelligence Community, 1945–1955* (New York: Oxford University Press, 1992). Diamond provides more details of the relationship between the CIA, the FBI, the foundations, and the new institutes.

14. See Joel Beinin's article in this volume ("The New McCarthyism: Policing Thought about the Middle East") for his discussion of Campus Watch, one of

the most notorious of the "monitoring" efforts; see also the American Association of University Professors (AAUP) response to the Academic Bill of Rights effort (proposed bills that have now been introduced in state legislatures in Georgia, Colorado, California, Ohio, and Indiana and the U.S. Congress would involve the state, the federal government, or both in oversight of curricula, teaching, and faculty hiring and promotion in both public and private institutions of higher education): http://www.aaup.org/statements/index.html. A powerful interest group effectively accused the Ford Foundation of supporting Palestinian terrorist groups. Both Ford and Rockefeller now require grantees to sign an agreement eschewing violence and its supporters. Initially, nine prominent universities refused to sign, complaining that the language was too broad and jeopardized campus film festivals, lectures, and photo displays about highly charged disputes and ran "up against the basic principle of protected speech on our campuses" (Daniel Golden, "Colleges Object To New Wording in Ford Grants," *Wall Street Journal*, May 4, 2004). A new "side letter" issued by the Ford Foundation outlining its commitment to academic freedom has reassured the nine universities and made it possible for them to accept Ford money once again. The letter, titled "Pursuing our Mission as a Responsible Philanthropic Institution," can be found in the appendix section and at http://www.fordfound. org/about/guideline.cfm.

15. "Presidio of Monterey: History of the Presidio of Monterey," Defense Language Institute Web site, http://www.dli.army.mil/content/about.htm.

16. From the mission statement of the Defense Language Institute Foreign Language Center, http://www.dliflc.edu/About%20DLIFLC/about_dliflc_ index.html. According to the history section on the same site, the U.S. Air Force met most of its foreign-language training requirements in the 1950s through contract programs at universities such as Yale, Cornell, Indiana, and Syracuse.

17. Clifford, testimony before the National Briefing on Language and National Security.

18. Kenneth W. Mildenberger, cited in Gilbert W. Merkx, "Plus Ça Change: Challenges to Graduate Education under HEA Title VI," in John N. Hawkins, (ed.), *International Education in the New Global Era: Proceedings of a National Policy Conference on the Higher Education Act, Title VI, and Fulbright-Hays Programs* (Los Angeles: UCLA, 1998), p. 76, http://www.isop.ucla.edu/ pacrim/title6/.

19. Donna Miles, "DoD Seeks People With Language Skills, Regional Expertise," American Forces Press Service, Feb. 3, 2005, http://www.vnis. com/story.cfm?textnewsid=1371.

20. "Stewart E. McClure: Chief Clerk, Senate Committee on Labor, Education, and Public Welfare (1949–1973)," Oral History Interviews, Senate Historical Office, Washington, D.C., sec. 4, p. 112, available on the Senate Web site: http://

www.senate.gov/artandhistory/history/oral_history/Oral_History_McClure.htm.

21. Lorraine McDonnell, Sue E. Berryman, and Douglas Scott, *Federal Support for International Studies: The Role of NDEA Title VI* (Santa Monica, CA: Rand, 1981), p. 3.

22. Richard D. Scarfo, "The History of Title VI and Fulbright-Hays," in Hawkins (ed.), *International Education in the New Global Era*, p. 23.

23. McClure, oral history, p. 118.

24. Sidney Charles Sufrin, *Administering the National Defense Education Act* (Syracuse, NY: Syracuse University Press, 1963), p. 45.

25. Scarfo, "History of Title VI and Fulbright-Hays," p. 24.

26. J. William Fulbright, "The Most Significant and Important Activity I Have Been Privileged to Engage In During My Years in the Senate," *Annals of the American Academy of Political and Social Science* 424 (1976), p. 2.

27. Scarfo, "History of Title VI and Fulbright-Hays," p. 24.

28. McDonnell, Berryman, and Scott, *Federal Support for International Studies*, p. 6.

29. Scarfo, "History of Title VI and Fulbright-Hays," p. 24.

30. Clifford testimony: "I think we have finally passed — we've left behind the events of — the ill-feeling that was created by the Vietnam War period, when there was such a huge distrust between government and academia, which led partly to the disinvestments in NDEA."

31. McDonnell, Berryman, and Scott, *Federal Support for International Studies*, pp. 6 and 7.

32. "The University on the Make," *Ramparts Magazine*, April 1966, available at http://www.cia-on-campus.org/msu.edu/msu.html.

33. Chris C. Mooney, "For Your Eyes Only," *Lingua Franca*, November 2000, available at http://www.chriscmooney.com/article_db.asp?id=295.

34. The second concerted effort is described in a letter written on AAS letterhead, dated January 30, 1973, and signed by Robert E. Ward, reporting on the extensive measures he had undertaken to enlist the aid of many well-connected people and organizations in defense of Title VI. For example, he arranged for the president of Association of American Universities (AAU) to send a strong letter of protest to President Nixon. "This letter emphasized the fact that the elimination of Title VI funds was a breach of the President's agreement in the Moynihan-Pusey correspondence of 1970 to support Title VI at the current rates until it was absorbed by the projected National Foundation on Higher Education — which, of course, has not yet come into existence" (p. 2). He noted that he had even invoked a Quaker connection, and, finally, that "short of collective seppuku on the White House lawn, this was all I could think of to do" (p. 3). The letter is in the files of the Middle East Studies Association.

35. According to the 1979 General Accounting Office (GAO) report, approximately one-third fewer language fellowships were awarded in 1974 than in 1973. In 1973, there were a total of 1,110, of which 136 were in Arabic, 2 in Hebrew, 1 in Kurdish, 17 in Persian, and 20 in Turkish. For 1974, the total was much less, under 700.

36. Scarfo, "History of Title VI and Fulbright-Hays," p. 24.

37. See Joel Beinin's article in this volume. Also, on the activities at the University of Arizona, see Paul Findley, *They Dare to Speak Out: People and Institutions Confront Israel's Lobby* (Westport, CT: Lawrence Hill and Company, 1985), pp. 181–212; other efforts can be found in Jonathan S. Kessler and Jeff Schwaber, *The AIPAC College Guide: Exposing the Anti-Israel Campaign on Campus* (Washington, D.C.: American Israel Public Affairs Committee, 1984); Colin Campbell, "Middle East Group Wants Anti-Defamation League to Disown List," *New York Times*, January 30, 1985, p. 9; Karen Winkler, "Political Tensions of Arab-Israeli Conflict Put Pressure on Scholars Who Study Middle East," *Chronicle of Higher Education*, March 27, 1985, p. 5.

38. *Strength through Wisdom: A Critique of U.S. Capability; A Report to the President from the President's Commission on Foreign Languages and International Studies.* U.S. Government Printing Office, Washington D.C., 1979, p. 5.

39. Making education consistent with the demands of a modern-day market was a major theme of the 1983 report on K–12 education, "A Nation at Risk: The Imperative for Educational Reform," written by the National Commission on Excellence in Education at the request of T.H. Bell (available at http://www.ed.gov/pubs/NatAtRisk/index.html. The report recommended longer course sequences. Also, "Federal allocations that did support this accumulation came under new critical scrutiny as the end of the cold war undermined the single most effective lobbyist argument in support of area studies on Capitol Hill. The military need for intelligence had always been the secret weapon for Title VI lobbyists — and when Ronald Reagan tried to kill the Department of Education, Caspar Weinberger, Secretary of Defense, protected international and area studies." David Ludden, "Area Studies in the Age of Globalization," January 25, 1998, p. 2 (http://www.sas.upenn.edu/~dludden/areast2.htm).

40. http://nsep.aed.org/aboutnsep.html.

41. For example, the intelligence strings attached to the Defense Intelligence Agency's Defense Academic Research Support Program (DARSP), which has funded foreign area research since 1981, prompted the Association of African Studies Programs, the Executive Council of the Latin American Studies Association, and nineteen directors of university area studies centers to issue a letter calling on universities not to respond to DARSP's request for contract proposals. The letter stated, "It is in the national interest of the United States to maintain a

clear boundary between military/intelligence activities of our government and foreign area scholarly research and programs of our universities." The Middle East Studies Association issued a formal resolution on November 25, 1985, expressing similar reservations. At the same time, it acknowledged that it was in the "public interest for members of the academic community to contribute responsibly to government efforts to improve the analysis and discussion of foreign policy and international security issues." The resolution concluded by exhorting MESA members "to reflect carefully upon their responsibilities to the academic profession prior to seeking or accepting funding from intelligence sources." Material on file at the MESA secretariat and published in the *Middle East Studies Bulletin* 16.1 (1986).

42. "National Security Education Program," http://www.ndu.edu/nsep.

43. Section 925. "Since adoption of the current requirement, approximately 73% of the scholarship (undergraduate) and fellowship (graduate) recipients (combined) have met the service requirement through federal employment, and 27% through employment in higher education" (p. 9 n.10). "However the pattern of service is distinctly different for undergraduate scholarship recipients vs. graduate fellowship recipients — 93% of scholarship recipients have met the requirement through federal employment vs. 50% of the fellowship recipients" (p. 9 n.11). "Thus far, it appears that graduate fellowship recipients are much more likely to meet their service requirement by taking positions in higher education" (p. 14). Jeffrey J. Kuenzi, "National Security Education Program: Background and Issues," updated January 21, 2005, http://www.fas.org/sgp/crs/ misc/RL31643.pdf.

44. *Foreign and Military Intelligence*, Book I of the Final Report of the Select Committee to Study Governmental Operations (Washington, D.C.: U.S. Government Printing Office, 1976), pp. 189–90.

45. Colin Campbell, "C.I.A. Grant Raises Questions on Research Rules at Harvard," *New York Times*, November 5, 1985.

46. *MESA Newsletter* 8.1 (1986), p. 8.

47. Alan Berger, "The C.I.A. at Harvard," *Boston Globe*, November 29, 1985, p. 22.

48. Other groups also sent letters, among them the American Council of Learned Societies, the Association for Asian Studies, and the Association of Concerned African Scholars.

49. NSEP Resolution, adopted by MESA's Board of Directors on October 28, 1992; presented to the membership at the annual business meeting on October 30, 1992; passed by the membership through referendum vote on March 31, 1993. *MESA Newsletter* 15.1 (1993), p. 12.

50. Stanley J. Heginbotham, "The National Security Education Program," *Items* 46.2–3 (1992), p. 22.

51. The South Asia Council of the Association for Asian Studies, quoted in David Wiley, "National Security Education Program: Who's Setting the agenda?" *Journal of the International Institute* 1.1 (1994), http://www.umich. edu/ ~iinet/journal/vol1no1/Wiley.html.

52. Ved Prakash Vatuk, "Big Brother in the Classroom: US Congress Authorizes CIA to Fund Language and Area Studies," *India Currents* 6.2 (1992), p. M5.

53. Letter from AAS President Tetsuo Najita to Senator Boren, March 1, 1993. On file at the MESA secretariat.

54. Although this has never been publicly discussed, it has been acknowledged by Fulbright staff in private communication. Fulbright does not post or broadcast a list of off-limits topics, but the organization's staff will advise informally about which topics are likely not to be approved and which methods are completely forbidden. Personal email communication, May 25, 2004. Board members of the American Research Center in Egypt (ARCE) are also aware of the problem, as their grant recipients have also encountered difficulties in obtaining research permits. Personal communication with the former ARCE president Charles D. Smith in Tucson, Arizona, May 22, 2004.

55. The Committee on Academic Freedom Abroad of the Middle East Studies Association became involved in the case, as did his employer, the University of California at Berkeley. He was released after a number of difficult months. This information is in the files of the Middle East Studies Association.

56. Paul Desruisseaux, "From Controversy to Quiet Prosperity, Federal Foreign-Study Effort Is a Survivor," *Chronicle for Higher Education*, April 7, 2000, http://chronicle.com/weekly/v46/i31/31a05901.htm.

57. "National Security Education Program (NSEP) Analysis of Federal Language Needs," NSEP Web site, http://www.ndu.edu/nsep/Federal_Language_ Needs_2001.htm.

58. Katherine McIntire Peters, "Lost in Translation," May 1, 2002, pp. 1–2, http://www.govexec.com/features/0502/0502s4.htm. For a comprehensive report, see Nancy L. Ruther, "The International and Foreign Language Human Capital Challenge of the U.S. Federal Government," Duke University Conference, January 23–25, 2003, http://www.duke.edu/web/cis/globalchallenges/ pdf/ruther.pdf.

59. This was most recently expressed in the 2003 testimony to Congress meant to justify NSEP's continuation: "The establishment of NSEP represented an important recognition that the nation's colleges and universities were not producing the quantity or quality of professionals equipped with the language and cultural skills needed to effectively address complex issues confronted by the U.S. in the post–cold war environment." "NSEP Report to Congress (September 2003)," p. 10, http://www.ndu.edu/nsep/NSEPRpt.pdf.

60. NFLC request for proposal guidelines for Russian, Chinese, and Persian languages: www.nflc.org/NFLIRussianSolicitation.pdf and www.nflc.org/nfli/ChineseFAQ.doc and www.councilnet.org.conf/Persian%ONFLI%20Solicitation.doc.

61. See, for example, a statement written by the MESA board of directors. "MESA Board of Directors Statement Re: National Flagship Language Initiative — Pilot Program (NFLI-P)," April 26, 2003, http://fp.arizona.edu/mesassoc/boardletters.htm#427NFLIP.

62. The CASA program is the preeminent intensive advanced Arabic program offered by any U.S. entity. According to the director of CASA, Mahmoud al-Batal, the program has accepted NSEP money indirectly through the National Foreign Language Center and the Arabic for Interactive Communication program at the University of Washington. In 2003, the program accepted funds from NSEP in support of four fellowships but with the stipulation that there be no service requirement attached to these fellowships. This agreement changed after the hardening of the service requirement by Congress in fall 2003; CASA would not accept the fellowships with the renewed (and explicitly security-related) service obligation. Instead the funds are used to develop teaching materials and enhance teacher training. Personal e-mail communication, August 4, 2004. Contrary to its intent, the service obligation continues to impede the development of the nation's linguistic strength.

63. See http://www.clubfed.com/youngfeds/2005/YF011205.htm.

64. Simon, "Beef Up the Country's Foreign Language Skills," p. A23.

65. Miles, "DOD Seeks People With Language Skills."

66. Press release: "e-LCTL Initiative," http://elctl.msu.edu.

67. African programs have also been criticized. The effort to control information through intimidation has affected other federal and nonfederal programs. See, for example, the accusations against the Ford Foundation (n.11).

68. United States House of Representatives, Committee on Education and the Workforce (108th Congress), Report on HR 3077: International Studies in Higher Education Act of 2003, October 8, 2003. (Referred to Senate Committee after being Received from House.) Full text available from http://thomas.loc.gov.

69. *Ibid.*

70. Many of these points have been articulated by Miriam Kazanjian, a consultant to the Coalition for International Education, in memos to the coalition and in letters to Congressional representatives on the CIE's behalf. Copies are on file at the MESA Secretariat in Tucson, Arizona.

71. Report on HR 3077.

72. For a discussion of the issue of balance and diversity, see David A.

Hollinger, "What Does It Mean to Be 'Balanced' in Academia?" Paper presented at the annual meeting of the American Historical Association, January 9, 2005.

73. Steven Heydemann, "Warping Mideast Judgments," *Chicago Tribune*, March 14, 2004, http://www.ssrc.org/programs/mena/MES_Opinions/heyde mann.page.

74. This and the previous quotation are from communications on file at the MESA secretariat.

75. "NYCLU Defends Academic Freedom at Columbia University," p. 4, http://www.nyclu.org/Bollinger_ltr_122004.html.

76. Lisa Hirschmann, "U. Senate Meets, Responds to MEALAC Debate: Bollinger Addresses Dismissal of Khalidi; Senate Debates Appropriate Response for Grievances," *Columbia Spectator*, February 28, 2005, http://www.columbia spectator.com/vnews/display.vART/2005/02/28/4222d6a8c1874.

77. C. Wright Mills, *White Collar*, 1951, quoted in John Lie, "Moral Ambiguity, Disciplinary Power, and Academic Freedom," *Bulletin of Concerned Asian Scholars* 29.1 (1997).

78. Statistics gathered in a survey conducted by the National Foreign Language Center. See http://www.nflc.org/security/natsecurity.asp and http://elctl.msu.edu.

79. "Alert university stakeholders (administrators, alumni, trustees, regents, parents of students, state/provincial and federal legislators) to the problems in Middle East studies and encourage them to address existing problems. We challenge these stakeholders to take back their universities" http://www.campus-watch.org/about.php.

80. Quoted in an article by Neve Gordon, "Why Some Israeli Professors Feel They Are the Victims of an Old-Fashioned Witch Hunt," http://hnn.us/ articles/9418.html, and Israel Academia Monitor, http://israel-academia-monitor. com/.

81. "NYCLU Defends Academic Freedom at Columbia University," p. 4.

82. National Security Education Program, "United States Civilian Linguist Reserve Corps Feasibility Study," http://www.ndu.edu/nsep/CivilianLinguist ReserveCorpsFeasibilityStudy.pdf.

83. Miles, "DoD Seeks People With Language Skills."

84. A group of forty American minority groups joined civil-liberties activists in expressing "grave concern" over an American government effort to record the number and national origin of Arab Americans living within the United States. "These actions are a violation of the public's trust in the census bureau, and a troubling reminder of one of our nation's darkest days, when the sharing of similar information resulted in the internment of Japanese Americans during World War II," read the group's statement, released August 13, 2004.

Will Rasmussen, "US Groups Query Census Action on Arab-Americans," *Daily Star* (Beirut), August 16, 2004, http://www.dailystar.com.lb/article.asp?edition_id=10&categ_id=2&article_id=7363.

85. Miles, "DoD Seeks People With Language Skills."

The New McCarthyism: Policing Thought about the Middle East

Joel Beinin

Since the September 11, 2001, terrorist attacks on the World Trade Center and the Pentagon, a coterie of supporters of George W. Bush's Manichaean view of the world — a group that can be called the American Likud — has spearheaded a campaign to delegitimize critical thought about the Middle East.[1] The Likud, Israel's largest party, champions a hawkish stand on Arab-Israeli issues, extensive Israeli settlement in the West Bank, a minimal, if any, Palestinian state, and free-market capitalism. Some of the American Likudniks are Israeli citizens; most are not. In either case, they argue, explicitly or implicitly, that U.S. interests in the Middle East are congruent with their conception of Israel's interests. In their view, Israel is uniquely capable of being the most reliable U.S. ally in the region. Hence, Washington should actively defend Israel rather than attempt to mediate between Israel and its Arab allies. Criticism of Israel's policies toward the Palestinians or of U.S. support for Israeli policies is, therefore, "anti-American" and immediately suspected of being anti-Semitic.

The principal players in this undertaking are Martin Kramer, the author of a hot-headed and poorly researched tract attacking the Middle East Studies Association published by the leading "pro-Israel" think tank, the Washington Institute for Near East Policy,[2] and Daniel Pipes, who directs his own private think tank, the Middle East Forum, and is the founder of Campus Watch, a now infamous Web site that targets Middle East scholars and programs. Kramer and Pipes have Ph.D.s in Middle East studies but have long been considered eccentric and marginal by much of the scholarly community.[3] They have therefore relocated from academia to think tanks with close ties to Israel's ruling circles. Somewhat less prominent, though equally persistent, is Stanley Kurtz, a contributing editor of *National Review Online* and a fellow at the Hoover Institution on War, Revolution and Peace, a veteran conservative think tank at Stanford University. Kurtz has a Ph.D. in anthropology with a specialization in South Asia but no Middle East credentials. Bit players include Jonathan Schanzer, sometime co-author, with Pipes, of columns in the *New York Post*; Jay Nordlinger, the managing editor of *National Review*; and Marc Rauch and David Horowitz of FrontPageMagazine.com. Horowitz is the most notorious of the erstwhile 1960s radicals who turned on their former associates with a vengeance.

The source of this group's influence is its connections to powerful political allies and patrons: militaristic nationalists like Secretary of Defense Donald Rumsfeld and Vice President Dick Cheney; the Christian Zionist electoral base of the Republican Party,[4] represented in George W. Bush's administrations by John Ashcroft (attorney general in the first administration), John Bolton (undersecretary of state for arms control and international security in the first administration and nominee for ambassador to the United Nations in the second), Tom DeLay (House of Representatives minority leader in the first administration and majority leader in the second), and the president himself; and military industries that promote the U.S.-Israel alliance as a business asset.

The American Likudniks and their allies have exploited the American people's understandable fears after 9/11 to intimidate and defame ordinary citizens, public figures, university faculty and staff members, and elected officials who have publicly criticized the Bush administration's war on Afghanistan, the prospect of an endless "war on terror," the war on Iraq, and the unprecedented level of U.S. indulgence of Israel's occupation of Palestine and repression of the Palestinian people. Because much of the corporate and even the public mass media has been colonized by conservative talk-show hosts and news commentators while most of the competition has timidly acquiesced, colleges and universities are among the few public institutions where intelligent political discourse remains possible in the United States. Consequently, they have been the object of intense policing to regulate what may be thought and said about the Middle East.

Scholars who study and teach the Middle East and the Muslim world have been singled out as disloyal purveyors of information and analysis detrimental to the national interest. Right-wing pundits have accused the entire Middle East Studies Association of North America (MESA), the largest organization of scholars who study the Middle East, of bearing some measure of responsibility for what befell the United States on September 11 because its members failed to warn the American public about the dangers of radical Islam.

This is not the first time right-wing fanatics have waged a campaign of vilification, guilt by association, guilt by ethnic or religious affiliation, and delegitimization of dissenting opinions. In the early years of the Cold War, the American people were whipped into an anti-Communist frenzy by demagogues led by the infamous Republican senator Joseph McCarthy and the House Committee on Un-American Activities (HUAC). Claiming to find Communist conspiracies in every corner of American life, McCarthy and HUAC conducted modern-day witch hunts in Hollywood, trade unions, the government, and the academy. McCarthy and his minions epitomized the trend in American political thought that conflates dissent with treason and celebrates anti-intellectualism as patriotism.

The McCarthyites deployed fear of a foreign enemy and an unfamiliar ideology to bully the American people into abandoning customary standards of civil liberties, academic freedom, and common sense. Intellectuals who insisted on a realistic analysis of the Soviet Union were decried as traitors; scholars of East Asia, such as Owen Lattimore, were blamed for "losing" China, and some of their careers were ruined.[5] Today, Middle East specialists are being subjected to similar accusations.

There are, of course, important differences between the two historical periods. One of the most salient is that, even if the extent of its aggressive intentions was often wildly inflated, the Soviet Union did have nuclear weapons and therefore the military capacity to destroy the United States. The Cold War was, in part, a struggle for influence between great powers of roughly the same order of magnitude.

Today, American military power is unmatched by any conceivable array of opposing forces. This is one of the reasons for the emergence of international terrorist groups that target the United States. Conventional warfare is not a viable option for them. Even if such groups have received support from states, they remain essentially nonstate actors with limited strategic capacity. Horrific as the terrorist strikes of September 11 were, such attacks cannot erode the commanding military power and political influence of the United States on a global scale. However, failure to understand the causes of such attacks and irresponsible reactions to them can diminish the country's global political standing.

The language and tactics of warfare — as in "war on terror" — impede rather than enhance our capacity to confront this challenge, even more than they did in the era of the Cold War. They easily become justifications for demonizing the world's 1.2 billion Muslims, undermining the democratic rights and physical security of Arab and Muslim Americans, and suspending critical judgment in addressing the crucial issues of war and peace, thus diminishing the credibility of the claim that democracy is superior to any other political system. An exemplary expression of this tendency was the counterdemonstrator at the massive protest march before the opening of the Republican National Convention in New York on August 29, 2004, who carried a poster saying "Islam Supports Kerry."[6]

Another difference is that the Middle East was only a minor factor in public discussion of U.S. foreign policy in the McCarthy era. Since the 1967 Arab-Israeli War, it has become ever more central. Concurrently, unlimited support for Israel emerged as a central component of the political agenda of a new force in American politics: the neoconservative movement.

The conjuncture of the 1967 Arab-Israeli War and the 1968 New York teachers' strike gave birth to neoconservatism. These events broke the alliance between broad sectors of the Jewish and African American communities that had been a salient component of the civil-rights struggles of the 1940s, 1950s, and 1960s. The 1967 war captivated many American Jews. Most of them embraced as never before what they perceived to be a heroic Israel battling for its existence against a genocidal Arab onslaught. A highly romanticized image of Israel, as depicted in Leon Uris's novel *Exodus* and its silver-screen version starring Paul Newman, became a keystone of American Jewish identity and restored Jewish pride after the Holocaust. Many Jews were outraged that some African American leaders and organizations sympathized with the Palestinians and other Arab peoples. The next year, a group of New York teachers, most of whom were Jewish, went on strike to resist demands for control of local schools by the communities where they were located, which were predominantly African American and Hispanic, causing deep and still unhealed rifts between the teachers and the communities.

Misguided concern for Israel and a narrow understanding of American Jewish interests pushed such formerly left-liberal Jews as Norman Podhoretz, the former editor of *Commentary*, Irving Kristol, the founding editor of *Public Interest*, and others to the forefront of the neoconservative movement, tying it closely to militant pro-Israelism. Responding to a fairly low but nonetheless significant level of criticism of Israel's post-1967 policies, the neoconservatives joined national American Jewish organizations in branding Middle East scholars and others with dissident views on the Arab-Israeli conflict "anti-Semites" or "self-hating Jews."[7]

With the outbreak of the second intifada in September 2000 and the installation of the Bush administration a couple of months later, and even more after September 11, such slanders proliferated exponentially, framed by a public discourse of fear, revenge, and crude assertions of American supremacy that made reasoned discussion of the Middle East exceedingly difficult.[8] The American Likudniks and their Christian Zionist allies transformed uncritical support for Israel from a political position into a religious dogma enshrined in public policy. To avoid being seen as allied with the devil, the national Democratic Party and its standard bearers — traditionally inclined to support Israel because of the significance of Jews in the party's base — vied with Republicans in adopting positions on Arab-Israeli matters that were widely considered detached from reality throughout the rest of the world. Yet there was little space in public discourse to suggest that this might have something to do with "why they hate us."

Pressure from private special-interest groups, not the state, as was the case in the 1950s, now represents the most immediate threat to academic freedom and freedom of speech. Since the beginning of the second intifada, alarmed by what they perceive as "the outbreak of anti-Israel activities on a number of campuses across North America," some national Jewish organizations have enhanced their efforts to delimit the boundaries of permissible discussion of the Middle East at colleges and universities. This activity is motivated in large part by a desire to keep eighteen- to twenty-nine-year-old American Jews in the "pro-Israel" camp as

these groups define it. Leaders of these organizations are dis-
tressed that many young Jews "reserve the right to question the
Israeli position" and "reject the notion that all Palestinians and
Muslims support terrorism."[9]

A final distinction between the McCarthy era and the present is
that in the 1950s the U.S. government had no choice but to rely on
research universities as the primary source of expertise on the
Soviet Union and the regions of Asia, Africa, and Latin America
that were contested during the Cold War. Therefore, despite the
general acquiescence of academia with the intellectual and institutional framework of the Cold War, there were occasional opposi-
tional voices, even in some very prominent places. The substantial
role of students and faculty members in the anti–Vietnam War
movement; the defection of most university-based Latin America
specialists from U.S. policy in the Reagan years, if not earlier; similar, if less widespread, defections among Africa and Middle East
specialists; and the "culture wars" of the 1980s and 1990s all
contributed to the rise of think tanks funded by right-wing and
corporate sources designed to constitute alternative sources of
knowledge unconstrained by the standards of peer review, tolerance for dissent, and academic freedom.

In the field of Middle East studies, the Washington Institute for
Near East Policy (WINEP), established in 1985, is undoubtedly the
most influential think tank.[10] Led and funded by people linked to
the American-Israel Public Affairs Committee (AIPAC), the leading Zionist lobbying organization, WINEP rose to prominence when
several of its associates entered the administration of President
George H. W. Bush. During the Clinton years, WINEP-affiliated
figures, most notably the former WINEP executive director Martin Indyk, were prominent managers of the Palestinian-Israeli
"peace process." The chief participant in the peace process of the
1990s, Dennis Ross, became executive director of WINEP after
he left the Clinton administration. In the past, WINEP adopted
the views of whatever Israeli government was in office. Since the
outbreak of the second intifada, support for the Likud has become
the normative "pro-Israel" position. This reflects the structural
shift to the right in many institutions of the American Jewish
community and mirrors developments in Israel, where the Labor
Party has been devastated by its association with the failed 1993
Oslo Accords and 2000 Camp David summit.

Daniel Pipes's Middle East Forum and the Jewish Institute for National Security Affairs promote even more hawkish views on Arab-Israeli matters than WINEP does. However, they are careful to describe their positions as promoting American interests: they support "strong ties with Israel, Turkey, and other democracies as they emerge," "human rights," "a stable supply and a low price of oil," and "the peaceful settlement of regional and international disputes."[11]

Defending Civilization

The effort to muzzle critics of the Bush administration's foreign policy was initially framed as a struggle to defend "Western civilization." The foundational texts of recent currents of civilizational anxiety include Samuel Huntington's widely read (and disputed) writings on "the clash of civilizations," a phrase Huntington lifted from Bernard Lewis — the right wing's emblem of politically correct Middle East scholarship.[12] Defending civilization — "the white man's burden," "*la mission civilisatrice*," or, more ominously, preserving the "purity of the Aryan race" — is a common trope in the array of justifications for militarism and imperial expansion. Representing the stakes as the survival of civilization rather than a debate about public policy leads easily to an alarmist, if not hysterical, tone and highly inflated rhetoric that characterizes those with dissenting views as beyond the pale.

For example, Americans for Victory Over Terrorism (AVOT) impugned the patriotism of anyone who opposed the war on Afghanistan and the Bush administration's foreign policy more generally. AVOT was founded in March 2002 by William Bennett — the former secretary of education and drug czar and the author of *The Book of Virtues*, an especially hypocritical moralist tract in view of the exposure of his addiction to gambling.[13] AVOT began as a subsidiary of the Project for the New American Century, a think tank distinguished, since its establishment in 1997, by its promotion of a U.S. war on Iraq in alliance with the now-discredited Ahmad Chalabi. It subsequently migrated to the conservative Claremont Institute. The principal funder of AVOT is Lawrence Kadish, the former chairman of the Republican Jewish Coalition, which seeks to bring Jews into the Republican Party.[14] Kadish has been one of the largest individual contributors to the Republican Party since George H.W. Bush became president; he is also a supporter of the Likud and of the construction of the illegal Har Homa (Jabal Abu Ghneim) settlement near Jerusalem, and a critic of the Oslo Accords.[15]

Bennett launched AVOT with an open letter in the *New York Times* describing the external and internal threats to the United States. According to the letter, the external threat comprised "radical Islamists and others," and the internal threat consisted of "those who are attempting to use this opportunity to promulgate their agenda of 'blame America first.'" AVOT's list of internal enemies included former President Jimmy Carter, whose offense was to criticize the notion of an "axis of evil" that President Bush advanced in his 2002 State of the Union address as "overly simplistic" and "counter-productive." Other internal enemies included the Democratic congressional representative and former presidential candidate Dennis Kucinich, of Cleveland, and the Democratic representative Maxine Waters, of Los Angeles.[16]

Defending civilization was also the theme of the first organized post–September 11 attempt to enforce the Bush administration's foreign-policy agenda by attacking critical thinking about the Middle East. In November 2001, the American Council of Trustees and Alumni (ACTA) issued a report titled "Defending Civilization: How Our Universities Are Failing America and What Can Be Done About It."[17] As the title suggests, ACTA maintained that criticism of the war in Afghanistan on campuses across the country was tantamount to undermining civilization and proof that American universities were "failing." ACTA argued that American universities had been brought to this sorry state by inadequate (meaning insufficiently celebratory) teaching of Western culture and American history. Consequently, students and faculty members did not understand what was at stake in the fight against terrorism and were impeding the defense of civilization by asking too many questions.

ACTA was co-founded by Lynne Cheney, the wife of Vice President Dick Cheney and a fellow of the American Enterprise Institute, a think tank that has enthusiastically supported the Middle East policy of the Bush administration. Former Democratic vice-presidential candidate and senator Joseph Lieberman, one of the most conservative voices in his party, was a member of ACTA's national council. Although she was no longer officially active in ACTA when the 2001 report was released, a lengthy passage by Ms. Cheney was quoted on its cover, giving the document the appearance of a quasi-official statement of government policy.

The original version of "Defending Civilization" named and quoted comments made by 117 university faculty and staff members and students in reaction to the September 11 attacks. ACTA's ire was aroused by my statement, "If Usama Bin Laden is confirmed to be behind the attacks, the United States should bring him before an international tribunal on charges of crimes against humanity."[18] Other remarks in the report's list of unacceptable statements included "Ignorance breeds hate" and "[T]here needs to be an understanding of why this kind of suicidal violence could be undertaken against our country."

ACTA's attack on American universities in the name of "defending civilization" was as much about suppressing any form of dissent from the military response to the September 11 attacks as it was about defending a traditional approach to teaching U.S. history. By smearing those who attempted to debate the efficacy of a war against Afghanistan and compiling a list of those who did not scrupulously follow the Bush administration, ACTA revealed its affinity with the McCarthyite tradition in American political life. After receiving considerable criticism for resuscitating the blacklist so infamously deployed in the McCarthy era, ACTA removed the names from the report's appendix but left the quotes and the institutions. Some of those named in the ACTA report were teachers and students of the Middle East and Central Asia. But like AVOT, ACTA did not discriminate by specifically targeting them in its effort to quash free speech and political debate. ACTA is an equal-opportunity defamer and considers anyone who criticizes the Bush administration's foreign policy an enemy of civilization.

Area Studies and Un-American Scholarship in the Age of Empire

The American Likudniks assumed responsibility for launching a more focused assault on Middle East scholars. The gist of their attack on Middle East scholars is that the Middle East Studies Association has been taken over by a crowd of postcolonial-studies/postmodernist extremists inspired by the late Edward Said's book *Orientalism*. These un-American radicals, they claim, have imposed an intellectual and political orthodoxy on the study of Islam and the Middle East. Martin Kramer's *Ivory Towers on Sand:*

The Failure of Middle Eastern Studies in America is the fullest expression of this argument. Kramer argues that Edward Said is responsible for what went wrong in American Middle East studies, and a good deal else besides.[19]

Why Kramer is so focused on Edward Said is unclear. Perhaps it is because Bernard Lewis, who exemplifies the style of scholarship that Said disparaged, was Kramer's teacher at Princeton University. In addition, Lewis is, along with P.J. Vatikiotis and the late Elie Kedourie, an intellectual patron of Tel Aviv University's Moshe Dayan Center for Middle Eastern and African Studies, a research center with ties to the Israeli diplomatic and military establishment. Kramer is a former director of the Moshe Dayan Center.

Said and Lewis had an ugly exchange in the *New York Review of Books* instigated by Lewis's harsh review of *Orientalism*.[20] Subsequently, Said overwhelmed Lewis in a public debate on the topic "The Scholars, the Media, and the Middle East" held at the annual MESA meeting in November 1986.[21] But Said was never a regular presence at MESA and did not even belong to the organization until he was made an honorary fellow in 1999. His appearance at its 1986 annual meeting was his first. He did not return until 1998, when he attended a plenary session dedicated to assessing the impact of *Orientalism* twenty years after its publication. Kramer attended that session and objected to its purpose in a manner that many in the audience, including myself, considered unprofessional and intemperate.

Said's *Orientalism* certainly did influence American Middle East studies, and rightly so. It is an important and intellectually impressive work. But it is not without flaws, and it was not received uncritically. Nor did it rule out other approaches and understandings of the Middle East. Kramer's claim that the wholesale adoption of Said's views by the leading members of MESA led to the failure of the entire edifice of American Middle East studies is contradicted by his own evidence. He cites a critical review of *Orientalism* published by the late Malcolm Kerr, a former MESA president, in MESA's *International Journal of Middle East Studies* — the leading scholarly journal in the field.[22] Kramer also quotes the former MESA president Nikki Keddie, who wrote that while *Orientalism* was "important and in many ways positive," it had had "some unfortunate consequences," among them that "Orientalism for many people is a word that substitutes for thought and enables people to dismiss certain scholars and their works.... It may not have been what Edward Said meant at all, but the term has become a kind of slogan."[23] These critical comments by former MESA presidents whose scholarship is highly regarded by their peers demonstrate that there are no orthodoxy regarding and no wholesale adoption of Said's ideas.

Kramer explicitly denigrates several scholars whose approach to modern Islam he deems faulty: John Esposito, John Voll, Richard Bulliet, and Fawaz Gerges. But a fair reading of their work reveals that, while they differ from Kramer's understanding of modern Islamic movements, their work does not reflect any significant intellectual influence of Edward Said, cultural studies, postcolonialism, or postmodernism — all things Kramer abhors. Similarly, Kramer pours scorn on Roger Owen, Philip Khoury, Robert Fernea, Elizabeth Warnock Fernea, Michael Hudson, Rashid Khalidi, and Augustus R. Norton for their interpretations of modern Arab politics. But, with the partial exception of Khalidi's *Palestinian Identity: The Construction of Modern National Consciousness*, their rather traditional, empiricist methods are also little influenced by Edward Said.[24] What is common to all these scholars is that, despite the variety of their work and their negligible affinities to post-anything, they are more critical of Israeli policy toward the Palestinians than the views commonly presented in the U.S. mass media and certainly more than Kramer and others like him are willing to tolerate.

The Israel Connection and Its History
The unstated, but never entirely concealed, agenda of shielding Israel from criticism links the post–September 11 campaign to monitor teaching and research on the Middle East to earlier efforts initiated after the 1967 Arab-Israeli War. The following narrative represents only the tip of a phenomenon that few have been willing to discuss publicly because doing so invites precisely the accusations of anti-Semitism or self-hatred that one seeks to discredit. After the 1967 war, the American Jewish Committee (AJC), whose mission includes "strengthen[ing] the basic principles of pluralism around the world, as the best defense against anti-Semitism and other forms of bigotry,"[25] the Anti-Defamation League (ADL), whose purpose is to expose and combat anti-Semitism, and AIPAC sounded alarms about the increasing influence of

"Arab propaganda" on university campuses and began to monitor the activities of students and teachers they considered "anti-Israel." They frequently suggested that criticism of Israel and Zionism bordered on or was equivalent to anti-Semitism.

During the 1970s, public criticism of Israel and Zionism increased, in large measure due to the activities of the newly formed Association of Arab-American University Graduates, Noam Chomsky, and a handful of others. However, it remained primarily limited to the academy. Even in colleges and universities, few non-Arab teachers or students had the mettle to face the scurrilous slanders routinely directed at those who opposed Israel's occupation of the West Bank, the Gaza Strip, the Sinai Peninsula, and the Golan Heights and supported the Palestinian people's right to self-determination. This began to change when Menachem Begin became the first Likud prime minister of Israel in 1977. The central component of the Likud, the former Herut Party, emerged out of the pre-1948 Irgun Zeva'i Le'umi, or National Military Organization (known by its Hebrew abbreviation, Etzel), commanded by Begin. The Etzel was considered a terrorist organization by both the British and mainstream Zionists. The expansion of Israeli settlements in the West Bank during the Begin regime (1977–83) signaled that occupation and annexation might become a long-term affair. Some Palestinian leaders in the occupied territories and abroad began to seek Israeli and Jewish partners for a struggle against Begin's policies. This posed a substantial threat to the likes of the AJC, the ADL, and AIPAC because it reduced the credibility of the charge of anti-Semitism aimed at critics of Israel. These and other American Jewish organizations who had adopted protecting Israel from criticism as their mission responded with a renewed campaign on college campuses.

One of the initial public sorties reflecting this more aggressive posture came from the Tucson Jewish Community Council. In 1981, the council charged that the outreach program (that is, activities aimed at the general public and K–12 teachers) of the University of Arizona's Near Eastern Center and its coordinator were guilty of anti-Israel bias.[26] An external investigating committee dismissed the charge. Unsatisfied with this outcome, the American Jewish Committee commissioned Gary S. Schiff to prepare a report surveying centers for Middle East studies at several universities. The Schiff report expressed concern about "possible bias in outreach programs dealing with the controversial issues that surround the Middle East." Schiff considered it ominous that federally funded fellowships were not available for the study of Hebrew, as they were for Arabic, Turkish, and Farsi because the U.S. government did not define Hebrew as a "critical language" (that is, a less commonly taught language whose study should be encouraged to enhance national security). Rather than draw the obvious conclusion that the government believed there was already an adequate number of Hebrew speakers in the U.S., he implied that some form of discrimination might be at work. Finally, Schiff was troubled about funding contributions from Arab states to centers for Middle East studies at universities such as Princeton and Georgetown. In retrospect, this seems ridiculous in the case of Princeton, which has had the reputation of being the most "pro-Israel" program in Middle East studies for the last quarter century. Schiff did not express any concern about the potentially deleterious effects of Jewish funding for chairs in Jewish studies.[27]

In November 1983, the New England regional office of the Anti-Defamation League, reacting to increased criticism of Israel following its invasion of Lebanon in 1982, distributed a booklet designed "to help Jewish students deal with anti-Zionist and anti-Semitic activities on college campus[es]."[28] Once again, there was no clear distinction between the two. The booklet lists "anti-Israel" organizations and individuals, with an emphasis on those in New England and northern California. The same year the national office of the ADL published *Pro-Arab Propaganda in America: Vehicles and Voices, A Handbook.* These were the first efforts to compile lists of university faculty and staff members whose opinions were not in accord with Zionist doctrine. They were not the last.

In 1983, a London monthly, *The Middle East,* reported: "AIPAC puts a lot of effort into monitoring anti-Israel speakers. Tapes and notes are collected and files compiled."[29] In 1984, AIPAC produced a 187-page college guide whose objective was to "expos[e] the anti-Israel campaign on campus."[30] A twelve-page questionnaire filled out by students (presumably those sympathetic to AIPAC's worldview) who volunteered to do so provided the basis for the information in the guide. Students were invited to "name any individual faculty who assist anti-Israel groups. How is this assistance offered? (If there is a Middle East Study Center, please elaborate on its impact on campus.)"[31]

MESA responded to these activities on the part of the ADL and AIPAC at its 1984 annual meeting, by passing, after a hot debate, a resolution describing the ADL and AIPAC's publications as "factually inaccurate and unsubstantiated" and "unbalanced." The resolution called on the ADL and AIPAC to "disavow and refrain from such activities."[32] This highly unusual and politically charged resolution signalled that a majority of MESA's most active members were no longer intimidated by the threat of being labeled anti-Semites when discussing the Arab-Israeli conflict. Thus MESA became a dubious institution for American Jewish organizations — such as the ADL and AIPAC — whose identity and status depend largely on uncritical support for Israel.

It is worth noting that the ADL, AIPAC, and organizations like them do not, in fact, speak for the majority of Jews in the United States. About half of American Jews belong to no Jewish organization whatsoever, some of them precisely because they do not wish to be associated with uncritical support for Israel. This phenomenon, which is especially pronounced among young Jews, prompted a major research effort to improve "Israel messaging," conducted by the Republican pollster Frank Luntz and funded primarily by the Andrea and Charles Bronfman Philanthropies. The resulting report, *Israel in the Age of Eminem: A Creative Brief for Israel Messaging*, argues that "Most traditional communications and marketing strategies are not reaching the vast majority of young Jews.... Strategies are relied upon that have worked in decades past, incorporating poor aesthetics, the use of long, detailed lists, one-sided sloganeering, overtly religious messages, and an assumption of a love of Israel. It will take new strategies and new tactics to engage this audience." The closest Luntz comes to considering the possibility that it may be Israel's actual policies that alienate young American Jews is acknowledging that "they reserve the right to question the Israeli position."[33]

The ADL went beyond merely monitoring institutions and individuals it considered "anti-Israel," "anti-Semitic," or both.[34] In April 1993, the San Francisco police seized over ten thousand files from the ADL's local office. They had been compiled from information provided by Roy Bullock, who had worked as a "fact finder" for the ADL since the 1960s. Bullock sold information to the ADL, the South African intelligence agency, and possibly the Israeli Mossad, and he occasionally worked for the FBI. He compiled dossiers on some ten thousand individuals and six hundred organizations labeled "pinkos," "right," "Arabs," "skins," and "ANC" (after the African National Congress). Among those subjected to surveillance were the San Francisco Labor Council, International Longshore Workers Union Local 10, the Oakland Educational Association, the National Association for the Advancement of Colored People, Irish Northern Aid, the International Indian Treaty Council, the faculty of Mills College, and the Asian Law Caucus. The San Francisco police department estimated that 75 percent of Bullock's information was obtained illegally. A police officer, Tom Gerard, had supplied Bullock with confidential information about his targets for an $8,000 fee. Gerard was indicted for illegal use of a police computer in 1994 and fled to the Philippines. The *San Francisco Chronicle* reports: "Ultimately, he pleaded no contest to a misdemeanor charge of illegally accessing government information."[35] The ADL made out-of-court cash settlements with the city of San Francisco, the Arab-American Anti-Discrimination Committee, and three individuals.

Notwithstanding the illegal overzealousness of the San Francisco office of the ADL, from the mid–1980s until the September 11 terrorist attacks, there were only sporadic efforts to defame individual Middle East scholars who were critical of Israel and the U.S.'s Middle East policy. An unknown number of professorial appointments and promotions was tainted by political pressure. Some department chairs, deans, and program directors were subjected to regular phone calls or letters from "supporters of Israel" complaining about the activities of faculty members under their supervision. But partly because of MESA's resistance to the agenda of the ADL and AIPAC, and partly because after the first intifada it became increasingly difficult to promote an uncritical view of Israel, there was no concerted campaign.

The New Campaign Against Freedom of Speech on Campus

The publication of Kramer's *Ivory Towers on Sand* by the Washington Institute for Near East Policy heralded the beginning of such a campaign and a new phase in the efforts to subject critical thinking in the field of Middle East studies to surveillance. Kramer and others like him were emboldened by their links to senior Bush administration officials, such as Richard Perle, the former chair of the Defense Policy Board; Paul Wolfowitz, the former Deputy Secretary of Defense; Douglas Feith, the former undersecretary of defense; and Elliott Abrams, the deputy national security advisor for global democracy. All were affiliated with WINEP, the Jewish Institute for National Security Affairs, the Project for the New American Century, and other conservative think tanks whose ambit extends beyond the Middle East.

Kramer and his allies have several assets that were unavailable to the AJC, the ADL, and AIPAC for their campaigns of defamation in the early 1980s, which largely failed to silence criticism of Israel and the U.S.'s Middle East policy in American universities. They have much more powerful political connections in the executive branch. September 11 and the wars against Afghanistan and Iraq rendered the Middle East a more prominent topic in public culture, albeit largely in a caricatured form, than ever before. Finally, the Internet enabled Kramer and his fellow travelers to reach a much broader audience.

The notorious Campus Watch Web site, established by Daniel Pipes, purports, in language removed from the site after it aroused a storm of criticism of its blatantly McCarthyite character, to "monitor and gather information on professors who fan the flames of disinformation, incitement, and ignorance."[36] Campus Watch declares that Middle East scholars "seem generally to dislike their own country and think even less of American allies abroad. They portray U.S. policy in an unfriendly light and disparage allies." The site also asserts, "Middle East Studies in the United States has become the preserve of Middle Eastern Arabs, who have brought their views with them. Membership in the Middle East Studies Association (MESA), the main scholarly association, is now 50 percent of Middle Eastern origin." Therefore, MESA is, Campus Watch implies, an unpatriotic and not truly American organization.

These assertions are false and brazenly bigoted. Expressing dissent from prevailing foreign policy is no indication of whether one likes the United States. Such dissent is in the tradition of democratic patriotism and has occasionally succeeded in mobilizing the public to correct catastrophic policy failures, such as the war in Vietnam. The majority of MESA members are not of Middle Eastern origin, and it would be of no consequence if they were. Casting aspersions on scholars, or anyone else for that matter, because of their national origin violates the fundamental spirit of American liberties and undermines the distinctive character of the United States as an immigrant society. The racist language in Campus Watch's statement of purpose is not a one-time slip of the tongue. Pipes has described Muslim immigrants to western Europe, in ambiguous language suggesting that he may or may not endorse such a description, as "brown-skinned peoples cooking strange foods and maintaining different standards of hygiene." He continues: "Muslim customs are more troublesome than most."[37]

In spring 2003, despite extensive opposition from a broad spectrum of individuals and organizations, including some Jewish groups, President Bush nominated Pipes to a seat on the board of directors of the federally funded United States Institute of Peace, whose mission is to sponsor research promoting peaceful conflict resolution. The president and his advisers appeared to make it a matter of principle to ignore the opposition to Pipes's nomination, but the Senate Committee on Health, Education, Labor, and Pensions declined to approve it. Nonetheless, the president partly had his way by appointing Pipes after the Senate had adjourned for the summer. Thus Pipes served on the board, but for less than a full term. This episode indicated that what had begun as an apparently arcane debate among scholars had assumed national political significance.

In June 2003, Stanley Kurtz testified before the House Committee on Education and the Workforce that "Title VI–funded programs in Middle Eastern Studies (and other area studies) tend to purvey extreme and one-sided criticisms of American foreign policy."[38] He urged legislators to take action to ensure "balance." Representative Peter Hoekstra obliged by using the occasion of the reauthorization of Title VI funding to introduce a bill called the International Studies in Higher Education Act (HR 3077).[39] The bill passed the House of Representatives unanimously in October 2003. However, the Senate Committee on Health, Education, Labor, and Pensions, emboldened by staunch opposition to the bill from senior Democratic Senators Kennedy and Harkin, did not report it to the full Senate, and the resolution died in committee. However, it resurfaced in the 109th Congress as HR 509. The promoters of this effort to disregard normal standards of academic freedom and freedom of speech seem likely to persist. This effort to limit scholarship, teaching, and public discussion of the Middle East is worth examining because it is representative of their agenda and tactics.

Title VI of the National Defense Education Act of 1958 and the Higher Education Act of 1965 provide about $95 million for graduate fellowships, language training and community outreach to one hundred eighteen centers for regional area studies. To this routine funding reauthorization, HR 3077 appended a proposal to establish the International Higher Education Advisory Board, which would have investigative powers "to study, monitor, apprise [*sic*] and evaluate" activities supported by Title VI. This advisory board would be charged with ensuring that government-funded academic programs "reflect diverse perspectives and represent the full range of views" on international affairs.[40] Three board members would be appointed by the Secretary of Education; two of those would represent government agencies with national security responsibilities (the CIA, the FBI, the Department of Homeland Security, and so on). The leaders of the House of Representatives and the Senate would each appoint two more.

As HR 3077's active supporters accepted Stanley Kurtz's contention that Middle East studies was dominated by an anti-America, anti-Israel cabal, it was clear that "diverse perspectives" in this context was code for limited criticism of American Middle East policy and of Israel. The bill was not motivated by concern about the activities of centers for Latin American or East Asian studies. The International Studies in Higher Education Act would have immediately affected only the seventeen federally funded national resource centers for Middle East studies at American universities. This is clearly a dangerous precedent that portends the possibility of direct government interference in teaching, public programs, and research.

Just as dangerous, but more immediately efficacious, was the private initiative of the Ford and Rockefeller foundations to add restrictive language to their grant stipulations. In January 2004, the Ford Foundation announced that it would withdraw funding from any university grantee that expended funds of any provenance to promote "violence, terrorism, or bigotry or the destruction of any State." The Rockefeller Foundation required that its grantees not "directly or indirectly engage in, promote or support other organizations or individuals who engage in or promote terrorist activity."[41] For the uninitiated, such language might seem

bizarre. What American university would actually promote terrorism? Is it plausible that previous Ford and Rockefeller grantees
did so? What activities would be covered by this language? If a
Palestinian student group called for the replacement of the state
of Israel with a secular, democratic state, would that constitute
calling for "the destruction of any State" and thereby threaten its
university's Ford Foundation grants?

This new language was a response to sensationalized reporting by the Jewish Telegraphic Agency news service and the Jewish
weekly *Forward*. Those organizations and their allies in Congress
— Representative Jerrold Nadler and Senator Charles Grassley —
claimed that the Ford Foundation had funnelled money to "anti-
Israel activity," for example by paying for Palestinian nongovernmental organizations to attend the 2001 World Conference
Against Racism, Racial Discrimination, Xenophobia and Related
Intolerance, in Durban, which adopted a resolution critical of
Israel, and that it had indirectly funded terrorist organizations.[42]
The Ford Foundation has funded several Palestinian NGOs, as
well as Rabbis for Human Rights, B'Tselem (The Israeli Information Center for Human Rights in the Occupied Territories), and
the New Israel Fund, for years. Because of the rightward drift of
American Jewish organizations, even funding Israeli human-rights
organizations — let alone Palestinian organizations of any sort —
is a suspect activity. In late 2003, the ADL, the AJC, and other
influential forces in the organized Jewish community, supported
by the *New York Sun*, whose editorial policy is unwavering support
for Israel, directed a sustained barrage of charges of anti-Semitism
against the Ford Foundation and made recommendations to the
foundation on its new policy. The new Ford and Rockefeller grant
language represented a capitulation to this attack out of fear of
being labeled anti-Semitic, a charge to which the Ford Foundation is particularly sensitive because its founder *was* a well-known
anti-Semite.

In April 2004, Roger Bowen, the general secretary of the
American Association of University Professors, and a prestigious
group of major research universities — Harvard, Yale, Princeton,
Cornell, Columbia, Stanford, the University of Pennsylvania,
Massachusetts Institute of Technology, and the University of Chicago — wrote letters to the Ford and Rockefeller foundations objecting to the new language and arguing that it violated "the basic

principle of protected speech on our campuses."[43] The letters implied that the universities might refrain from applying for Ford or Rockefeller grants if the language was not altered. Columbia and the University of Chicago delayed accepting new Ford Foundation grants, and the University of Michigan expressed its reservations and sought to insert a clause in its agreement with Ford stipulating that the new language was not meant to curtail academic freedom.

As the American Association of University Professors reports, "in July [2004], Susan Berresford, president of the Ford Foundation, responded to Bowen's letter, assuring him that the foundation does 'not intend to interfere with the speech of faculty.' She added, 'Our grant letter relates to the official speech of the university and to speech that the university explicitly endorses.'"[44] At the time of this writing, the final language of the grant acceptance letters was undetermined.

After lengthy negotiations, the foundations retreated from a broad interpretation of their new funding guidelines and explicitly endorsed academic freedom and open debate. But even though the Ford and Rockefeller foundations relented to some extent, the experience has had a chilling effect, because it demonstrated that they could be intimidated by unfounded accusations of anti-Semitism. Program officers have become more cautious and spent more time demonstrating their bona fides. Some grants that would once have passed with little difficulty have not been made for what appear to be political reasons. The entire affair has become part of the architecture of the constraints on university campuses and in intellectual circles more broadly regarding Middle East issues.

"The New Anti-Semitism"

Academic freedom and open debate on Middle East–related issues were very badly served by the widely reported remarks of Harvard University President Lawrence Summers, who was the Secretary of the Treasury in the Clinton administration. At the start of the 2002–2003 academic year, addressing a student prayer meeting, he stated that harsh criticisms of Israel were "anti-Semitic in their effect if not their intent."[45] Summers was referring to a petition signed by six hundred Harvard and MIT faculty and staff members and students calling on the university to divest its funds from companies doing business in Israel, as a protest against Israel's continuing occupation of the West Bank, the Gaza Strip, and East Jerusalem.

Similar efforts with different formulations of the target were subsequently launched at over forty colleges and universities. A year later, two Catholic orders — the Sisters of Loretto and the Sisters of Mercy of Detroit — filed a shareholder resolution asking the Caterpillar Corporation to investigate the misuse of its equipment by the Israeli armed forces, who have employed Caterpillar bulldozers to destroy Palestinian homes and orchards and to kill American peace activist Rachel Corrie.[46] The Catholic groups were asked to file the resolution by the California-based group Jewish Voice for Peace. The resolution failed but received 4 percent of the vote at the April 2004 annual meeting of the Caterpillar Corporation — a very high number for a measure opposed by the board of directors.[47] On July 2, 2004, the General Assembly of the Presbyterian Church (USA) voted to start "phased and selective divestment of its nearly $8 billion portfolio from select companies that profit from sales of products or services that cause harm to Palestinians or Israelis or both."[48] Following in the footsteps of the Presbyterians, on February 21, 2005, the central committee of the World Council of Churches, which represents more than three hundred forty churches, denominations, and fellowships in over one hundred countries and territories, recommended a policy of "phased, selective divestment from multinational corporations involved in the [Israeli] occupation" of the West Bank and the Gaza Strip to encourage peace between Israel and Palestine.[49] In May 2005, *Ekklesia* reported that the Church of England's "Ethical Investment Advisory Group will be examining whether the £197,000 of shares currently held in Caterpillar are consistent with the Church's ethical investment policy, which prohibits investment in arms companies or companies making 'weapons platforms' such as naval vessels or tanks."[50]

In the face of the willingness of such a broad range of religious and political organizations and individuals to consider some form of divestment from corporations that do business in Israel as a means to protest the Israeli occupation of the West Bank, the Gaza Strip, and East Jerusalem and to hasten peace, Lawrence Summers's effort to shut down these protests by dismissing them as anti-Semitic has no intellectual basis. One need not support the substance of such demands for divestment to discern the difference between anti-Semitism and even the most vehement criticism of Israel. Whatever one thinks of demands for divestment, they are directed at specific policies of the state of Israel and are not inherently anti-Semitic.[51]

Nevertheless, arguments to the contrary by the president of one of the country's most prestigious institutions of higher learning and the weak-kneed response to intimidation by the Ford and Rockefeller foundations seem to have authorized others to go on the political offensive without fear of being criticized as boorish enemies of academic freedom. Campus Watch, the *New York Sun*, the Democratic candidate for mayor of New York Anthony Weiner, and several Jewish organizations raised a storm of protest when Columbia University named Rashid Khalidi to a newly established endowed chair, making him the Edward Said Professor of Arab Studies. This eventually escalated to a broad attack on the entire Department of Middle East and Asian Languages and Cultures. The tendentious claims of the university's critics were exemplified by the campus Hillel rabbi's concern that Jewish students "felt a 'slant' against Israel both in the classroom and in extracurricular activities."[52]

It is unclear why students' emotional reaction to information or analysis presented in a classroom has any bearing on its factual accuracy or intellectual legitimacy. Undoubtedly, many white student supporters of Jim Crow practices at universities throughout the American South in the 1960s were distressed to learn that these practices were illegal and despised by many Americans. This did not make them any less so. And university administrations have no business interfering with legal extracurricular student activities.

While Columbia's administration stood firm on Khalidi's appointment, in late 2004 the university president Lee Bollinger capitulated to pressure from the same circles by appointing an ad hoc grievance committee to look into charges of intimidation of Jewish students and anti-Semitism among professors of Middle East studies, based on an unreleased documentary, *Columbia Unbecoming*, produced by a pro-Israel propaganda organization, the David Project. The primary target of the campaign was the professor Joseph Massad. The committee report, released on March 31, 2005, cleared the Department of Middle East and Asian Languages and Cultures and the accused professors of all charges. The sole exception, based on tendentious evidence contradicted by eyewitnesses, was the allegation that in one instance Professor Massad exceeded the "commonly accepted bounds" of behavior.[53]

Nonetheless, newspapers across the spectrum of opinion, from the *New York Sun* to the *Village Voice* to the *New York Times*, criticized Columbia for conducting a whitewash.[54] The *New York Times* editorial, while agreeing that the evidence provided to the ad hoc committee "seem[s] to indicate that the controversy ... has been overblown," added that the panel's mandate should have included "the quality and fairness of teaching" because "most student complaints were not really about intimidation, but about allegations of stridently pro-Palestinian, anti-Israeli bias on the part of several professors." In other words, the *New York Times* called on university administrations to vet courses for their political content.

Politically motivated groups, using evidence that was not made available to the public, pressured a major university into investigating its faculty based on criteria completely alien to academic procedures. Most of those who complained about professors were not students in their classes (and some were not students at all). As the Ad Hoc Report notes, some faculty members apparently recruited students to spy on their colleagues. But this was of less concern to the New York media than Columbia's failure to prevent the teaching of courses critical of Israel, irrespective of the scholarly validity of the courses' content.

One reason that such violations of standards of free speech, academic freedom, and normal academic procedures has been tolerated is that the Anti-Defamation League, the Zionist Organization of America, the American Jewish Committee, and the Hillel foundation (the parent body of the largest Jewish student organization) have sought to convince federal legislators and others that there is a wave of anti-Semitism on American campuses. If this were the case, then perhaps it would be justifiable to bend academic norms to stem the tide.

The ADL's annual audit of anti-Semitic activity in America detected a 24 percent increase in anti-Semitic activities on U.S. college campuses in 2002.[55] However, the entire increase in incidents of anti-Semitism on U.S. campuses, according to the ADL's own statistics, amounted to twenty-one actions. Among these were several high-profile incidents, most of them motivated by opposition to Israel's policies toward the Palestinians. Paradoxically, by failing to make a clear distinction between anti-Semitism, which should always and everywhere be opposed, and anti-Zionism, which is a legitimate political opinion, the ADL and like-minded organizations exposed American Jews to attack by identifying them with Israel and its policies.

In spring 2003, several Republican senators and their aides met with representatives of the ADL, the American Jewish Committee, the Zionist Organization of America, and Hillel. Shortly thereafter, the third-ranking Republican member of the U.S. Senate, Rick Santorum, announced that he planned to introduce so-called ideological diversity legislation that would cut federal funding to colleges and universities that permitted professors, students, and student organizations to openly criticize Israel. Like the ADL and some other organizations that purport to represent American Jews, Santorum considers criticism of Israel equivalent to anti-Semitism. Santorum did not formulate his announcement into a bill by the end of 108th Congressional session.[56]

The Politics of Diversity

The activities of AVOT, ACTA, Martin Kramer, Daniel Pipes, Stanley Kurtz, Campus Watch, the ADL, and the AJC bear the marks of a concerted campaign. The principals are committed to Ariel Sharon's understanding of the Middle East, the core proposition of which, in the post–September 11 period, is that the late Yasser Arafat and the Palestinian Authority were equivalent to Osama bin Laden and al-Qa'eda. George W. Bush clearly embraced that view. The effect of this campaign has been to open the door to a host of political initiatives that imperil free discussion of the Middle East and potentially much more.

Most of the people who have attacked the Middle East Studies Association and other Middle East policy dissidents spend their days in think tanks, where they hobnob with foreign-policy makers and mass-media opinion makers. They mainly write Op-Eds and policy think pieces. They do not, for the most part, engage in the primary recognized activities of scholars: teaching and research. But having failed to win in the marketplace of ideas, these people seek to use the power of the state to suppress wayward thinking. In doing so, they have claimed to advocate balance and diversity — things no reasonable person would oppose. But these are relative, and therefore political, terms. The center of any debate depends on where the margins are drawn. If committed fanatics prepared to employ unscrupulous tactics are permitted to drive political discourse to the extreme right, as they have attempted to do in the name of balance, then the center will have been completely redefined. This, of course, has long been the objective of those who brought the Bush administration to power and applies to issues well beyond Middle East policy.

Consequently, this is a political fight, not merely a scholarly debate. The battle for ideas is surely a component of this struggle, but academic freedom is likely to be severely attenuated if the professoriat restricts itself to that arena. Even if they act only in self-defense, students and scholars who want to preserve their right to think, speak, and write critically about the Middle East, and potentially much more, need to expose those who assault our liberties and take the case for academic freedom and freedom of speech to the public.

There are good reasons to expect that such a struggle can be won. There is no case on record in which an investigation of university teaching on the Middle East has actually revealed substantial bias. The investigations of the University of Arizona and Columbia University affirmed the propriety of the behavior of the faculty members concerned in all essential respects. The only thing the American Likudniks have been able to demonstrate conclusively is that they do not agree with the views of many scholars of the Middle East. Given the debacle in Iraq, which the advice of Bernard Lewis and others scholars of his bent were influential in promoting and justifying, it might be reasonable to conclude that such thinkers' knowledge of the modern Middle East is less useful than that of the scholars they disparage.[57]

NOTES

1. An earlier version of this essay was published as "The New American McCarthyism: Policing Thought About the Middle East," *Race and Class* 46.1 (2004), pp. 101–15.

2. Martin S. Kramer, *Ivory Towers on Sand: The Failure of Middle Eastern Studies in America* (Washington, D.C.: Washington Institute for Near East Policy, 2001).

3. See these reviews of Daniel Pipes's work: Ira M. Lapidus, review of *Slave Soldiers and Islam: Genesis of a Military System, Journal of Interdisciplinary History* 12.4 (1982), pp. 716–18; Fred Halliday, review of *In the Path of God: Islam and Political Power, Political Science Quarterly* 99.3 (1984), pp.583–84; Bryan S. Turner, "State, Religion, and Minority Status: A Review Article," *Comparative Studies in Society and History* 27.2 (1985), pp. 304–11; Raymond Hinnebusch, review of *Greater Syria: The History of an Ambition, American Historical Review* 96.5 (1991), p. 1589; Mary C. Wilson, review of *Greater Syria: The History of an Ambition, British Journal of Middle Eastern Studies* 20.2 (1993), pp. 256–57; and Sussan Siavoshi, review of *The Hidden Hand: Middle East Fears of Conspiracy, International Journal of Middle East Studies* 30.2 (1998), pp. 272–74. See also Roger Hardy's review of Martin Kramer, *Arab Awakening and Islamic Revival: The Politics of Ideas in the Middle East, International Affairs* 73.1 (1997), pp. 191–92.

4. Christian Zionism denotes a current of evangelical Protestantism that views the state of Israel as the forerunner of the reestablishment of the Kingdom of David and a herald of the second coming of Christ. According to this belief system, Israel must be supported absolutely, especially in its claims to the biblical territories of the West Bank and East Jerusalem, because the Jews must possess all the land promised by God before Christ can return. The major Christian Zionist political organizations are the Christian Coalition of America, founded by Pat Robertson; the Moral Majority, founded by Jerry Falwell; the Unity Coalition for Israel, which claims to represent forty million people; the Religious Roundtable, led by Ed McAteer; and Stand for Israel, co-founded by Ralph Reed.

5. The best history of McCarthyism is Ellen Schrecker, *Many Are the Crimes: McCarthyism in America* (Boston: Little, Brown, 1998). On scholars and the "loss" of China, see Robert P. Newman, *Owen Lattimore and the "Loss" of China* (Berkeley: University of California Press, 1992).

6. I observed the counterdemonstrator on the corner of Seventh Avenue and 34th Street.

7. I have been called a self-hater too many times to remember since I returned to the United States in 1973 after living in Israel. A recent and extraordinarily excessive example of this form of attack is the Self-Hating and/or Israel Threatening List, which lists nearly seven thousand disapproved Jews. See http://www.masada2000.org/shit-list.html.

8. Of course there are anti-Semites among those who criticize Israel and American Middle East policy — neo-Nazis, supporters of the Aryan Nation, and so on — and many radical Islamic groups deploy anti-Semitic language and imagery, much of it derived from European political discourses. But accusations of anti-Semitism or self-hatred directed at prominent critics of American

Middle East policy, such as the late Edward Said, Rashid Khalidi, Naseer Aruri, Noam Chomsky, Phyllis Bennis, Tony Judt, Barbara Lubin, Zachary Lockman, and Stephen Zunes, are totally baseless.

9. Frank Luntz, *Israel in the Age of Eminem: A Creative Brief for Israel Messaging* (Andrea and Charles Bronfman Philanthropies, March 2003), pp. 3, 7, 16.

10. Joel Beinin, "Money, Media and Policy Consensus: The Washington Institute for Near East Policy," *Middle East Report* no. 180 (1993), pp. 10–15.

11. Web site of the Middle East Forum, http://www.meforum.org/.

12. Samuel P. Huntington, "The Clash of Civilizations?" *Foreign Affairs* 72.3 (1993), pp. 22–49, and *The Clash of Civilizations and the Remaking of World Order* (New York: Simon and Schuster, 1996). The phrase comes from Bernard Lewis, "The Roots of Muslim Rage," *Atlantic Monthly* 266.3 (1990), pp. 47–60.

13. Joshua Green, "The Bookie of Virtue," *Washington Monthly*, June 2003, http://www.washingtonmonthly.com/features/2003/0306.green.html.

14. Jim Lobe, "The War on Dissent Widens," AlterNet, March 12, 2002, www.alternet.org/story/12612.

15. "Lawrence Kadish (with Susan)," www.motherjones.com/news/special_reports/mojo_400/38_kadish.html, March 5, 2001.

16. All quotes from the AVOT full-page advertisement, *New York Times*, March 12, 2002. See also Jim Lobe, "The War on Dissent Widens," Alternet, March 12, 2002. http://www.alternet.org/story/12612.

17. Jerry L. Martin and Anne D. Neal, "Defending Civilization: How Our Universities Are Failing America and What Can Be Done About It" (Washington, D.C.: American Council for Trustees and Alumni, November 2001).

18. *Ibid.*

19. For a fuller discussion of Martin Kramer and others in his camp, see ch. 7 of Zachary Lockman, *Contending Visions of the Middle East: The History and Politics of Orientalism* (Cambridge: Cambridge University Press, 2004).

20. Bernard Lewis, "The Question of Orientalism," *New York Review of Books* 29.11 (June 24, 1982), pp. 49–56; Edward W. Said and Oleg Grabar, with a reply by Bernard Lewis, "Orientalism: An Exchange," *New York Review of Books* 29.13 (August 12, 1982), pp. 44–48.

21. The full text of the exchange, with the remarks of Christopher Hitchens and Leon Wieseltier, was published as "The MESA Debate: The Scholars, the Media, and the Middle East" in *Journal of Palestine Studies* 16.2 (1987), pp. 85–104.

22. Kramer, *Ivory Towers on Sand*, p. 36.

23. *Ibid.*, p. 37.

24. Rashid Khalidi, *Palestinian Identity: The Construction of Modern National Consciousness* (New York: Columbia University Press, 1977).

25. Mission statement of the American Jewish Committee, http://www.ajc. org/WhoWeAre/MissionAndHistory.asp.

26. President's Report Concerning the Outreach Program of the Near Eastern Center (undated and unpublished, my personal files).

27. Gary S. Schiff, *Middle East Centers at Selected American Universities: A Report Presented to the American Jewish Committee* (Washington, D.C.: Academy for Educational Development, 1981), pp. 5–7.

28. Jordan Millstein, letter to "Zionist Activist/Student," November 7, 1981, accompanying the booklet (unpublished, my personal files).

29. "The Secret Strategy of the Israeli Lobby," *The Middle East*, December 1983, p. 29.

30. Jonathan S. Kessler and Jeff Schwaber, *The AIPAC College Guide: Exposing the Anti-Israel Campaign on Campus* (Washington, D.C.: American-Israel Public Affairs Committee, 1984).

31. American-Israel Public Affairs Committee, *The AIPAC College Guide: A Survey of Political Activism (Campus Survey)*, 1984.

32. Middle East Studies Association of North America, *Resolution of the Board of Directors to be Discussed at the Business Meeting*, 1984.

33. Luntz, *Israel in the Age of Eminem*, p. 7.

34. Bob Egelko, "Jewish Defense Group Settles S.F. Spying Suit," *San Francisco Chronicle*, February 23, 2002; Dan Evans, "Paper Trail of Deceit," *San Francisco Examiner*, April 1, 2002.

35. Egelko, "Jewish Defense Group Settles S.F. Spying Suit."

36. The Campus Watch Web site is www.campus-watch.org.

37. Daniel Pipes, "The Muslims Are Coming! The Muslims Are Coming!" *National Review*, November 19, 1990, http://www.danielpipes.org/article/198.

38. "Statement of Stanley Kurtz," June 19, 2003, http://www.house.gov/ ed_workforce/hearings/108th/sed/titlevi61903/kurtz.htm. Much of this testimony recapitulates Kramer's book.

39. The information in the next two paragraphs comes partly from a report on the status of HR 3077 in National Coalition for History, "*Washington Update*" 10.7 (February 20, 2004), http://h-net.msu.edu/cgi-bin/logbrowse. pl?trx= vx&list=H-NCH&month=0402&week=c&msg=6TVRRgan222jFnJdLseTV g&user=&pw=.

40. See appendix for details and text.

41. Daniel Golden, "Colleges Object to New Wording in Ford Grants," *Wall Street Journal*, May 4, 2004.

42. In fall 2003, Edwin Black wrote a four-part series of articles titled "Funding Hate" for the Jewish Telegraphic Agency, available at www.jta.org/ ford.asp. *Forward* featured the series prominently; see, for example, Edwin

Black, "Ford Foundation Aided Groups Behind Biased Durban Parley," October 17, 2003, http://www.featuregroup.com/fgarchive/forward.com.

43. Golden, "Colleges Object to New Wording in Ford Grants."

44. Marjorie J. Censer, "Academics Protest Ford and Rockefeller Grant Terms," *Academe* 90.5 (2004), http://www.aaup.org/publications/Academe/2004/04so/04soNB.htm#2.

45. Lawrence Summers, "Address at Morning Prayers," Memorial Church, Cambridge, MA, September 17, 2002, http://president.harvard.edu/speeches/2002/morningprayers.html.

46. For more information see http://www.rachelcorrie.org.

47. For the text of the resolution at the Caterpillar Corporation annual meeting of April 14, 2004, see http://www.jewishvoiceforpeace.org. On the campaign to persuade Caterpillar to stop selling equipment to Israel more generally, see http://www.catdestroyshomes.org/. On the Presbyterian Church's actions, see Alexa Smith, "Nuns Squeeze Caterpillar: PC(USA) Isn't Only Group Studying Bulldozer Sales to Israel," Presbyterian News Service, August 2, 2004, see http://www.pcusa.org/pcnews/2004/04342.htm.

48. Alexa Smith, "Taking Stock of Taking Stock: Church Researching 'Selective' Divestment in Israel-Related Firms," Presbyterian News Service, August 2, 2004, http://www.pcusa.org/pcnews/2004/04341.htm.

49. *Christian Post*, February 23, 2005. On line at http://www.christianpost.com/article/church/1931/Section/World.Council.of.Churches.Recommends.Mideast.Selective.Divestment/l.htm.

50. "Church of England debates withdrawal of Caterpillar investments," *Ekklesia*, May 17, 2005, http://www.ekklesia.co.uk/content/news_syndication/article_050517cofe.shtml.

51. For a nuanced approach to what constitutes anti-Semitism and a refutation of the notion that criticism of Israel and Zionism constitutes anti-Semitism, see Henri Picciotto and Mitchell Plitnick (eds.), *Reframing Anti-Semitism: Alternative Jewish Perspectives* (Oakland, CA: Jewish Voice for Peace, 2004), which includes Judith Butler's influential essay "No, It's Not Anti-Semitic."

52. Adam Dickter, "Columbia Probing Mideast Studies: Presidential Panel, Meeting in Secret, Has Heard Testimony about Anti-Israel Activity," *The Jewish Week*, April 16, 2004.

53. The full text of the committee report, Professor Massad's statement to the committee, and his response to the report are available at http://www.columbia.edu/cu/news/05/03/al_hoc_grievance_committee_report.html.

54. Jacob Gershman, "Faculty Committee Largely Clears Scholars," *New York Sun*, March 31, 2005; "Intimidation at Columbia," *New York Times*, April 7, 2005; Nat Hentoff, "Columbia Whitewashes Itself," *Village Voice*, April 8, 2005.

55. Anti-Defamation League, "ADL Releases New Figures on Anti-Semitic Incidents: More Than 1,500 Acts Reported Across U.S. in 2002; Campus Figures Up 24 Percent," March 26, 2003, http://www.adl.org/presrele/asus_12/4243_12.asp.

56. Timothy Starks, "Universities Resist Efforts to Require Ideological Diversity on Campuses," *New York Sun,* April 15, 2003.

57. Robert Blecher, "Free People Will Set the Course of History: Intellectuals, Democracy and American Empire," *Middle East Report Online*, March 2003, http://www.merip.org/mero/interventions/blecher_interv.html.

APPENDIX

American Association of University Professors: 1940 Statement of Principles on Academic Freedom and Tenure (with 1970 Interpretive Comments)*

In 1940, following a series of joint conferences begun in 1934, representatives of the American Association of University Professors and the Association of American Colleges (now the Association of American Colleges and Universities) agreed on a restatement of the principles set forth in the "1925 Conference Statement on Academic Freedom and Tenure." This restatement is known as the "1940 Statement of Principles on Academic Freedom and Tenure."

The "1940 Statement" is printed below, followed by interpretive comments developed by representatives of the American Association of University Professors and the Association of American Colleges in 1969. The governing bodies of the two associations, which met in November 1989 and January 1990, adopted several changes in language in order to remove gender-specific references from the text.

The purpose of this statement is to promote public understanding and support of academic freedom and tenure and agreement upon procedures to ensure them in colleges and universities. Institutions of higher education are conducted for the common good and not to further the interest of either the individual teacher or

---

* Http://www.aaup.org/statements/Redbook/1940stat.htm. This is a slightly abridged version. In addition to some slight formatting changes, the list of endorsers and the endnotes were removed.

the institution as a whole. The common good depends upon the free search for truth and its free exposition.

Academic freedom is essential to these purposes and applies to both teaching and research. Freedom in research is fundamental to the advancement of truth. Academic freedom in its teaching aspect is fundamental for the protection of the rights of the teacher in teaching and of the student to freedom in learning. It carries with it duties correlative with rights. [1]

Tenure is a means to certain ends; specifically: (1) freedom of teaching and research and of extramural activities, and (2) a sufficient degree of economic security to make the profession attractive to men and women of ability. Freedom and economic security, hence, tenure, are indispensable to the success of an institution in fulfilling its obligations to its students and to society.

Academic Freedom
a. Teachers are entitled to full freedom in research and in the publication of the results, subject to the adequate performance of their other academic duties; but research for pecuniary return should be based upon an understanding with the authorities of the institution.

b. Teachers are entitled to freedom in the classroom in discussing their subject, but they should be careful not to introduce into their teaching controversial matter which has no relation to their subject. [2] Limitations of academic freedom because of religious or other aims of the institution should be clearly stated in writing at the time of the appointment. [3]

c. College and university teachers are citizens, members of a learned profession, and officers of an educational institution. When they speak or write as citizens, they should be free from institutional censorship or discipline, but their special position in the community imposes special obligations. As scholars and educational officers, they should remember that the public may judge their profession and their institution by their utterances. Hence they should at all times be accurate, should exercise appropriate restraint, should show respect for the opinions of others, and should make every effort to indicate that they are not speaking for the institution. [4]

Academic Tenure

After the expiration of a probationary period, teachers or investigators should have permanent or continuous tenure, and their service should be terminated only for adequate cause, except in the case of retirement for age, or under extraordinary circumstances because of financial exigencies.

In the interpretation of this principle it is understood that the following represents acceptable academic practice:

1. The precise terms and conditions of every appointment should be stated in writing and be in the possession of both institution and teacher before the appointment is consummated.

2. Beginning with appointment to the rank of full-time instructor or a higher rank, [5] the probationary period should not exceed seven years, including within this period full-time service in all institutions of higher education; but subject to the proviso that when, after a term of probationary service of more than three years in one or more institutions, a teacher is called to another institution, it may be agreed in writing that the new appointment is for a probationary period of not more than four years, even though thereby the person's total probationary period in the academic profession is extended beyond the normal maximum of seven years. [6] Notice should be given at least one year prior to the expiration of the probationary period if the teacher is not to be continued in service after the expiration of that period. [7]

3. During the probationary period a teacher should have the academic freedom that all other members of the faculty have. [8]

4. Termination for cause of a continuous appointment, or the dismissal for cause of a teacher previous to the expiration of a term appointment, should, if possible, be considered by both a faculty committee and the governing board of the institution. In all cases where the facts are in dispute, the accused teacher should be informed before the hearing in writing of the charges and should have the opportunity to be heard in his or her own defense

by all bodies that pass judgment upon the case. The teacher should be permitted to be accompanied by an advisor of his or her own choosing who may act as counsel. There should be a full stenographic record of the hearing available to the parties concerned. In the hearing of charges of incompetence the testimony should include that of teachers and other scholars, either from the teacher's own or from other institutions. Teachers on continuous appointment who are dismissed for reasons not involving moral turpitude should receive their salaries for at least a year from the date of notification of dismissal whether or not they are continued in their duties at the institution. [9]

5. Termination of a continuous appointment because of financial exigency should be demonstrably bona fide.

1940 Interpretations
At the conference of representatives of the American Association of University Professors and of the Association of American Colleges on November 7–8, 1940, the following interpretations of the 1940 *Statement of Principles on Academic Freedom and Tenure* were agreed upon:

1. That its operation should not be retroactive.

2. That all tenure claims of teachers appointed prior to the endorsement should be determined in accordance with the principles set forth in the 1925 *Conference Statement on Academic Freedom and Tenure*.

3. If the administration of a college or university feels that a teacher has not observed the admonitions of paragraph (c) of the section on Academic Freedom and believes that the extramural utterances of the teacher have been such as to raise grave doubts concerning the teacher's fitness for his or her position, it may proceed to file charges under paragraph 4 of the section on Academic Tenure. In pressing such charges, the administration should remember that teachers are citizens and should be accorded the freedom of citizens. In such cases the administration must assume full responsibility, and the American Association of University Professors and the Association of American Colleges are free to make an investigation.

1970 Interpretive Comments

Following extensive discussions on the "1940 Statement of Principles on Academic Freedom and Tenure" with leading educational associations and with individual faculty members and administrators, a joint committee of the AAUP and the Association of American Colleges met in 1969 to reevaluate this key policy statement. On the basis of the comments made, and the discussions that ensued, the joint committee felt the preferable approach was to formulate interpretations of the statement in terms of the experience gained in implementing and applying it for over thirty years and of adapting it to current needs.

The committee submitted to the two associations for their consideration the following interpretive comments. These interpretations were adopted by the Council of the American Association of University Professors in April 1970 and ratified at the fifty-sixth annual meeting as association policy.

In the thirty years since their promulgation, the principles of the 1940 *Statement of Principles on Academic Freedom and Tenure* have undergone a substantial amount of refinement. This has evolved through a variety of processes, including customary acceptance, understandings mutually arrived at between institutions and professors or their representatives, investigations and reports by the American Association of University Professors, and formulations of statements by that association either alone or in conjunction with the Association of American Colleges. These comments represent the attempt of the two associations, as the original sponsors of the 1940 *Statement*, to formulate the most important of these refinements. Their incorporation here as Interpretive Comments is based upon the premise that the 1940 *Statement* is not a static code but a fundamental document designed to set a framework of norms to guide adaptations to changing times and circumstances.

Also, there have been relevant developments in the law itself reflecting a growing insistence by the courts on due process within the academic community which parallels the essential concepts of the 1940 *Statement*; particularly relevant is the identification by the Supreme Court of academic freedom as a right protected by the First Amendment. As the Supreme Court said in *Keyishian v. Board of Regents,* 385 U.S. 589 (1967), "Our Nation is deeply committed to safeguarding academic freedom, which is of transcendent value to all of us and not merely to the teachers concerned. That freedom is therefore a special concern of the First Amendment, which does not tolerate laws that cast a pall of orthodoxy over the classroom."

The numbers refer to the designated portion of the 1940 *Statement* on which interpretive comment is made.

1. The Association of American Colleges and the American Association of University Professors have long recognized that membership in the academic profession carries with it special responsibilities. Both associations either separately or jointly have consistently affirmed these responsibilities in major policy statements, providing guidance to professors in their utterances as citizens, in the exercise of their responsibilities to the institution and to students, and in their conduct when resigning from their institution or when undertaking government-sponsored research. Of particular relevance is the *Statement on Professional Ethics*, adopted in 1966 as Association policy. (A revision, adopted in 1987, may be found in AAUP, Policy Documents and Reports, 9th ed. [Washington, D.C., 2001], 133–34.)

2. The intent of this statement is not to discourage what is "controversial." Controversy is at the heart of the free academic inquiry which the entire statement is designed to foster. The passage serves to underscore the need for teachers to avoid persistently intruding material which has no relation to their subject.

3. Most church-related institutions no longer need or desire the departure from the principle of academic freedom implied in the 1940 *Statement*, and we do not now endorse such a departure.

4. This paragraph is the subject of an interpretation adopted by the sponsors of the 1940 *Statement* immediately following its endorsement which reads as follows:

If the administration of a college or university feels that a teacher has not observed the admonitions of paragraph (c) of the section on Academic Freedom and believes that the extramural utterances of the teacher have been such as to raise grave doubts concerning the teacher's fitness for his or her position, it may proceed to file charges under paragraph 4 of the section on Academic Tenure. In pressing such charges, the administration should remember that teachers are citizens and should be accorded the freedom of citizens. In such cases the administration must assume full responsibility, and the American Association of University Professors and the Association of American Colleges are free to make an investigation.

Paragraph (c) of the section on Academic Freedom in the 1940 *Statement* should also be interpreted in keeping with the 1964 "Committee A Statement on Extramural Utterances" (*Policy Documents and Reports*, 32), which states inter alia: "The controlling principle is that a faculty member's expression of opinion as a citizen cannot constitute grounds for dismissal unless it clearly demonstrates the faculty member's unfitness for his or her position. Extramural utterances rarely bear upon the faculty member's fitness for the position. Moreover, a final decision should take into account the faculty member's entire record as a teacher and scholar."

Paragraph 5 of the *Statement on Professional Ethics* also deals with the nature of the "special obligations" of the teacher. The paragraph reads as follows:

As members of their community, professors have the rights and obligations of other citizens. Professors measure the urgency of other obligations in the light of their responsibilities to their subject, to their students, to their profession, and to their institution. When they speak or act as private persons they avoid creating the impression of speaking or acting for their college or university. As citizens engaged in a profession that depends upon freedom for its health and integrity, professors have a particular obligation to promote conditions of free inquiry and to further public understanding of academic freedom.

Both the protection of academic freedom and the requirements of academic responsibility apply not only to the full-time probationary and the tenured teacher, but also to all others, such as part-time faculty and teaching assistants, who exercise teaching responsibilities.

5. The concept of "rank of full-time instructor or a higher rank" is intended to include any person who teaches a full-time load regardless of the teacher's specific title.

6. In calling for an agreement "in writing" on the amount of credit given for a faculty member's prior service at other institutions, the *Statement* furthers the general policy of full understanding by the professor of the terms and conditions of the appointment. It does not necessarily follow that a professor's tenure rights have been violated because of the absence of a written agreement on this matter. Nonetheless, especially because of the variation in permissible institutional practices, a written understanding concerning these matters at the time of appointment is particularly appropriate and advantageous to both the individual and the institution.

7. The effect of this subparagraph is that a decision on tenure, favorable or unfavorable, must be made at least twelve months prior to the completion of the probationary period. If the decision is negative, the appointment for the following year becomes a terminal one. If the decision is affirmative, the provisions in the 1940 *Statement* with respect to the termination of service of teachers or investigators after the expiration of a probationary period should apply from the date when the favorable decision is made.

The general principle of notice contained in this paragraph is developed with greater specificity in the *Standards for Notice of Nonreappointment*, endorsed by the Fiftieth Annual Meeting of the American Association of University Professors (1964). These standards are:

Notice of nonreappointment, or of intention not to recommend reappointment to the governing board, should be given in writing in accordance with the following standards:

(a) *Not later than March 1 of the first academic year of service*, if the appointment expires at the end of that year; or, if a one-year appointment terminates during an academic year, at least three months in advance of its termination.

(b) *Not later than December 15 of the second academic year of service*, if the appointment expires at the end of that year; or, if an initial two-year appointment terminates during an academic year, at least six months in advance of its termination.

(c) At least twelve months before the expiration of an appointment after two or more years in the institution.

Other obligations, both of institutions and of individuals, are described in the *Statement on Recruitment and Resignation of Faculty Members*, as endorsed by the Association of American Colleges and the American Association of University Professors in 1961.

8. The freedom of probationary teachers is enhanced by the establishment of a regular procedure for the periodic evaluation and assessment of the teacher's academic performance during probationary status. Provision should be made for regularized procedures for the consideration of complaints by probationary teachers that their academic freedom has been violated. One suggested procedure to serve these purposes is contained in the *Recommended Institutional Regulations on Academic Freedom and Tenure*, prepared by the American Association of University Professors.

9. A further specification of the academic due process to which the teacher is entitled under this paragraph is contained in the *Statement on Procedural Standards in Faculty Dismissal Proceedings*, jointly approved by the American Association of University Professors and the Association of American Colleges in 1958. This interpretive document deals with the issue of suspension, about which the 1940 Statement is silent.

The 1958 *Statement* provides: "Suspension of the faculty member during the proceedings is justified only if immediate harm to the faculty member or others is threatened by the faculty member's continuance. Unless legal considerations forbid, any such suspension should be with pay." A suspension which is not followed by either reinstatement or the opportunity for a hearing is in effect a summary dismissal in violation of academic due process.

The concept of "moral turpitude" identifies the exceptional case in which the professor may be denied a year's teaching or pay in whole or in part. The statement applies to that kind of behavior which goes beyond simply warranting discharge and is so utterly blameworthy as to make it inappropriate to require the offering of a year's teaching or pay. The standard is not that the moral sensibilities of persons in the particular community have been affronted. The standard is behavior that would evoke condemnation by the academic community generally.

Union of Concerned Scientists:

Restoring Scientific Integrity in

Policy Making*

On February 18, 2004, over sixty leading scientists — Nobel laureates, leading medical experts, former federal agency directors, and university chairs and presidentss — signed the statement below, voicing their concern over the misuse of science by the Bush administration.

Successful application of science has played a large part in the policies that have made the United States of America the world's most powerful nation and its citizens increasingly prosperous and healthy. Although scientific input to the government is rarely the only factor in public policy decisions, this input should always be weighed from an objective and impartial perspective to avoid perilous consequences. Indeed, this principle has long been adhered to by presidents and administrations of both parties in forming and implementing policies. The administration of George W. Bush has, however, disregarded this principle.

When scientific knowledge has been found to be in conflict with its political goals, the administration has often manipulated the process through which science enters into its decisions. This has been done by placing people who are professionally unqualified or who have clear conflicts of interest in official posts and on scientific advisory committees; by disbanding existing advisory committees; by censoring and suppressing reports by the government's own scientists;

*Http://www.ucsusa.org/global_environment/rsi/page.cfm?pageID=1320. This is a slightly abridged and reformatted version of the text published on the Web site of the Union of Concerned Scientists. The statement accompanied a detailed report released on February 2004 and updated on July 2004.

and by simply not seeking independent scientific advice. Other administrations have, on occasion, engaged in such practices, but not so systematically nor on so wide a front. Furthermore, in advocating policies that are not scientifically sound, the administration has sometimes misrepresented scientific knowledge and misled the public about the implications of its policies.

For example, in support of the president's decision to avoid regulating emissions that cause climate change, the administration has consistently misrepresented the findings of the National Academy of Sciences, government scientists, and the expert community at large. Thus in June 2003, the White House demanded extensive changes in the treatment of climate change in a major report by the Environmental Protection Agency (EPA). To avoid issuing a scientifically indefensible report, EPA officials eviscerated the discussion of climate change and its consequences.

The administration also suppressed a study by the EPA that found that a bipartisan Senate clean air proposal would yield greater health benefits than the administration's proposed Clear Skies Act, which the administration is portraying as an improvement of the existing Clean Air Act. "Clear Skies" would, however, be less effective in cleaning up the nation's air and reducing mercury contamination of fish than proper enforcement of the existing Clean Air Act.

Misrepresenting and suppressing scientific knowledge for political purposes can have serious consequences. Had Richard Nixon also based his decisions on such calculations he would not have supported the Clean Air Act of 1970, which in the following 20 years prevented more than 200,000 premature deaths and millions of cases of respiratory and cardiovascular disease. Similarly, George H.W. Bush would not have supported the Clean Air Act Amendments of 1990 and additional benefits of comparable proportions would have been lost.

The behavior of the White House on these issues is part of a pattern that has led Russell Train, the EPA administrator under Presidents Nixon and Ford, to observe, "How radically we have moved away from regulation based on independent findings and professional analysis of scientific, health and economic data by the responsible agency to regulation controlled by the White House and driven primarily by political considerations."

Across a broad range of policy areas, the administration has undermined the quality and independence of the scientific advisory system and the morale of the government's outstanding scientific personnel:

- Highly qualified scientists have been dropped from advisory committees dealing with childhood lead poisoning, environmental and reproductive health, and drug abuse, while individuals associated with or working for industries subject to regulation have been appointed to these bodies.
- Censorship and political oversight of government scientists is not restricted to the EPA, but has also occurred at the Departments of Health and Human Services, Agriculture, and Interior, when scientific findings are in conflict with the administration's policies or with the views of its political supporters.
- The administration is supporting revisions to the Endangered Species Act that would greatly constrain scientific input into the process of identifying endangered species and critical habitats for their protection.
- Existing scientific advisory committees to the Department of Energy on nuclear weapons, and to the State Department on arms control, have been disbanded.
- In making the invalid claim that Iraq had sought to acquire aluminum tubes for uranium enrichment centrifuges, the administration disregarded the contrary assessment by experts at Livermore, Los Alamos and Oak Ridge National Laboratories.

The distortion of scientific knowledge for partisan political ends must cease if the public is to be properly informed about issues central to its well being, and the nation is to benefit fully from its heavy investment in scientific research and education. To elevate the ethic that governs the relationship between science and government, Congress and the Executive should establish legislation and regulations that would:

- Forbid censorship of scientific studies unless there is a reasonable national security concern;

- Require all scientists on scientific advisory panels to meet high professional standards; and
- Ensure public access to government studies and the findings of scientific advisory panels.

To maintain public trust in the credibility of the scientific, engineering and medical professions, and to restore scientific integrity in the formation and implementation of public policy, we call on our colleagues to:
- Bring the current situation to public attention;
- Request that the government return to the ethic and code of conduct which once fostered independent and objective scientific input into policy formation; and
- Advocate legislative, regulatory and administrative reforms that would ensure the acquisition and dissemination of independent and objective scientific analysis and advice.

HR 3077:

The International Studies in

Higher Education Act

This appendix provides the context for and relevant language of HR 3077. It also includes a sample of statements by its supporters and opponents.

Context

In September 2003, the U.S. House of Representatives unanimously passed HR 3077, the International Studies in Higher Education Act. The intent of the act is to reauthorize and amend the International Education Programs, Title VI, funding through Fiscal Year 2009.[1] Title VI funds are currently provided to one hundred twenty-three National Resource Centers, of which seventeen study the Middle East. Area-studies centers typically receive three-year grants and use the funding for fellowships, language programs, community outreach, lecture series, and symposiums.

Due to intense criticism of HR 3077, the U.S. Senate has yet to vote to authorize a companion bill. The controversy revolves around whether the United States government should monitor and control federally funded foreign-language and area-studies programs through an oversight committee composed of political appointees vested with sweeping powers of investigation. The primary concern is that government intervention in education will replace professional standards by arbitrary political ones. A related issue is that area-studies centers that refuse to cooperate with such a board could lose their funding.[2] Area studies, in other words, finds itself in the unenviable position of being between the hammer of intervention and the anvil of privatization. For these reasons, HR 3077 is an important case study in the threats to academic freedom after September 11.[3]

Language

HR 3077's most controversial aspect is the establishment of an advisory board to review the institutions that accept Title VI funding. According to the final language of the bill, the advisory board would "provide advice, counsel and recommendations to the Secretary [of Education] and the Congress on international education issues for higher education."[4] The purpose of the board is to

- provide expertise in the area of national needs for proficiency in world regions, foreign languages, and international affairs;

- make recommendations that will promote the excellence of international education programs and result in the growth and development of such programs at the postsecondary education level that will reflect diverse perspectives and the full range of views on world regions, foreign language, and international affairs; and

- advise the Secretary [of Education] and the Congress with respect to needs for expertise in government, the private sector, and education in order to enhance America's understanding of, and engagement in, the world.[5]

The legislation stated that the board is to be

independent of the Secretary [of Education] and the other offices and officers of the Department [of Education]. Except as provided in this subsection and subsection (f), the recommendations of the International Advisory Board shall not be subject to review or approval by any officer of the Federal Government. Nothing in this title shall be construed to authorize the International Advisory Board to mandate, direct, or control an institution of higher education's specific instructional content, curriculum, or program of instruction. The Board is authorized to study, monitor, apprise [sic] and evaluate a sample of activities supported under this title in order to provide recommendations to the Secretary [of Education] and the Congress for the improvement of programs under the title and to ensure programs meet the purposes of the title. The recommendations of the Board may address any area in need of improvement, except that any recommendation of specific legislation to Congress shall be made only if the President deems it necessary and expedient.[6]

The board is to be composed of seven members, all political appointees. Of the three selected by the Secretary of Education, two would be representatives from "national security agencies." The House and Senate majority and minority leaders are to select the remaining four members, with each body appointing two members.[7]

Supporters and Detractors

The most outspoken supporters of the proposed advisory board are a group of conservatives who support the politics of the Israeli right wing and some major Jewish organizations. Stanley Kurtz, a research fellow at Stanford University's Hoover Institution on War, Revolution and Peace, testified before the House Subcommittee on Select Education in June 2003 in favor of the advisory board and has written several articles on Title VI in which he consistently cites and praises fellow conservatives Daniel Pipes and Martin Kramer.[8] Indeed, the targeting of Title VI was first broached in Kramer's book *Ivory Towers on Sand*. Kramer is a fellow at the conservative think tank the Washington Institute for Near East Policy (WINEP), set up by the American Israel Public Affairs Committee.[9]

Opponents of HR 3077 include the American Association of University Professors (AAUP), the American Anthropological Association (AAA), the Middle East Studies Association (MESA), the American Council on Education (ACE), and the American Civil Liberties Union (ACLU).[10] ACE, which represents nineteen associations and councils, also developed a series of "talking points" designed to refute the assertions in Stanley Kurtz's testimony to the House.[11]

NOTES

The information and references in this appendix are based on a research report prepared by Osamah Khalil.

1. Current Title VI funding is $95 million annually, reflecting an increase of $20 million after September 11, 2001. See Jennifer Jacobson, "The Clash Over Middle East Studies," *Chronicle of Higher Education*, February 6, 2004.

2. Daniel Pipes, "Defund Middle East Studies," *New York Sun*, February 24, 2004.

3. See Michelle Goldberg, "Osama University?" *Salon.com*, November 6,

2003; Kimberly Chase, "Speaking in 'approved' tongues," *Christian Science Monitor*, March 11, 2004; Chris Hedges, "Casting Mideast Violence in Another Light," *New York Times*, April 20, 2004; Alisa Solomon, "The Ideology Police," *Village Voice*, February 25, 2004; Nikhil Aziz, "Campus Insecurity," *Public Eye* 18.1 (2004); Anders Stringberg, "The New Commissars," *American Conservative*, February 2, 2004.

4. United States House of Representatives, Committee on Education and the Workforce (108th Congress), Report on HR 3077: International Studies in Higher Education Act of 2003, October 8, 2003 (referred to Senate Committee after being received from House). Full text available from http://thomas.loc. gov.

5. HR 3077, RFS, Sec. 6.

6. *Ibid.*

7. The final language of the legislation submitted to the Senate does not identify these agencies. However, the committee report says: "These agencies may include, but not be limited to, the Department of Defense, the Department of Homeland Security, the Department of State, the National Security Administration, and the Central Intelligence Agency."

8. Stanley Kurtz, "Anti-Americanism in the Classroom," *National Review Online*, May 16, 2002; "Ivory Scam," *National Review Online*, May 29,2002; and "Balancing the Academy," *National Review Online*, September 23, 2002.

9. Richard Morin and Claudia Deane, "Mideast Studies Professors Get Failing Grade," *Washington Post*, October 30, 2001. See Joel Beinin's article in this volume for further information.

10. AAUP Statement, "Proposed International Advisory Board, in H.R. 3077, the International Studies in Higher Education Act," http://www.aaup. org/govrel/hea/2003/Internatadvise.htm; AAUP Letter to Representative Judd Gregg, Chairman of the Committee on Health, Education, Labor and Pensions, Committee on Health, Education, Labor and Pensions, March 4, 2004, http://www.aaup.org/govrel/hea/2004/HR3077Coallet.htm; AAA Letter to Senator John Warner, Chairman, Senate Health, Education, Labor and Pensions Committee from Elizabeth Brumfiel, President, AAA, February 19, 2004, http://www.aaanet.org/gvt/act_area_studies_board_title_ vi.htm; MESA, http://fp.arizona.edu/mesassoc/Bulletin/Pres%20Addresses/ Anderson.htm. Other academic associations that opposed the advisory board included the Association of Asian Studies (http://www.aasianst.org/title6. htm); National Council for Languages and International Studies (http://www.languagepolicy. org/nclistviltr.html); the College Art Association (http://www.collegeart.org/ caa/advocacy/alerts/alertjan04.html); the Association of Professional Schools of International Affairs (http://www.apsia.org/ apsia/publications/HR_3077.pdf);

the American Federation of Teachers (http://www.aft.org/pubs-reports/on_campus/ 2004/mayjune/washwire. htm); and the Texas Foreign Language Association(http://www.tfla.info/advocacy.htm)ACLU,http:// www.aclu.org/FreeSpeech/ FreeSpeech.cfm?ID= 14952&c=42. The Friends Committee on National Legislation (FCNL), a public-interest lobby founded by members of the Religious Society of Friends, also opposed the legislation: http://www.fcnl.org/issues/ item.php?item_id=962 &issue_id=67.

11. American Council on Education, "Letter Regarding The International Studies in Higher Education Act," October 21, 2003, http://www.acenet.edu/ washington/letters/2003/10oct/3077.cfm, and "Talking Points Refuting Stanley Kurtz's Attack On HEA-Title VI Area Centers," http://www.acenet.edu/ washington/letters/2002/07july/titlevi.talking.points.cfm. Among the groups represented by ACE are the National Education Association and the National Humanities Alliance.

American Israel Public Affairs Committee
American Jewish Committee
American Jewish Congress
Anti-Defamation League
B'nai B'rith International
Hadassah, the Women's Zionist Organization
   of America, Inc.
Jewish War Veterans of the U.S.A.
Union of Orthodox Jewish Congregations

March 15, 2004
The Honorable [FULL NAME]
United States Senate
Washington, DC 20510

Dear Senator [LAST NAME]:

We strongly support H.R. 3077, the International Studies in
Higher Education Act, which the House of Representatives passed
by a large bipartisan majority on October 21, 2003. We urge the
Senate to incorporate similar provisions into the Higher Education Act reauthorization, or to enact a similar measure as a free-
standing bill. In our view, these provisions will help the federal
program for funding international studies centers fulfill its fundamental purposes and, at the same time, will enhance intellectual
freedom and academic debate.

Title VI of the Higher Education Act provides federal funds to
selected international studies and foreign language centers at universities across the country. Congress enacted Title VI to help
meet vital national needs — such as training experts for national
security and other government service, and educating the public
on international affairs.

Evidence shows that a considerable number of centers funded
under Title VI have failed to serve the basic objectives of the program — namely to support American security and foreign policy
interests. These centers discourage students from serving in the

national security arena and have even refused to cooperate with the National Security Education Program, which funds foreign language students who intend to work for national security related agencies after graduation.

In particular, a significant number of Title VI Middle East centers — rather than encouraging academic objectivity — follow a political agenda, with scholars uncritically promoting a positive image of Palestinians, Arabs, and the Islamic world, while ignoring or denigrating Israel. We are concerned that, before September 11, Middle East scholars at these centers apparently avoided focusing on Islamist terrorism — instead characterizing fanatical Islamism as a movement for democratic reform. Consequently, Middle East centers failed to detect and alert us to the rising threat. Amazingly, even today almost no academics at these centers study this ominous phenomenon.

In addition, scholars who have studied this issue have documented that, too often, Middle East centers exclude scholars with other perspectives — thereby stifling discourse on critical issues. The large influx of Saudi and other foreign funding to some Title VI Middle East centers casts further doubt on their independence and objectivity.

For these reasons, Middle East centers funded under Title VI generally have failed to produce the kind of realistic depiction and analysis of this pivotal region that students, the public, and the government need.

We are particularly troubled that government-funded centers disseminate one-sided views to an audience far wider than the college campus — through outreach programs to K–12 teachers, educators, and the general public that are an integral part of the Title VI funding program.

H.R. 3077 is narrowly tailored to begin addressing critical flaws in the Title VI program — without restricting academic freedom. The bill provides: (1) When the Secretary of Education ("Secretary") chooses which international studies centers will receive Title VI funds, s/he should take into account whether a center's activities advance national interests and foster debate from diverse perspectives; (2) Title VI off-campus outreach programs must represent "diverse perspectives" and be "reflective of the full range of views on the subject matter;" and (3) a bipartisan International Higher Education Advisory Board is created to make recommendations to Congress and the Secretary for improving the Title VI program.

Far from stifling academic freedom, H.R. 3077 seeks to enhance intellectual freedom and debate in international studies. It specifically provides that one criterion for selecting Title VI centers would be the extent to which they foster debate from different perspectives.

H.R. 3077 deliberately gives the new Advisory Board very narrow authority — its only power would be to make recommendations to the Secretary and the Congress for improving the overall Title VI program and ensuring that it meets its program objectives. The legislation gives the Advisory Board no input concerning individual institutions of higher learning — let alone individual scholars. Furthermore, H.R. 3077 explicitly declares that the Board has no authority to "mandate, direct, or control" curriculum or instructional content.

The government has a duty to assure that the funds it expends are used to serve the purposes for which Congress allocated them. Every government program needs basic accountability to provide that assurance. Title VI currently has no such accountability — H.R. 3077 would remedy that significant deficiency.

Of course, even after enactment of this measure, international studies centers would remain free to present one-sided views and to exclude alternative viewpoints. Such centers, however, would be less likely to continue receiving Title VI funding — an appropriate outcome for those programs that choose not to advance the purposes for which Title VI tax dollars are provided.

For these compelling reasons, we urge your support for this important legislative initiative.

Respectfully submitted,

American Israel Public Affairs Committee
American Jewish Committee
American Jewish Congress
Anti-Defamation League
B'nai B'rith International
Hadassah, The Women's Zionist Organization of America
Jewish War Veterans of the U.S.A.
Union of Orthodox Jewish Congregations

October 21, 2003

RE: H.R. 3077

Dear Representative:

On behalf of the undersigned organizations, I write to express support for H.R. 3077, the International Studies in Higher Education Act, with one specific exception noted below.

We are pleased that H.R. 3077 renews the HEA Title VI international education programs and makes several key improvements. The events of recent years have underscored in untold ways the importance of international education expertise to our national well being. This bill renews the existing and highly successful Title VI international education programs and makes several important improvements to them.

Our enthusiasm for the legislation is strongly tempered by some of the specific provisions surrounding the proposed International Education Advisory Board. We support the creation of a well-structured advisory board for the Title VI international education programs because we believe that such a body will be a forum for discussions about international education and will contribute fresh ideas for improvements in federal policies and programs. However, we are very concerned that, as drafted, the proposed Advisory Board does not meet this standard and may have unintended consequences.

We believe the current legislation leaves open the possibility that the Advisory Board could intrude into the academic conduct and content of higher education and could impinge on institutional decisions about curriculum and activities. Indeed, the powers vested in the proposed Advisory Board make it more of an investigative, rather than an advisory, body.

In response to our concerns, several important changes were made in the structure and authority of the Advisory Board during committee consideration and we are grateful for these modifications. We will continue to work with the members and staff of the Education and the Workforce Committee to address our remaining concerns. We hope that as this bill moves through the legislative process that the Advisory Board provisions will be modified in such a way that we can offer unqualified support for this legislation.

We appreciate the leadership of Select Education Subcommittee Chairman Peter Hoekstra and Ranking Member Rubén Hinojosa, as well as the efforts of Education and the Workforce Committee Chairman John Boehner and Ranking Member George Miller in moving this legislation forward and in responding to the concerns that we have raised.

Thank you for considering our views and moving this important piece of legislation in such a timely fashion.

Sincerely,

David Ward
President, American Council on Education

On behalf of:
American Association of State Colleges and Universities
American Council on Education
American Council on International Intercultural Education
American Councils for International Education: ACTR/ACCELS
Association of American Universities
Association of International Education Administrators
Committee on Institutional Cooperation Senior International
    Officers
Council for Christian Colleges and Universities
Council of Directors of National Resource Centers for Foreign
Language and Area Studies
Council of Graduate Schools
Forum on Education Abroad
NAFSA: Association of International Educators
National Association of College and University Business Officers
National Association of State Universities and Land-Grant
    Colleges

National Association of Student Personnel Administration
National Council of Organizations of Less Commonly Taught
    Languages
National Education Association
National Humanities Alliance

AMERICAN ASSOCIATION OF UNIVERSITY PROFESSORS
AMERICAN BOOKSELLERS FOUNDATION FOR FREE
    EXPRESSION
AMERICAN LIBRARY ASSOCIATION
ASSOCIATION OF AMERICAN UNIVERSITY PRESSES
FEMINISTS FOR FREE EXPRESSION
NATIONAL COALITION AGAINST CENSORSHIP
PEACEFIRE
PEN AMERICAN CENTER

March 4, 2004

Judd Gregg, Chairman
Committee on Health, Education, Labor and Pensions
428 Dirksen Senate Office Building
Washington, DC 20510–6300

Dear Senator Gregg and Members of the Committee:

We write to express our concerns about HR 3077, the International Studies in Higher Education Act of 2003, passed by a voice vote in the House of Representatives last fall and now under consideration in your committee. Specifically, our concern centers on §633 of the legislation, which establishes an International Advisory Board, and raises serious issues because of its potential to suppress certain views, chill dissent, and restrict academic discourse.

Ostensibly, the purpose of §633 is to create an advisory board to "promote the excellence of international education programs," a laudable goal. However, the institutional mechanism it would create threatens to undermine, not enhance, the excellence of federally-funded international education programs and the respect they command.

By granting the advisory board the authority to "monitor," "evaluate," and "make recommendations," the legislation creates a real risk that academic programs funded by the federal government will become, or be perceived as, politically driven. This concern is heightened by the fact that all members of the advisory board are appointed by politicians.

Members of the House and Senate, and even the Secretary of Education, are not the logical choices to select an academic advisory board. Their concerns are necessarily different from those of the academic community, and in some ways potentially antithetical to the academic mission. Leaving aside the serious issue of academic freedom, the injection of political considerations into the content of higher education can only serve to undermine its integrity.

Two of the most vocal proponents of the legislation, Daniel Pipes and Stanley Kurtz, take no pains to conceal that the purpose of the advisory board is to influence the content of funded programs to meet political objectives. Specifically, they object to the views and writings of the late Edward Said, whose work is widely read in mid-east studies programs. In his Congressional testimony, Kurtz characterized Said as "anti-American."

Said, while critical of American policies, is regarded by many experts on the middle east as an important scholar and thinker. To dismiss him as "un-American" grossly and unjustly oversimplifies his body of work. Said was, if nothing else, prolific; he wrote 20 books and hundreds of articles, and his work has been subjected to critical analyses many times over.

Even if he were not esteemed, he was surely within his rights to advance his views, no matter how unpopular. There are sharp divisions of thought among mid-east scholars. And contemporary faculty are surely within their rights to assign and discuss his or any other relevant work. It bears noting that academic readings are rarely simply accepted uncritically; rather a central purpose of higher education is to teach students the practice of critical analysis.

A higher education advisory board whose implicit mission is to review academic programs for their slant on specific issues and views is a form of censorship. At the point at which colleges and universities cannot teach about politically sensitive issues without Congressional oversight, we will have abandoned our commitment to freedom of speech, thought, and inquiry.

All sides in this dispute have the right to advance their views in the marketplace of ideas. Open and vigorous discussion and debate are the basic tools of a free society. It is un-American, in the most basic sense, to suppress disputed or unpopular ideas, or to engage in "thought-control," no matter how subtle.

The Supreme Court long ago warned against the impulse to "burn the house to roast the pig." We suggest that §633 could do just that, by undermining basic First Amendment principles in the name of preserving freedom. We strongly urge you to leave decisions about curricular content where they belong, in the capable hands of the academic community.

Sincerely,

Joan E. Bertin, Executive Director
National Coalition Against Censorship

Mark F. Smith, Director of Government Relations
American Association of University Professors

New York Civil Liberties Union: Letter to Columbia University President Lee Bollinger in Defense of Academic Freedom*

December 20, 2004

Mr. Lee C. Bollinger
President, Columbia University
New York, New York 10027

Dear President Bollinger:

We are writing with respect to the current controversy at Columbia University arising out of a film, entitled "Columbia Unbecoming." This controversy deeply implicates issues of academic freedom and civil discourse on campus. We recognize your distinguished academic career as a First Amendment scholar and your professional and personal commitment to freedom of speech and to what you have variously described in your writings as the "ethic of tolerance" and the "virtue of magnanimity."[1]

---

*On April 6, 2005, the NYCLU released another long and detailed letter responding to the report released by a special ad hoc committee appointed by President Lee Bollinger to investigate the charges against several faculty members by the David Project, a Boston-based pro-Israel advocacy group. "NYCLU Calls Columbia Committee Report Inadequate," http://www.nyclu.org/bollinger_pr_050705.html.

Accordingly, we do not presume to lecture you on the principles and importance of academic freedom. Nevertheless, we feel compelled to address this matter because of its seriousness as a public controversy and because of the need — in circumstances such as this when fundamental principles as well as the university itself are under attack — to lend our voice in defense of academic freedom and to express our long-standing commitment to ideological diversity, pluralism and tolerance upon which any community of scholars and any system of intellectual discourse must ultimately rest.

The New York Civil Liberties Union (NYCLU) believes that it is vitally important to foster an academic environment conducive to the free exchange of ideas. We further believe that, in order to foster such an environment, freedom of thought and expression must be scrupulously protected even when, in doing so, protection is bestowed upon ideas that are deeply offensive to a distinct segment of the community. We recognize that, as Provost Alan Brinkley has observed, "... students have a right to learn in an atmosphere that permits an open exchange of ideas." We do not, however, regard these rights of students, correctly understood, as incompatible with principles of academic freedom. Moreover, when one closely scrutinizes the assertion of student rights as set forth in the film and when one considers the film's accusations directed at the conduct of certain Columbia professors in failing to provide an appropriate classroom atmosphere, the line between ideological content and conduct seems to blur significantly and one is left with the distinct impression that these accusations are really about the content of academic lectures and writings. Thus, in the end, the attempt by some outside the academy to transform these accusations into a demand for the termination of a scholar or other sanctions reduces to a direct attack upon principles of academic freedom. Our reasons for reaching this conclusion are amplified below. Our suggestions as to how the University should respond to this attack upon academic freedom are also set forth below.

I.

The facts of the controversy, as we understand them, are as follows. The David Project has produced a film[2] that contains accusations that Columbia professors — particularly from the Middle East Asian Languages and Cultures (MEALAC) Department — have taken positions that are seriously critical of policies pursued by the Israeli government and have engaged in the intimidation of students "when they voiced pro-Israel views."[3] And, according to the Columbia Spectator, "[o]ne professor featured in the film is Professor Joseph Massad."

Two episodes involving Professor Massad's interactions with students are apparently identified in the film. One involves an alleged exchange outside the classroom between Professor Massad and Tomy Schoenfeld, a former member of the Israel Defense Forces, in which Mr. Schoenfeld reportedly asked Professor Massad a question and the Professor responded that he would not answer the question until Mr. Schoenfeld revealed "How many Palestinians [he had] killed."[4] The second episode involves an exchange between a student, Noah Liben, who was defending the treatment of Sephardic Jews by the Ashkenazi majority in Israel and who concluded this discussion by asking whether Professor Massad understood the student's point. Professor Massad allegedly answered that he did not understand the point that the student was trying to make and, according to Mr. Liben, the Professor "smirked" during the student-teacher exchange. In the film, and elsewhere,[5] Professor Massad is further accused, in his lectures and writings, of describing the State of Israel as "a racist state that does not legitimately represent Jews."

The accusations set forth in the film have provoked a variety of responses. Congressman Anthony Weiner has called upon Columbia University to terminate Professor Massad's appointment. New York City Councilmember Michael Nelson has threatened to have the City Council investigate the academic environment at Columbia. The New York *Sun* has written an editorial criticizing Columbia and urging the University to "fire Mr. Massad . . . and to discipline Mr. [Rashid] Khalidi for the errors in his book." The New York *Daily News* issued a more moderate statement but its editorial, nevertheless, grudgingly described academic freedom as a "guise" rather than recognizing its important instrumental value.[6] It has been further reported that potential donors to Columbia have read accounts of this controversy and have threatened to withhold funding unless Columbia responds adequately to the accusations set forth in the David Project film. On the other hand, many scholars within the university and around the country have rallied to the defense of the professors who were accused of misconduct in the film.

Moreover, Professor Massad has issued a detailed and vigorous response to the accusations. Professor Massad asserts that the David Project film is part of a "witch-hunt [that] aims to stifle pluralism, academic freedom and the freedom of expression on university campuses"; that such a campaign is "pressuring the university to abandon proper academic procedures for evaluating scholarship"; and that "the major strategy " of those engaged in this campaign is to "equate criticism of Israel with anti-Semitism." As to the specific accusations set forth by students in the film, Professor Massad asserts that Tomy Schoenfeld was not a student of his and he does not recall ever having met Mr. Schoenfeld. As for his exchanges with Noah Liben, Professor Massad asserts that he "remember[s] having [had] a friendly rapport with Noah" characterized by ongoing communications between Professor and student long after the incidents which were described in the film. Moreover, Professor Massad states that "the lie that the film propagates claiming that I would equate Israel with Nazi Germany is abhorrent." Professor Massad further asserts: "I have never made such a reprehensible equation."

II.

It is the obligation of a university to create and to maintain an environment conducive to academic freedom. This obligation which is owed by the university to its scholars and students is necessary to protect diversity of discourse and experimentation even if such intellectual pursuits are provocative, unorthodox and controversial. Accordingly, faculty members must retain broad latitude to think as they will and to write as they think and to suffer no recriminations, from outside the academy, for the content of their scholarship.

This does not mean that such scholarship is immune from criticism. Within the university community, academic judgments such as tenure and promotion can and should rest upon the content and quality of one's scholarship. It is to be expected, therefore, that such scholarship will be critically scrutinized within the academy. Moreover, members of the academic community and even those that are outside the academy who believe that an academic writing or lecture is wrong-minded have every right to respond, on the merits, with a public refutation of the perceived error. But the appropriate response must be substantive. It must be on the merits. And critics outside the academy must avoid seeking to support their substantive arguments with threats and sanctions. This requirement is in keeping with the concept of the academic campus as a paradigmatic marketplace of ideas where the appropriate response to bad ideas cannot be coerced silence but must instead, involve "more speech" to refute and correct the unwisdom of the original expression.[7]

Accordingly, while those outside the university community remain free to criticize academic scholarship, it is entirely inappropriate for potential donors to try to use the power of the purse to dictate the content of scholarship or the composition of a university's faculty or one of its departments. As Arthur Lovejoy, one of the founders of the American Association of University Professors has observed: "the distinctive social function of the scholar's trade cannot be fulfilled if those who pay the piper are permitted to call the tune."[8] Similarly, it is also inappropriate for public officials to try to intrude into the academic processes with threats of sanctions or investigations. We learned this in *Sweezy v. New Hampshire*, 354 U.S. 234 (1957) where Justice Frankfurter's concurring opinion correctly observed that "political power must abstain from intrusion into this activity of [academic] freedom, pursued in the interest of wise government and the people's well-being except for reasons that are exigent and obviously compelling."[9] The observations of Professor Lovejoy and the experience of *Sweezy* reinforce the importance of a central principle of academic freedom. That principle holds that academic judgments regarding the content of curriculum and the composition of the faculty reside, as a matter of academic self-governance, within the academy and that intrusion into these matters by those outside the academy must be vigorously resisted.

III.

In extolling the importance of academic freedom we do not mean to suggest that professors bear no responsibility to treat their students with civility and respect. As noted above, Provost Alan Brinkley has correctly observed that "students have a right to learn in an atmosphere that permits an open exchange of ideas." So understood, students have the right to express their own views. They have the right to criticize the professors for the content of their scholarship, for the nature of their pedagogical style or for what they perceive to be a lack of open-mindedness. They can advance such criticism in student newspapers, in off-campus publications, at rallies, in student surveys, in private conversations and in evaluations of instructors that are routinely submitted by students at the conclusion of a course. They can even advance such criticism in class if permitted by the professor to do so. In this way, the commitment to civil discourse is entirely compatible with principles of academic freedom.

But, in asserting their right to criticize, students must also understand the limitations of such rights. The classroom is a bounded educational environment. It is not, except at the invitation of the professor, an open forum for students to express any views that they wish at any time. It is not, except at the invitation of a professor, an opportunity for those not enrolled in a course to attend and participate in classroom discussions. Additionally, students cannot expect, through the use of a grievance procedure[10] or otherwise that the university administrators will call professors to account for the content of their lectures or their ideological assertions within the classroom.

Moreover, the right of students to an appropriate learning environment does not immunize them from ideas that they find provocative or disturbing or even offensive. Students can expect to be treated with respect. They cannot expect that their views and opinions will be unchallenged. And they cannot expect that their professors will trim the cut of their convictions so as not to offend the sensibilities of their students. The notion of a system of free expression embraces the commitment to speech that is wide-open, unfettered and robust. Such robust expression requires that teachers and students alike must remain persons "of fortitude able to thrive in a hardy climate." *Craig v. Harney*, 331 U.S. 367, 376 (1947).

IV.

As suggested above, the claims of incivility of professors in their treatment of students seem, in this case, to be inextricably bound to the ideological disputes between certain professors and the students advancing these claims. We reach this conclusion for several reasons. First, the episodes identified by the students do not appear to involve situations where the allegations of uncongeniality were unrelated to substantive or ideological conversations taking place within the classroom.[11] Second, we suspect that this controversy would not have acquired the attention that it has received had it been simply about the rudeness of professors or their intolerance of other points of view. This film would not have provoked the sort of controversy that has now developed had it not arisen in the context of the deeply divisive political controversy involving Israel and Palestinians.

So understood, the attack upon Professor Massad and others in the MEALAC Department is fundamentally about their scholarship and political expression. Thus, the criticism of these academics must be seen for what it is: an assault upon principles of academic freedom and upon political speech.

V.

In a December 6 letter to you, Provost Brinkley advanced three recommendations for your consideration: First, in the belief that the grievance procedures available to students "are not sufficiently robust to deal effectively with controversies of this kind," Provost Brinkley recommended that "all schools work carefully at their existing grievance procedures" and that they develop more effective procedures, if necessary. Second, Provost Brinkley recommended that all "schools make a major effort to educate students, faculty and administrators on what the procedures are and how they can be used." Third, Provost Brinkley recommended the appointment of an *ad hoc* committee to entertain and investigate student complaints including the current complaints directed at the MEALAC Department. In a December 8 memorandum to the Columbia community you endorsed and implemented the third recommendation.

Where, as here, the accusations from students about the conduct of certain professors remain deeply contested, a serious investigation of those claims may well be useful to determine the truthfulness of the competing claims. Nevertheless, we have grave reservations about an *ad hoc* committee engaging such an investigation. First, where, as here, the accusations with respect to professorial conduct are so inextricably bound with ideological disagreements, we fear that holding professors to account for their statements runs a severe risk of intrusion by administrators into academic content and political ideology. Accordingly, in a controversy as politically charged as is this one, we are concerned that the investigation, if not undertaken with appropriate sensitivity toward academic freedom, will descend into an inquisition into the ideological or political views of the professors who have been accused. Finally, we are troubled that in discussing the need for more effective procedures for the consideration of student grievances, Provost Brinkley seemed to ignore the substantive limitations, discussed above,[12] respecting the right of students to an appropriate learning environment. We are concerned that unless students understand those limitations the grievance procedures will become, at best, a source of misunderstanding and, worse still, a license for censorship.

VI.

We also note from conversations that we have had with undergraduate students at Columbia that some have suggested, by way of a resolution of this controversy, that Columbia should insist on more ideological balance within the MEALAC Department. This is a seductive but ultimately flawed recommendation.

It is flawed because it is fundamentally at odds with the marketplace theory of free expression. Under that theory, balance is loosely but imperfectly achieved through the self-corrective mechanism of "more speech" as a response to bad ideas. And if we abandon that theory because it is not really working in practice we are left with the question as to whom we would trust to make the decision that the ideological composition of a particular department is balanced. Because judgments about "balance" are inevitably so subjective, efforts to achieve balance almost always fail. Thus, for example, for about 20 years we tried to achieve "balance" within the broadcast media by adopting a "fairness doctrine." But a few years ago the "fairness doctrine" was abandoned as a failure. The FCC concluded that fairness had the net effect of reducing the volume and quality and diversity of expression.[13] Moreover, trying to impose balance from outside the Department might well violate academic freedom principles of self-governance. Would those who urge balance within the MEALAC Department go to the University of Chicago and tell the economics department that it needs to be more balanced? The point is that the marketplace model rather than the model insisting on balance seems more effective at provoking intellectual creativity and in achieving pluralism and diversity. Under that model, one must look beyond a particular department or even a particular university to acquire a full exposure to the diversity of expression.

VII.

For all of these reasons, we call upon the University to respond appropriately to this assault on academic freedom. This response can and should involve several initiatives. First, we urge that you make clear to the public that academic judgments about members of the faculty must be left to the academy and that the attempted intrusion by donors or by politicians into this matter is entirely inappropriate. Second, you should use your office to educate the Columbia community about the importance and value of academic freedom and of freedom of speech on campus. Third, you should use your office to educate the Columbia student body about the nature of the learning environment to which they are entitled and about the limitations of that entitlement including the fact that they are not immune from hearing provocative or disagreeable or even offensive ideas from instructors or fellow students. You might inform students that they have a right to criticize their professors for what they regard as errors in scholarship or politics or even pedagogical style. But students have no right to initiate administrative investigations designed to call professors to account for their substantive views.

Finally, we urge the University to do what it can do best. It can convene a symposium to explore fully the real issues that have provoked this controversy. The University has the capacity to bring to the symposium table those representing a broad array of perspectives and viewpoints on this divisive topic and it can use the vehicle of "more speech" to address the current disagreements that so obviously exist.

We would be happy to meet with you to discuss any and all of these issues.

Sincerely,

Arthur Eisenberg
Donna Lieberman
Udi Ofer

cc: Provost Alan Brinkley

NOTES

1. Bollinger, "The Tolerant Society: A Response to Critics," 90 *Columbia Law Review* 979, 984 (1990). We may have some reservations with respect to the conceptual model that you advance in your 1990 *Columbia Law Review* piece. But that is the subject of another discussion and a very different letter.

2. The David Project is a Boston-based non-profit organization. The film is entitled "Columbia Unbecoming." The film has apparently been screened for interested Columbia students and Columbia officials and for the press and for certain public officials and some others. But it has apparently not been released for public exhibition. The authors of this letter have not seen the film. Assertions about its content, as set forth in this letter, are therefore derived from secondary sources including Columbia undergraduate students who have seen the film.

3. *Columbia Spectator*, November 4, 2004.

4. According to *Jewish Week*, October 29, 2004, Mr. Schoenfeld described this encounter as occurring "at an off-campus lecture … three years ago."

5. The *New York Sun*, Nov. 4, 2004. The *New York Sun* further describes Professor Massad as "the most outspoken critic of Israel and Zionism at Columbia … [who] argues that Israel is a racist state that does not legitimately represent Jews. He supports a one-state solution to the Middle East conflict…."

6. The *Daily News* editorial stated, *inter alia*, that "Columbia's Department of Middle East and Asian Languages and Cultures … has built a steady reputation for having a faculty that enforces some rather distasteful views under the guise of academic freedom." *Daily News*, Editorial, October 21, 2004.

7. *See*, Milton, *Areopagitica*.

8. *See*, Lovejoy, "Professional Association or Trade Union?" 24 *AAUP Bull.* 409, 414 (1938), quoted in Rabban, "Does Academic Freedom Limit Faculty Autonomy," 66 *Texas Law Review* 1405, 1413 (1988).

9. 354 U.S. at 262. In this regard, Justice Frankfurter quoted from a South African statement on open universities:

"It is the business of a university to provide that atmosphere which is most conducive to speculation, experiment and creation. It is an atmosphere in which there prevail 'the four essential freedoms' of a university — to determine for itself on academic grounds who may teach, what may be taught, how it shall be taught, and who may be admitted to study." *Sweezy*, 354 U.S. at 263.

10. In our view grievance procedures which allow administrators to call professors to account for conduct or even "speech acts" must be limited to circumstances where professors engage in behavior unrelated to the content of their lectures or writings.

11. The episode involving Tomy Schoenfeld did not involve a student of Professor Massad and did not take place within a classroom at all.

12. *Supra*, Section III.

13. This outcome should not have been surprising. Consider the term "fair and balanced" as used by Fox News in its self-promotion. It may well be that Roger Ailes and Bill O'Reilly believe that Fox broadcasts are "fair and balanced," but a great many people do not share that view. And if one were to ask the public to evaluate the fairness and balance of a wide range of news outlets from the *New York Post* to the *New York Times* you would get wildly different assessments.

Ford Foundation

Memorandum on Grant Language

TO: Ford Foundation Grantees

FROM: Alison R. Bernstein
      Melvin L. Oliver
      Bradford K. Smith

DATE: January 8, 2004

SUBJECT: Ford Foundation Policies

This memorandum describes important changes in Ford Foundation policy and practice that are now reflected in new language in our standard grant letter. We made these changes in response to heightened concerns among the public and policymakers about violence, terrorism, and bigotry and the possible misuse of philanthropic money for these purposes. We hope they make clear the values and assumptions that underlie our work together.

Ford's support for your work reflects our shared intent to strengthen democratic values, reduce poverty and injustice, promote international cooperation, and advance human achievement. The Foundation encourages initiatives by those living and working closest to where problems are located; promotes collaboration among the nonprofit, government and business sectors; and ensures participation by men and women from diverse communities and at all levels of society. We are dedicated to the pursuit of excellence, respectful debate and dialogue, and non-violent problem solving.

While your grant letter may have been issued before the new grant letter language was introduced, we hope that you will understand the need for the changes and accept the new language which is outlined below.

Violence, terrorism, bigotry, and the destruction of any state

We have added the following new language to our standard grant agreement letter: "By countersigning this grant letter, you agree that your organization will not promote or engage in violence, terrorism, bigotry or the destruction of any state, nor will it make sub-grants to any entity that engages in these activities." This prohibition applies to all of the organization's funds, not just those provided through a grant from Ford.

In addition, the grant letter now includes explicit language explaining that Ford may cease funding for failure to comply with terms of the grant letter and of the grant itself: "Failure to comply with the terms of this letter may result in immediate cessation of funding and/or support from the Foundation. In addition, if your organization expends or commits any part of the grant funds for purposes or activities other than the purposes and activities for which this grant is made, your organization must repay to the Foundation an amount equal to the amount of grant funds so expended for other purposes or activities."

Monitoring and oversight

We have always taken seriously the monitoring of grants — to ensure that we learn together, make necessary adjustments in strategy, and ensure that grantees are spending our funds according to approved budgets. We recently added several measures to improve our understanding of grantee finances and to make clear the right we have always had and sometimes exercised, to audit or investigate the use of our funds.

Now, our standard grant agreement letter will state explicitly: "The Foundation is authorized to conduct audits, including on-site audits, at any time during the term of the grant, and within four years after completion of the grant." Beyond this, Ford has reinforced its oversight process with an expanded program of systematic grant audits. At our request, the international accounting firm KPMG has constructed a risk matrix that Ford will use to determine which grants we will audit under the expanded program.

We appreciate the hard work you do and the many challenges inherent in it and look forward to working with you in the months and years ahead. If you have any questions about the changes outlined in this memo or other matters related to your work with us, please feel free to talk with your program officer or with other Foundation staff. And, thank you for your partnership with us.

Pursuing our mission as a responsible philanthropic institution

The Ford Foundation's goals are to strengthen democratic values, reduce poverty and injustice, promote international cooperation and advance human achievement. The Foundation pursues these goals in a variety of regions and countries, some of which are areas of violence and conflict. Wherever we work, the Foundation supports a broad range of people and institutions worldwide who share our dedication to fairness, justice, and a sense of mutual responsibility for humankind and the well being of the natural world around us.

As we pursue the Foundation's goals, we take all reasonable measures to fulfill our responsibilities as a tax exempt charitable organization. In particular, we want to make sure that our funds are used for the intended charitable purposes and do not support terrorist or other illegal activities. Because we appreciate the important work that our grantees do around the world, some in extremely difficult environments, we strive to fulfill our oversight responsibilities without creating undue burdens for them or being unduly intrusive into their affairs.

To ensure the appropriate use of our grant funds and compliance with U.S. anti-terrorism laws, the Foundation has extensive procedures for making and monitoring grants. These include the following:

1. **A pre-grant review** of a proposed grantee organization and its programs by a program officer who discusses the proposed work with the prospective grantee and assesses the organization's capacity to undertake it.

2. **Legal review** of proposed grants and of the written submissions by the prospective grantee.

3. **Compliance with U.S. Anti-Terrorism Financing Rules.** Under applicable law, the Foundation and other charitable organizations in the United States face penalties and potential criminal liability if grant funds are used to support acts of terrorism or to support persons or organizations that have been identified as terrorists or terrorist groups, including on lists published by the United States government. The Foundation respects the government's need to take appropriate steps to prevent the financing of terrorism and is committed to doing its part to ensure that its funds are not used for this purpose. At the same time, we are sensitive to the burdens placed on our grantees in responding to requests for information and to the importance of avoiding the creation of unwarranted suspicion.

To ensure its compliance with the law, the Foundation checks the names of grantee and potential grantee organizations, their boards of directors, and executive directors against nine publicly available lists: the OFAC Specially Designated Nationals and Blocked Persons lists, the United Nations Consolidated list, the EU Terrorism list, the INTERPOL Most Wanted list, and four FBI lists. These checks are made when the Foundation first seriously considers a grant, before formally approving a grant, before the Foundation approves any payment to the grantee, and every day for each of the Foundation's roughly 4,000 active grantees.

The Foundation recognizes there can be mistakes on the list or the list checking can create "false positives" (i.e. names that appear to match in whole or in part with names on a list, but that after inquiry prove not to be the same person or organization). We make every effort to identify false positives and have found no instance in which a grantee or a principal of a grantee has been identified as a terrorist or having links to terrorism. The Foundation is committed to working with its grantees to address any issues that may arise during this process.

4. **A countersigned grant letter** from the grantee, which establishes a range of grant conditions. In 2003, the Foundation

introduced the following provision in its standard grant letter. "By countersigning this grant letter, you agree that your organization will not promote or engage in violence, terrorism, bigotry or the destruction of any State, nor will it make subgrants to any entity that engages in these activities."

The new grant letter language is consistent with the Foundation's core values and makes explicit what has always been implicit in our relationships with grantees — namely, that we do not want to support organizations whose conduct is antithetical to our objectives of promoting peace, justice, tolerance and understanding. In these times and given the highly charged places in which we do some of our work, we believe it is important to make clear, in non-technical language, to our grantees around the world and to the public to which we are accountable where we stand and what we expect of organizations that receive our support.

The vast majority of grantees have accepted the new language. A few organizations, mainly universities, have raised questions and we have made every effort to answer their concerns and to clarify the application of the grant language to their organization's particular mission and activities. In response to a question as to the bearing, if any, of the new language on academic freedom, we took the opportunity to reaffirm our commitment to freedom of expression, including academic freedom. The following statement contains the basic points we have made to provide clarification to universities:

> The Ford Foundation supports and endorses the principle of academic freedom. We recognize that it entails the expression by faculty, students and other individuals on campus of a broad range of views and opinions, which, in some cases, may be controversial, unpopular, or offensive. We value and support free and open debate. We do not intend to interfere with discussions in classrooms, faculty publications, student remarks in chat rooms, or other speech that express the views of the individuals. Our grant letter relates only to the official speech and conduct of the university and to speech or conduct that the university explicitly endorses; it is not intended to change the academic values of the university, nor to interfere in student admissions, faculty appointments, curriculum and academic program development, or establishment of research programs.

5. **One or more site visits** by a program officer during the term of a grant.

6. **The requirement that grantees submit periodic financial and narrative reports** during the grant term, which are reviewed by a program officer and a grants administrator for compliance with the term of the grant.

7. **A new and expanded worldwide program of grantee audits,** instituted in 2003, for which the Foundation engaged an international accounting firm to help in the selection of grantees to be audited.

Bibliography

Aidi, Hishaam D., "Slavery, Genocide and the Politics of Outrage: Understanding the New 'Racial Olympics,'" *Middle East Report* 234 (2005), pp. 40–55.

Akram, Susan M., and Kevin R. Johnson, "The Targeting of Arabs and Muslims," in Elaine C. Hagopian (ed.), *Civil Rights in Peril: The Targeting of Arabs and Muslims* (Chicago: Haymarket, 2004).

American Association of University Professors, "1915 Declaration of Principles on Academic Freedom and Academic Tenure," in *Policy Documents and Reports*, 9th ed. (Washington, D.C.: American Association of University Professors, 2001).

———, "1925 Conference Statement on Academic Freedom and Tenure," *AAUP Bulletin* 11 (1925), pp. 100–101.

———, "1940 Statement of Principles on Academic Freedom and Tenure with 1970 Interpretive Comments," in *Policy Documents and Reports*, 9th ed. (Washington, D.C.: American Association of University Professors, 2001).

———, "Academic Freedom and National Security in a Time of Crisis," *Academe* 89.6 (2003).

———, "Committee A Statement on Extramural Utterances," in *Policy Documents and Reports*, 9th ed. (Washington, D.C.: American Association of University Professors, 2001).

———, "Joint Statement on Rights and Freedoms of Students," in *Policy Documents and Reports*, 9th ed. (Washington, D.C.: American Association of University Professors, 2001).

———, *Policy Documents and Reports*, 9th ed. (Washington, D.C.: American Association of University Professors, 2001).

Atkinson, Richard C., "Academic Freedom and the Research

University," repr. in *Proceedings of the American Philosophical Society* 148.2 (2004), pp. 195–204.

Beinin, Joel, "Money, Media and Policy Consensus: The Washington Institute for Near East Policy," *Middle East Report* no. 180 (1993), pp. 10–15.

Bingham, Lisa B., "Employee Free Speech in the Workplace: Using the First Amendment as Public Policy for Wrongful Discharge Actions," *Ohio State Law Journal* 55.2 (1994), pp. 341–92.

Bok, Derek, *Universities in the Marketplace: The Commercialization of Higher Education* (Princeton, NJ: Princeton University Press, 2003).

Bradley, Richard, *Harvard Rules: The Struggle for the Soul of the World's Most Powerful University* (New York: HarperCollins, 2005).

Brubacher, John S., and Willis Rudy, *Higher Education in Transition: A History of American Colleges and Universities, 1636–1968* (New York: Harper and Row, 1968).

Butler, Judith, "Explanation and Exoneration, or What We Can Hear," in *Precarious Life: The Powers of Mourning and Violence* (London: Verso, 2004).

———, "No, It's Not Anti-Semitic," *London Review of Books*, August 21, 2003.

Byrne, J. Peter, "Academic Freedom: A 'Special Concern of the First Amendment,'" *Yale Law Journal* 99 (1989), pp. 251–340.

Chomsky, Noam, *Hegemony or Survival: America's Quest for Global Dominance* (New York: Metropolitan, 2003).

Cohen, Arthur M., *The Shaping of American Higher Education: Emergence and Growth of the Contemporary System* (San Francisco: Jossey-Bass, 1998).

Cohen, Robert, "This Was Their Fight and They Had to Fight It: The FSM's Nonradical Rank and File," in Robert Cohen and Reginald E. Zelnik (eds.), *The Free Speech Movement: Reflections on Berkeley in the 1960s* (Berkeley: University of California Press, 2002).

Cohen, Robert, and Reginald E. Zelnik (eds.), *The Free Speech Movement: Reflections on Berkeley in the 1960s* (Berkeley: University of California Press, 2002).

Cole, Jonathan R. "Academic Freedom Under Fire," *Daedulus* 135.2 (2005), pp. 1–13.

Conference of Representatives of the University of Cape Town and the University of the Witwatersrand, *The Open Universities in South Africa* (Johannesburg: Witwatersrand University Press, 1957).

Cooley, Thomas M., and Walter Carrington, *A Treatise on the Constitutional Limitations which Rest upon the Legislative Powers of the States of the American Union*, 8th ed. (Boston: Little, Brown, 1927).

Cumings, Bruce, "Boundary Displacement: Area Studies and International Studies During and After the Cold War," *Bulletin of Concerned Asian Scholars* 29.1 (1997), pp. 6–26.

Dewey, John, "Academic Freedom," in *The Middle Works, 1899–1924*, ed. Jo Ann Boydston, vol. 2, *1902–1903* (Carbondale: Southern Illinois Press, 1976).

Diamond, Sigmund, *Compromised Campus: The Collaboration of Universities with the Intelligence Community, 1945–1955* (New York: Oxford University Press, 1992).

Douglass, John Aubrey, *The California Idea and American Higher Education: 1850 to the 1960 Master Plan* (Stanford: Stanford University Press, 2000).

Elliott, Orrin Leslie, *Stanford University: The First Twenty-Five Years* (Stanford: Stanford University Press, 1937).

Farsoun, Samih, "The Roots of the American Anti-Terrorism Crusade," in Elaine C. Hagopian (ed.), *Civil Rights in Peril: The Targeting of Arabs and Muslims* (Chicago: Haymarket, 2004).

Findley, Paul, *They Dare to Speak Out: People and Institutions Confront Israel's Lobby* (Westport, CT: Lawrence Hill and Co., 1985).

Finkin, Matthew W., "Intramural Speech, Academic Freedom, and the First Amendment," *Texas Law Review* 66 (1988), pp. 1323–49.

Foner, Eric, *The Story of American Freedom* (New York: Norton, 1998).

Forrest, Barbara, and Glenn Branch, "Wedging Creationism into the Academy," *Academe* 91.1 (2005), pp. 37–41.

Forrest, Barbara, and Paul R. Gross, *Creationism's Trojan Horse: The Wedge of Intelligent Design* (Oxford: Oxford University Press, 2004).

Frank, Thomas, *What's the Matter with Kansas? How Conservatives Won the Heart of America* (New York: Metropolitan, 2004).

Friedman, Lawrence M., *The Republic of Choice: Law, Authority, and Culture* (Cambridge, MA: Harvard University Press, 1990).

Fulbright, J. William, "The Most Significant and Important Activity I Have Been Privileged to Engage In During My Years in the Senate," *Annals of the American Academy of Political and Social Science* 424 (1976), pp. 1–5.

———, "The War and Its Effects: The Military-Industrial-Academic Complex," in Herbert I. Schiller (ed.), *Super-State: Readings in the Military-Industrial Complex* (Urbana: University of Illinois Press, 1970).

Furner, Mary O., "Advocacy and Objectivity: A Crisis in the Professionalization of American Social Science, 1865–1905" (Lexington: University Press of Kentucky, 1975).

Gardner, David P., *The California Oath Controversy* (Berkeley: University of California Press, 1967).

Geiger, Roger L., "The American University at the Beginning of the Twenty-First Century: Signposts on the Path to Privatization," in Robert McC. Adams (ed.), *Trends in American and German Higher Education* (Cambridge, MA: American Academy of Arts and Sciences, 2002).

———, *Knowledge and Money: Research Universities and the Paradox of the Marketplace* (Stanford, CA: Stanford University Press, 2004).

———, *Research and Relevant Knowledge: American Research Universities Since World War II* (New York: Oxford University Press, 1993).

Glendon, Mary Ann, *Rights Talk: The Impoverishment of Political Discourse* (New York: Free Press, 1991).

Gorenberg, Gershom, *The End of Days: Fundamentalism and the Struggle for the Temple Mount* (Oxford: Oxford University Press, 2002).

Gould, Eric, *The University in a Corporate Culture* (New Haven, CT: Yale University Press, 2003).

Gouldner, Alvin, *The Future of Intellectuals and the Rise of the New Class* (Scranton, PA: HarperCollins, 1979).

Hagopian, Elaine C. (ed.), *Civil Rights in Peril: The Targeting of Arabs and Muslims* (Chicago: Haymarket, 2004).

Haskell, Thomas L., "Justifying the Rights of Academic Freedom in the Era of 'Power/Knowledge,'" in Louis Menand (ed.), *The*

Future of Academic Freedom (Chicago: University of Chicago Press, 1996).

Hedges, Chris, "Soldiers of Christ II: Feeling the Hate with the National Religious Broadcasters," *Harpers*, May 2005.

Heginbotham, Stanley J., "The National Security Education Program," *Items* 46.2–3 (1992), pp. 30–43.

Hofstadter, Richard, and Walter P. Metzger, *The Development of Academic Freedom in the United States* (New York: Columbia University Press, 1955).

Hollinger, David A., "What Does It Mean to Be 'Balanced' in Academia?" Paper presented at the annual meeting of the American Historical Association, January 9, 2005.

Hook, Sidney, "Past and Future: The Long View," in Hook (ed.), *In Defense of Academic Freedom* (New York: Pegasus, 1971).

Huntington, Samuel P., "The Clash of Civilizations?" *Foreign Affairs* 72.3 (1993), pp. 22–49.

———, *The Clash of Civilizations and the Remaking of World Order* (New York: Simon and Schuster, 1996).

Jackson, Jim, "Express and Implied Contractual Rights to Academic Freedom in the United States," *Hamline Law Review* 22 (1999), pp. 467–500.

Jackson, Shannon, *Professing Performance: Theatre in the Academy from Philology to Performativity* (Cambridge, UK: Cambridge University Press, 2004).

Joughin, Louis (ed.), *Academic Freedom and Tenure: A Handbook of the American Association of University Professors* (University of Wisconsin Press, 1969).

Kerr, Clark, *The Uses of the University* (Cambridge, MA: Harvard University Press, 2001).

Kirp, David L., *Shakespeare, Einstein, and the Bottom Line: The Marketing of Higher Education* (Cambridge, MA: Harvard University Press, 2003).

Kramer, Martin S., *Ivory Towers on Sand: The Failure of Middle Eastern Studies in America* (Washington, D.C.: Washington Institute for Near East Policy, 2001).

Krimsky, Sheldon, *Science in the Private Interest: Has the Lure of Profits Corrupted Biomedical Research?* (Lanham, MD: Rowman and Littlefield, 2003).

Lakoff, George, *Don't Think of an Elephant!: Know Your Values and Frame the Debate; The Essential Guide for Progressives* (White

River Junction, VT: Chelsea Green Publishing, 2004).

Leslie, Stuart W., *The Cold War and American Science: The Military-Industrial-Academic Complex at MIT and Stanford* (New York: Columbia University Press, 1993).

Lewis, Bernard, "The Question of Orientalism," *New York Review of Books* 29.11 (June 24, 1982), pp. 49–56.

———, "The Roots of Muslim Rage," *Atlantic Monthly* 266.3 (1990), pp. 47–60.

Lie, John, "Moral Ambiguity, Disciplinary Power, and Academic Freedom," *Bulletin of Concerned Asian Scholars* 29.1 (1997), pp. 30–33.

Lockman, Zachary, *Contending Visions of the Middle East: The History and Politics of Orientalism* (Cambridge: Cambridge University Press, 2004).

Lovejoy, Arthur O., "Academic Freedom," in Edwin R.A. Seligman (ed.), *Encyclopedia of the Social Sciences* (New York: Macmillan, 1930).

Lowell, Abbott Lawrence, "Report for 1916-17," in Henry Aaron Yeomans, *Abbott Lawrence Lowell, 1856–1943* (Cambridge, MA: Harvard University Press, 1948).

Lowen, Rebecca S., *Creating the Cold War University: The Transformation of Stanford* (Berkeley: University of California Press, 1997).

Lynch, Rebecca Gose, "Pawns of the State or Priests of Democracy? Analyzing Professors' Academic Freedom Rights Within the State's Managerial Realm," *California Law Review* 91.4 (2003), pp. 1061–1108.

MacIver, Robert M., *Academic Freedom in Our Time* (New York: Columbia University Press, 1955).

Marcuse, Herbert, "Repressive Tolerance," in Robert Paul Wolff, Barrington Moore Jr., and Herbert Marcuse, *A Critique of Pure Tolerance* (Boston: Beacon Press, 1969).

McCumber, John, *Time in the Ditch: American Philosophy and the McCarthy Era* (Evanston, IL: Northwestern University Press, 2001).

McDonnell, Lorraine, Sue E. Berryman, and Douglas Scott, *Federal Support for International Studies: The Role of NDEA Title VI* (Santa Monica, CA: Rand, 1981).

McDougall, Walter A., "Technocracy and Statecraft in the Space Age—Toward the History of a Saltation," *American Historical*

Review 87.4 (1982), pp. 1010–40.

Meiklejohn, Alexander, *Political Freedom: The Constitutional Powers of the People* (New York: Harper, 1960).

Menand, Louis (ed.), *The Future of Academic Freedom* (Chicago: University of Chicago Press, 1996).

Merkx, Gilbert, "Plus Ça Change: Challenges to Graduate Education under HEA Title VI," in John N. Hawkins (ed.), *International Education in the New Global Era: Proceedings of a National Policy Conference on the Higher Education Act, Title VI, and Fulbright-Hays Programs* (Los Angeles: UCLA, 1998).

Mertz, Elizabeth, "The Burden of Proof and Academic Freedom: Protection for Institution or Individual?" *Northwestern University Law Review* 82 (1988), pp. 492–539.

"The MESA Debate: The Scholars, the Media, and the Middle East," *Journal of Palestine Studies* 16.2 (1987), pp. 85–104.

Metzger, Walter P., "The 1940 Statement of Principles on Academic Freedom and Tenure," *Law and Contemporary Problems* 53.3 (1990), pp. 3–77.

———, *Academic Freedom in the Age of the University* (New York: Columbia University Press, 1961).

———, "The Age of the University," in Richard Hofstadter and Walter Metzger, *The Development of Academic Freedom in the United States* (New York: Columbia University Press, 1955).

———, "Profession and Constitution: Two Definitions of Academic Freedom in America," *Texas Law Review* 66 (1988), pp. 1265–1322.

Mill, John Stuart, "On Liberty," in *Utilitarianism*, ed. Mary Warnock (New York: World Publishing Co., 1971).

Mitchell, Timothy, *Rule of Experts: Egypt, Techno-Politics, Modernity* (Berkeley: University of California Press, 2002).

Morriss, Andrew P., "Exploding Myths: An Empirical and Economic Reassessment of the Rise of Employment At-Will," *Missouri Law Review* 59.3 (1994), pp. 679–774.

Nash, Gary, Charlotte Crabtree, and Ross E. Dunn, *History on Trial: Culture Wars and the Teaching of the Past* (New York: Knopf, 1997).

Newfield, Christopher, *Ivy and Industry: Business and the Making of the American University, 1880–1980* (Durham, NC: Duke University Press, 2003).

Newman, Frank, Lara Couturier, and Jamie Scurry, *The Future of*

Higher Education: Rhetoric, Reality, and the Risks of the Market (San Francisco: Jossey-Bass, 2004).

Newman, Robert P., *Owen Lattimore and the "Loss" of China* (Berkeley: University of California Press, 1992).

Noble, David F., *America by Design: Science, Technology, and the Rise of Corporate Capitalism* (Oxford: Oxford University Press, 1979).

Ortega y Gasset, José, *Mission of the University* (New Brunswick: Transaction, 1992).

Peirce, Charles S., "The Fixation of Belief," in *Values in a Universe of Chance: Selected Writings of Charles S. Peirce*, ed. Philip P. Wiener (Stanford: Stanford University Press, 1958).

Pincoffs, Edmund L. (ed.), *The Concept of Academic Freedom* (Austin: University of Texas Press, 1975).

Poskanzer, Steven G., *Higher Education Law: The Faculty* (Baltimore: John Hopkins University Press, 2002).

Post, Robert, "Between Governance and Management: The History and Theory of the Public Forum," *UCLA Law Review* 34 (1987), pp. 1713–1835.

Post, Robert C., "Academic Freedom and the 'Intifada Curriculum,'" *Academe* 89.3 (2003), pp. 16–20.

———, "The Constitutional Concept of Public Discourse: Outrageous Opinion, Democratic Deliberation, and *Hustler Magazine v. Falwell*," *Harvard Law Review* 103.3 (1990), pp. 601–86.

———, *Constitutional Domains: Democracy, Community, Management* (Cambridge, MA: Harvard University Press, 1995).

———, "Constitutionally Interpreting the FSM Controversy," in Robert Cohen and Reginald E. Zelnik (eds.), *The Free Speech Movement: Reflections on Berkeley in the 1960s* (Berkeley: University of California Press, 2002).

———, "Democratic Constitutionalism and Cultural Heterogeneity," *Australian Journal of Legal Philosophy* 25 (2000), pp. 185–204.

———, "Equality and Autonomy in First Amendment Jurisprudence," *Michigan Law Review* 95 (1997), pp. 1517–41.

———, "Foreword: Fashioning the Legal Constitution: Culture, Courts, and Law," *Harvard Law Review* 117.1 (2003), pp. 4–112.

———, "Reconciling Theory and Doctrine in First Amendment Jurisprudence," *California Law Review* 88.6 (2000), pp. 2353–74.

————, "Subsidized Speech," *Yale Law Journal* 106.1 (1996), pp. 151–95.

Price, David H., *Threatening Anthropology: McCarthyism and the FBI's Surveillance of Activist Anthropologists* (Durham, NC: Duke University Press, 2004).

Rabban, David M., "A Functional Analysis of Individual and Institutional Academic Freedom Under the First Amendment," *Law and Contemporary Problems* 53.3 (1990), pp. 227–301.

————, "Academic Freedom," in Leonard W. Levy, Kenneth L. Karst, and Dennis J. Mahoney (eds.), *Encyclopedia of the American Constitution* (New York: Macmillan, 1986).

————, "Can Academic Freedom Survive Postmodernism?" *California Law Review* 86 (1998), pp. 1377–89.

————, "Does Academic Freedom Limit Faculty Autonomy?" *Texas Law Review* 66 (1988), pp. 1405–29.

Rhoades, Gary, "Capitalism, Academic Style, and Shared Governance," *Academe* 91.3 (2005), pp. 38–42.

Rodgers, Daniel T., *Contested Truths: Keywords in American Politics Since Independence* (Cambridge, MA: Harvard University Press, 1998).

Rourke, Francis E., and Glenn E. Brooks, *The Managerial Revolution in Higher Education* (Baltimore: Johns Hopkins University Press, 1966).

Said, Edward W., "Identity, Authority, and Freedom: The Potentate and the Traveler," in Menand (ed.), *The Future of Academic Freedom*.

Said, Edward W., and Oleg Grabar, with a reply by Bernard Lewis, "Orientalism: An Exchange," *New York Review of Books* 29.13 (August 12, 1982), pp. 44–48.

Scarfo, Richard D., "The History of Title VI and Fulbright-Hays," in John N. Hawkins (ed.), *International Education in the New Global Era: Proceedings of a National Policy Conference on the Higher Education Act, Title VI, and Fulbright-Hays Programs* (Los Angeles: UCLA, 1998).

Schauer, Frederick, *Free Speech: A Philosophical Enquiry* (Cambridge, UK: Cambridge University Press, 1982).

Schrecker, Ellen, *Many Are the Crimes: McCarthyism in America* (Boston: Little, Brown, 1998).

————, *No Ivory Tower: McCarthyism and the Universities* (New York: Oxford University Press, 1986).

Scott, Joan W., "Academic Freedom as an Ethical Practice," in
Louis Menand (ed.), *The Future of Academic Freedom* (Chicago:
University of Chicago Press, 1996).

Searle, John R., "Two Concepts of Academic Freedom," in
Edmund L. Pincoffs (ed.), *The Concept of Academic Freedom*
(Austin: University of Texas Press, 1975).

Shils, Edward, "Do We Still Need Academic Freedom?" *American
Scholar* 62.2 (1993), pp. 187–209.

Simpson, Christopher, *Universities and Empire: Money and Politics
in the Social Sciences During the Cold War* (New York: New
Press, 1998).

Slaughter, Sheila, and Gary Rhoades, *Academic Capitalism and the
New Economy: Markets, State, and Higher Education* (Baltimore:
Johns Hopkins University Press, 2004).

Smith, Stacy E., "Who Owns Academic Freedom? The Standard
for Academic Free Speech at Public Universities," *Washington
and Lee Law Review* 59 (2002), pp. 299–360.

Stone, Geoffrey R., *Perilous Times: Free Speech in Wartime from the
Sedition Act of 1798 to the War on Terrorism* (New York: Norton,
2004).

Sufrin, Sidney Charles, *Administering the National Defense Education Act* (Syracuse, NY: Syracuse University Press, 1963).

Tribe, Laurence, *American Constitutional Law*, 2nd ed. (Mineola,
NY: Foundation Press, 1988).

Van Alstyne, William, "Academic Freedom and the First Amendment in the Supreme Court of the United States: An Unhurried Historical Review," *Law and Contemporary Problems* 53.3
(1990), pp. 79–154.

Van Alstyne, William, "The Specific Theory of Academic Free-
dom and the General Issue of Civil Liberty," in Pincoffs (ed.),
The Concept of Academic Freedom (Austin: University of Texas
Press, 1975).

von Helmholtz, Hermann, "On Academic Freedom in German
Universities," repr. in *Science and Culture: Popular and Philo-
sophical Lectures*, ed. David Cahan (Chicago: University of
Chicago Press, 1995).

Washburn, Jennifer, *University, Inc.: The Corporate Corruption of
American Higher Education* (New York: Basic Books, 2005).

Watson, James D., *The Double Helix: A Personal Account of the Discovery of the Structure of DNA* (New York: Touchstone, 1996).

Westmeyer, Paul, *A History of American Higher Education* (Spring-field, IL: Thomas, 1985).

Wiegman, Robyn (ed.), *Women's Studies on Its Own: A Next Wave Reader in Institutional Change* (Durham, NC: Duke University Press, 2002).

Wiley, David, "National Security Education Program: Who's Setting the Agenda?" *Journal of the International Institute* 1.1 (1994), pp. 3–5.

Williams, Bernard, *Truth and Truthfulness: An Essay in Genealogy* (Princeton, NJ: Princeton University Press, 2002).

Wright, Erik Olin, *Classes* (London: Verso, 1985).

Zelnik, Reginald E., "On the Side of the Angels: The Berkeley Faculty and the FSM," in Robert Cohen and Reginald E. Zelnik (eds.), *The Free Speech Movement: Reflections on Berkeley in the 1960s* (Berkeley: University of California Press, 2002).

Contributors

Joel Beinin is Professor of Middle East History at Stanford University. His research and writing focus on workers, peasants, and minorities in the modern Middle East and on Israel, Palestine, and the Arab-Israeli conflict. His most recent book is *Workers and Peasants in the Modern Middle East*. He served as president of the Middle East Studies Association of North America in 2002.

Judith Butler is Maxine Elliot Professor of Rhetoric and Comparative Literature at the University of California at Berkeley. She is the author of several books on feminist theory, cultural politics, and critical philosophy, including, most recently, *Precarious Life: Politics, Violence, Mourning*.

Beshara Doumani is Associate Professor of History at the University of California at Berkeley. His work focuses on the social and cultural history of the Middle East during the late Ottoman period. He is the author of *Rediscovering Palestine: Merchants and Peasants in Jabal Nablus, 1700–1900* and the editor of *Family History in the Middle East: Household, Property and Gender*.

Kathleen J. Frydl is Assistant Professor of History at the University of California at Berkeley. She received her Ph.D. from the University of Chicago in history, and she worked at the National Research Council before joining the Berkeley faculty. Her work focuses on modern U.S. political history with an emphasis on state power as expressed and negotiated through institutions. She wrote her dissertation about the GI Bill of the Second World War. She occasionally writes in the third person and wonders if this undermines any claim she might have to be taken seriously.